1 MONTH OF
FREE
READING

at

www.ForgottenBooks.com

By purchasing this book you are
eligible for one month membership to
ForgottenBooks.com, giving you
unlimited access to our entire
collection of over 1,000,000 titles via
our web site and mobile apps.

To claim your free month visit:

www.forgottenbooks.com/free75244

ISBN 978-0-428-97788-7
PIBN 10075244

IMPORTANCE

OF

RELIGIOUS OPINIONS.

TRANSLATED FROM THE FRENCH

[by, Mary Wollstonecraft]

OF

MR. NECKER.

***

LONDON:

\text{PRINTED FOR J. JOHNSON, N}^{\circ}\text{ 72, ST. PAUL'S}

CHURCH-YARD.

M.DCC.LXXXVIII.

ADVERTISEMENT.

IN rendering this Work into Engliſh ſome Liberties have been taken by the Tranſlator, which ſeemed neceſſary to preſerve the Spirit of the Original.

CONTENTS.

CHAP. I.

CHAP. II.

CHAP. III.

CHAP. IV.

CHAP. V.

CHAP.

CONTENTS.

CHAP.

CONTENTS.

CHAP. XI.

CHAP. XII.

CHAP. XIII.

CHAP. XIV.

CHAP. XV.

CHAP. XVI.

CHAP.

CONTENTS.

CHAP. XVII.

CHAP. XVIII.

INTRO-

INTRODUCTION.

MY thoughts having been detached
from the ftudy and difquifition of
thofe truths which have the political good
of the ftate for their object; and being no
longer obliged to fix any attention on thofe
particular arrangements of the public intereft, which are neceffarily connected with
the operations of government; I found
myfelf abandoned, as it were, by all the
important concerns of life. Reftlefs and
wandering in this kind of void, my foul,
ftill active, felt the want of employment.

I fome-

I fometimes formed the defign of tracing my ideas of men and characters; I imagined that long experience in the midft of thofe active fcenes which difcover the paffions, had taught me to know them well; but elevating my views, my heart was filled with a different ambition, and a defire to reconcile the fublimeft thoughts with thofe meditations from which I was conftrained to withdraw myfelf. Guided by this fentiment, I remarked, with fatisfaction, that there exifted a natural connection between the different truths which contribute to the happinefs of mankind. Our prejudices and our paffions frequently attempt to difunite them; but to the eye of an attentive obferver, they have all one common origin. From a fimilar affinity, the general views of adminiftration, the fpirit of laws, morality, and religious opinions, are clofely connected; and it is by carefully preferving an alliance fo beautiful, that we raife a rampart round thofe works, which are deftined for the profperity of ftates and the tranquillity of nations.

One.

One could not have taken an active part in the adminiftration of public affairs; or made it the object of ftedfaft attention; one could not have compared the feveral relations of this great whole, with the natural difpofitions of minds and characters; nor indeed obferved men in a perpetual ftate of rivalry and competition, without perceiving, how much the wifeft governments need fupport from the influence of that invifible fpring which acts in fecret on the confciences of individuals. Thus whilft I am endeavouring to form fome reflections on the importance of religious opinions, I am not fo far removed from my former habit of thinking as may, at the firft glance, be imagined; and as in writing on the management of finances, I omitted no argument to prove that there is an intimate connexion between the efficacy of governments, and the wifdom with which they are conducted; between the virtue of princes, and the confidence of their fubjects, I think I am ftill proceeding in the fame train of fentiment and reflection, when ftruck with

that

that spirit of indifference which is fo general, : I endeavour to refer the duties of men
to those principles which afford them the
moft natural fupport.

After having ftudied the interefts of a
great nation, and run over the circle of our
political focieties, we approach nearer perhaps to thofe fublime ideas which bind'
the general ftructure of mankind to that
infinite and Almighty Being, who is the
firft grand caufe of all, and univerfal mover
of the univerfe. In the rapid courfe of an
active adminiftration, indeed one cannot
indulge fimilar reflections; but they are
forming and preparing themfelves in the
midft of the tumult of bufinefs, and the
tranquillity of retirement enables us to
ftrengthen and extend them.

The calm which fucceeds hurry and
confufion, feems the feafon moft favourable
to meditation; and if any remembrance, or
retrofpective views of what is paft fhould
infpire you with a kind of melancholy, you
will

will be involuntarily led back to contemplations which border on thofe ideas with
which you have been long converfant. It
is thus the mariner, after having renounced
the dangers of the fea, fometimes feats
himfelf on the beach, and there, a more
tranquil obferver, confiders attentively the
boundlefs ocean, the regular fucceffion of
the waves, the impreffion of the winds,
the flux and reflux of the tide, and that
magnificent firmament, where, during the
night, among lights innumerable, he diftinguifhes the lucid point, which ferves as a
guide to the navigators.

It is in vain, in thofe high ftations under
government, to intereft yourfelf about the
happinefs of mankind in general; it is in
vain, that, penetrated with a juft refpect for
the important duties of office, a public
character fhall dare to take in hand the
caufe of the people, and inceffantly apply
himfelf to the defence of the weak, in oppofition to the attacks of the powerful; he
foon perceives how bounded are his abili-

ties,

ties, and how limited are thofe, even of
fovereignty itfelf. Pity for the diftreffes of
the individual is checked by the law of
civil rights; benevolence by juftice; and
liberty by its own abufes: you perpetually
behold merit ftruggling with patronage,
honour with fortune, and patriotifm with
the intereft of the individual. There is no
fuch thing as real difintereftednefs in the
paffions, only by fits and ftarts; unlefs
great circumftances, or vigorous virtue in
an adminiftration, forcibly renewed the
idea of public good, a general langour
would take place in every mind, and fociety
itfelf would appear one confufed mafs of
oppofite interefts, which the' fupreme authority keeps within bounds for the maintenance of peace, without any inquietude
about real harmony, or any revolution favourable to the manners or happinefs of
the public.

From the midft of thefe clafhings and
contradictions, continually recurring, a mi-
nifter, poffeffed of a reflecting mind, is inceffantly

ceffantly called back to the idea of imperfection; he will, undoubtedly, be forry,
when he fees the great difproportion which
exifts between his duty and his powers; and
he will fometimes grieve and be difcouraged,
at perceiving the obftacles he muft furmount,
and the difficulties he muft overcome: he
raifes, with labour and care, banks on the
ftrand, the waters fwell, their courfe becomes more rapid, and the firft precautions
rendered infufficient, oblige him to have recourfe to new works, which, thrown down
in their turn, hurry on a continued fucceffion of fruitlefs toil and ufelefs attempts.
What then would be the confequence, if
once the falutary chain of religious fentiments were broken? What would be the
event, if the action of that powerful fpring
were ever entirely deftroyed? You would
foon fee every part of the focial ftructure
tremble from its foundation, and the hand of
government unable to fuftain the vaft and
tottering edifice.

B 4   The

The fovereign, and the laws which are the interpreters of his wifdom, fhould have two grand obje

cts, the maintenance of public order, and the increafe of private happinefs. But to accomplifh both, the aid of religion is abfolutely neceffary. The fovereign cannot influence the happinefs of individuals, but by a general folicitude; becaufe the fentiments which fpring from the different chara

cters of men, or merely from the circumftances of their refpe

ctive fituations, are independent of him. Neither can he enfure the prefervation of public order, but by rules and inftitutions, which are only applicable to actions, and to thofe actions pofitively proved. It is neceffary alfo that the laws fhould extend their influence to fociety in a uniform manner; they fhould always have a tendency to diminifh the number of diftin

ctions, fhades, and modifications, that are to be found in the actions of men; in fhort, to prevent thofe abufes infeparably attendant on arbitrary decifions.

Such

Such are the bounds of fovereign authority, and fuch the neceffary developement of
its means and powers. Religion, to attain
the fame ends, employs other motives effentially different: firft, it is not in a vague
and general manner, that fhe influences the
happinefs of mankind; it is by addreffing
all men individually; by penetrating the
heart of every human being, and pouring
into it confolation and hope; by prefenting
to the imagination every thing that can infenfibly lead it captive; by taking poffeffion
of mens fentiments; by occupying their
thoughts; and by availing herfelf of this
dominion over them, to fuftain their courage,
and to afford them comfort under their af-
flictions and difappointments. In this manner religion concurs to maintain good order,
by means abfolutely diftinct from thofe of
government; for fhe not only governs our
actions, but even our fentiments: it is with
the errors and inclinations of each man in
particular, that fhe feeks to combat. Religion, in demonftrating the prefence of the
Deity, on all occafions, however fecret, exercifes

ercifes an habitual authority over the con‑
fciences of men; fhe feems to affift them
under the perturbations of fear, and yet at‑
tends them in their flight; fhe equally no‑
tices their intentions, projects, and repent‑
ance; and in the method which fhe takes,
feems as undulating and flexible in all her
motions, as the empire of the law appears
immoveable and conftrained.

I fhould not, at prefent, extend thefe re‑
flections any further; but, if religion, in
fome meafure, completes the imperfect work
of legiflation; if it ought to fupply the in‑
fufficiency of thofe means which govern‑
ment is under the neceffity of adopting,
the fubject I propofe to treat of feems not
foreign to thofe objects of meditation, which
the ftudy of adminiftration ought to com‑
prehend.

I well know, that it is impoffible to ex‑
plain the importance of religion, without,
at the fame time, fixing the attention on
the grand truths on which it depends; and

you

you muſt alſo frequently touch on many ſubjeçts that are cloſely connected with the deepeſt metaphyſics. We are, at leaſt, obliged to ſeek for a defence againſt thoſe arguments which ſap the foundation of the moſt neceſſary opinions ; by which the moſt impaſſioned ſentiments have been diſcouraged ; by which ſome would reduce man to a vegetable, make the univerſe the reſult of chance, and morality a ſtate trick.

As ſoon as I diſcovered how far my ſubject was likely to lead me, I felt myſelf intimidated ; but I could not allow this to be a ſufficient reaſon for relinquiſhing my undertaking ; and ſince the greater part of the philoſophers of the preſent age are united in oppoſition to thoſe opinions, which the light of nature ſeems to have rendered ſacred, it is become indiſpenſably neceſſary, to admit to the combat all that offer ; nay, even to ſelect a champion from the main body of the army, when all the ſtrong ones are already gone over to the camp of the enemy.

There

There is nothing which seems to engrofs the attention of mankind more than meta-phyfical enquiries, for it is by thinking alone they can be fathomed; the light gained by acquired knowledge is, in fome meafure, loft in thofe obfcure depths which it is neceffary to found, and that immenfe fpace which it is neceffary to traverfe. Thus, it were better, perhaps, that each fhould enter by chance into thefe labyrinths, where the paths, already traced, lead to no one determined point. I have, befides, often obferved, that, even for thofe re-fearches, where the helps of fcience are moft ufeful, we ought to fet a certain value on the particular excurfion of each genius, which feeks out for itfelf a way, and which, indebted to nature alone for its peculiar for-mation, preferves in its progrefs a character of its own; it is then, and then only, that we are not invefted with the diftinguifhing marks of flavifhnefs of thinking; but when, by devoting ourfelves to reflection, we coin-cide with the opinions of others, this con-formity has nothing of fervility in it, and

the

the marks of imitation are not even recognized.

In vain would man refift the impreffion of truth; in vain would he defend himfelf by a ridiculous indifference for ancient opinions; there never could be an idea more worthy to occupy our meditations, there never could be an idea, on which we might be more-fully permitted to expatiate, according to our knowledge and penetration, than that fublime one of a Supreme Being, and the relation we bear to him: an idea, which though far removed from us by its immenfity, every moment ftrikes the foul with admiration, and infpires the heart with hope.

It appears to me, that there are interefts which may be confidered as patriotic by intelligent and feeling beings; and while the inhabitants of the fame country, and the fubjects of the fame prince, employ themfelves diligently in one common plan of defence, the citizens of the world ought to be be inceſſantly anxious to give every new and poſſible ſupport to thoſe exalted opinions on which the true greatneſs of their exiſtence is founded, which preſerves the imagination from that frightful ſpectacle of an exiſtence without origin, of action without liberty, and futurity without hope. Thus after having, as I think, proved myſelf a citizen of France, by my adminiſtration, as well as my writings, I wiſh to unite myſelf to a fraternity ſtill more extended—that of the whole human race: it is thus, without diſperſing our ſentiments, we may be able neverthelefs to communicate ourſelyes a great way off, and enlarge in ſome meaſure the limits of our circle: glory be to our thinking faculties for it! To that ſpiritual portion of ourſelves which can take in the paſt, dart into futurity, and intimately aſſociate itſelf with the deſtiny of men of all countries, and of all ages. Without doubt, a veil is thrown over the greater part of thoſe truths, to which our curioſity would willingly attain; but thoſe which a beneficent God has permitted us to ſee, are amply ſufficient for

our

our guide and inftruction; and we cannot, for a continuance divert our attention without a fpecies of flothful negligence, and a total indifference to the fuperior interefts of man. How little is every thing indeed, when put in competition with thofe meditations, which give to our exiftence a new extent, and which, in detaching us from the duft of the earth, feem to unite our fouls to an infinity of fpace, and our duration of a day to the eternity of time! Above all, it is for you to determine, who have fenfibility—who feel the want of a Supreme Being, and who feek to find in him that fupport fo neceffary to your weaknefs, that defender and that affurance, without which painful inquietude will be perpetually tormenting you, and troubling thofe foft, tender affections which conftitute your happinefs.

However, I muft fay, there never perhaps was a period, when it was more effentially neceffary to recall to the minds of men, the importance of religious fentiments;

ments; at prefent they are but prejudices, if we may credit the fpirit of licentioufnefs and levity; the laws dictated by fafhion; and more particularly effential fince we have had philofophical inftructions, which excite the various deviations of vanity, and rally the wanderings of the imagination.

There is not any form of religion, undoubtedly, to which ideas more or lefs myftical have not been annexed; and of which the evidence has not been in proportion to the dictatorial language, and authoritative tone, which has been made ufe of in teaching and defending it; as fuch, one might at any given period have been tempted to difpute about particular parts of worfhip, which different nations have adopted; but it is principally in the prefent age, that a certain clafs of men has fprung up, diftinguifhed for their wit and talents; and who, intoxicated by the facility with which they have gained a victory, have extended their ambition, and had the daring courage to attack the referved body

of

of that army of which the front ranks had already given way.

This ftruggle between perfons, one of whom would imperioufly rule by faith alone, whilft the other thinks he has a right to reject with difdain every thing that has not been demonftrated, will always be a fruitlefs combat ; and only ferve to nourifh blind averfion and unjuft contempt. Some feek to wound their adverfaries, others to humble them ; in the mean time the good of mankind, and the true benefit of fociety, are abfolutely loft fight of ; yes, the real love of ufeful truths, the impartial fearch after them, and the defire of pointing them out, thefe fentiments, fo amiable and fo truly laudable, feem to be entirely unknown. I fee, permit me to fay it, I fee at the two ex-tremities of the arena, the favage inquifitor, and the inconfiderate philofopher ; but nei-ther the faggots lighted by the one, nor the derifions of the other, will ever diffufe any falutary inftruction ; and in the eyes of a rational man, the intolerance of monks

C adds

adds no more to the dominion of true religious fentiments, than the jefts of a few
licentious wits have effected a triumph in
favour of philofophy.

It is between thefe oppofite opinions, and
in the midft of wanderings equally dangerous, that we muft attempt to mark out our
way; but as all the opinions of men are
fubject to change; at prefent, when their
minds are more averfe to the maxims of
intolerance, it is religion itfelf that principally needs fupport; and fuch is the daily
diminution of it, that means fupplying the
deficiency feem to be already publicly preparing.   For fome time paft we have heard
of nothing but the neceffity of compofing
a moral catechifm, in which religious principles fhould not be introduced, as re-
fourfes that are now out of date, and when
it is time they were difcarded.   Without
doubt thefe principles might be more effectually attacked, could they ever be reprefented as totally ufelefs for the maintenance of public order; and if the cold
leffons

4

leffons of a political philofophy could be fubftituted for thofe fublime ideas, which, by the fpiritual tie of religion, binds the heart and mind to the pureft morality. Let us now examine if we fhould gain any thing by the exchange; let us fee, if the means they propofe to employ can be put in competition with thofe which ought to be made ufe of; and, if they are more folid, and more efficacious; let us fee, if this new doctrine, which is recommended, will produce in the foul the fame degree of con- folation; if it is calculated for thofe hearts which are poffeffed of fenfibility; and, above all, let us attentively confider, if it can be fuitable to the meafure of intelli- gence, and the focial fituation of the greater part of mankind. In fhort, in confidering the various queftions, which in any man- ner, relate to the important fubject we have undertaken to treat, let us not be afraid to refift, as well as we can, the foolifh ambi- tion of thofe, who, availing themfelves of the fuperiority of their underftanding, wifh to deprive man of his dignity, to place him

on

on a level with the duft under his feet, and make his forefight a punifhment :—melancholy and deplorable deftiny ! from which, however, we are permitted to feek to defend ourfelves ; cruel and difaftrous opinion ! which tears up by the roots every thing which furrounds it, which relaxes the moft neceffary bands, and, in an inftant, deftroys the moft delightful charm of life.

O thou God unknown !——but whofe beneficient idea has ever filled my foul, if thou ever throweft a look on thofe efforts which man makes to approach thee, fuftain my refolution, enlighten my underftanding, raife my thoughts, and rejeft not the defire I have to unite ftill more, if poffible, the order and happinefs of fociety, with the intimate and perfeft conception of thy divinity, and the lively idea of thy fublime exiftence.

O F

OF THE

IMPORTANCE

OF

RELIGIOUS OPINIONS.

CHAP. I.

On the Connection of Religious Principles with public Order.

WE know not diſtinctly the origin of moſt political ſocieties; but as ſoon as hiſtory exhibits men united in a national body, we perceive, at the ſame time, the eſtabliſhment of public worſhip, and the application of religious ſentiments, to the

main-

maintenance of good order and fubordination. Religious fentiments, by the fanction
of an oath, bind the people to the magiftrates, and the magiftrates to their engagements; they infpire a reverential refpect for the
obligations contracted between fovereigns;
and thefe fentiments, ftill more authoritative than difcipline, attach the foldier to
his commander; in fhort, religious opinions, by their influence on the manners of individuals, have produced an infinite number of illuftrious actions and
inftances of heroical difintereftednefs, of
which hiftory has tranfmitted us the remembrance. But as we have feen a philofophy fpring up among nations the moft
enlightened, anxioufly employed in depriving religion of all that merited refpect, differtations on times far removed from us,
and the various fyftems that they would
endeavour violently to affociate with religion, would become an endlefs fource of
controverfy. It is then, by reafoning alone,
by that exercife of the mind, which be-

longs

longs equally to all countries and all ages, that we can fupport the caufe which we have taken in hand to defend. There is, perhaps, fomething weak and fervile in our wifhing to draw affiftance from ancient opinions; reafon ought not, like vanity, to adorn herfelf with old parchments, and the difplay of a genealogical tree; more digni-fied in her proceeding, and proud of her immortal nature, fhe ought to derive every thing from herfelf; fhe fhould difregard paft times, and be, if I may ufe the phrafe, the contemporary of all ages.

It was referved, particularly for fome wri-ters of our age, to attack even the utility of religion ; and to feek to fubftitute, inftead of its active influence, the inanimate inftruc-tion of a political philofophy. Religion, fay they, is a fcaffold fallen into ruins, and it is high time to give to morality a more folid fup-port. But what fupport will that be? we muft, in order to difcover, and form a juft idea of it; diftinctly confider the dif-ferent motives of action on which depend

C 4. the

the relations that fubfift between men; and it will be neceffary to eftimate, afterwards, the kind and degree of affiftance which we may reafonably expect from a like fupport.

It appears to me, that in renouncing the efficacious aid of religion, we may eafily form an idea of the means that they will endeavour to make ufe of to attach men to the obfervance of the rules of morality, and to reftrain the dangerous exceffes of their paffions. They would, undoubtedly, place a proper value on the connection which fubfifts between private and general intereft; they would avail themfelves of the authority of laws, and the fear of punifh-ment; and they would confide ftill more in the afcendancy of public opinion, and the ambition, that every one ought to have, of gaining the efteem and confidence of his fellow-creatures.

Let us examine feparately thefe different motives; and firft, attentively confidering the union of private with public intereft,

let

let us fee if this union is real, and if we
can deduce from fuch a principle any moral
inftruction truly efficacious.

Society is very far from being a perfect
work; we ought not to confider as an harmonious compofition the different relations
of which we are witneffes, and particularly
the habitual contraft of power and weaknefs, of flavery and authority, riches and
poverty, of luxury and mifery; fo much
inequality; fuch a motly piece could not
form an edifice refpectable for the juftnefs
of its proportions.

Civil and political order is not then excellent by its nature, and we cannot perceive its agreement, till we have deeply
ftudied, and formed to ourfelves thofe reflections which legiflators had to make, and
the difficulties that they had to furmount.
It is then only, with the affiftance of the
moft attentive meditation, that we difcover
how thofe particular relations, which are
eftablifhed by focial laws, form, neverthelefs,

lefs, that fyftem of equilibrium, which is moft proper to bind together an immenfe diverfity of interefts ; but a great obftacle to the influence of political morality is, the neceffity of giving, for the bafis of the love of order, an abftract and complicated idea. What effect on vulgar minds would the fcientific harmony of the whole have, oppofed daily to the fentiment of injuftice and inequality, which arifes from the afpect of every part of the focial conftitution, when we acquire the knowledge of it, in a manner folitary and circumfcribed ; and how limited is the number of thofe, who can continually draw together all the fcattered links of this vaft chain !

It could not be avoided, in the beft regulated focieties, that fome fhould enjoy, without labour or difficulty, all the conveniencies of life ; and that others, and far the greater number, fhould be obliged to earn, by the fweat of their brow, a fubfiftence the moft fcanty, and a recompenfe the moft confined. It is not to be prevented, that fome will
find,

find, when oppreſſed by ſickneſs, all the aſſiſtance which officious tenderneſs and ſkill can afford; whilſt others are reduced to partake, in public hoſpitals, the bare relief that humanity has provided for the indigent. We cannot prevent ſome from being in a ſituation to laviſh on their families all the advantages of a complete education; whilſt others, impatient to free themſelves from a charge ſo heavy, are conſtrained to watch eagerly for the firſt appearance of natural ſtrength, to make their children apply to ſome profitable labour. In ſhort, we cannot avoid perpetually contraſting the ſplendour of magnificence with the tatters which miſery diſplays. Such are the effects, inſeparable from the laws, reſpecting property. Theſe are truths, the principles of which I have had occaſion to diſcuſs in the work which I compoſed on adminiſtration and political œconomy; but I ought to repeat them here, ſince they are found cloſely connected with other general views. The eminent power of property is one of the ſocial inſtitutions, the influence of which

has

has. the greateft extent; this confideration was applicable to the commerce of grain; it ought to be prefent to the mind, in dif-quifitions on the duties of adminiftration; and it is ftill more important, when the queftion is to be examined, what kind of moral inftruction may be proper for man-kind?

In effect, if it appertains to the effence of the laws of right, conftantly to introduce and maintain an immenfe difparity in the diftribution of property; were it an effential part of thefe laws, to reduce the moft nu-merous clafs of citizens, to that which is fimply the moft neceffary; the inevitable refult of fuch a conftitution would be, to nourifh, amongft men, a fentiment of habi-tual envy and jealoufy. Vainly would you demonftrate, that thefe laws are the only ones capable of exciting labour, animating induftry, preventing diforder, and oppofing obftacles to arbitrary acts of authority; all thefe confiderations fufficient, we grant, to fix the opinion and the will of the legiflator,

ator, would not ftrike in the fame manner the man thrown on the earth, without pro-perty, without refources, and without hopes; and he will never render free homage to the beauty of the whole, when there is nothing for him but deformity, abjectnefs, and contempt.

Men, in moft of their political reafon-ings, are deceived by refemblances and ana-logies: the intereft of fociety is certainly compofed of the interefts of all its mem-bers; but it does not follow from this ex-plication, that there is an immediate and conftant correfpondence between the ge-neral and private intereft; fuch an approxi-mation, could only be applicable to an imaginary focial ftate; and which we might reprefent as divided into many parts, of which the rich would be the head, and the poor the feet and hands: but political fociety is not one and the fame body, except under certain relations, whilft, relatively to other interefts, it partakes in as many ramifications of them as there are individuals,

Thefe

Thofe confiderations, to which we annex an idea of general intereft, would be very often fufceptible of numberlefs obfervations; but the principles, we are accuftomed to receive and tranfmit, in their moft common acceptation; and we difcover not the mixt ideas which compofe them, but at the moment when we analyze the principles, in order to draw confequences from them, in like manner as we perceive not the variety of colours in a ray of light, till the moment we divide them by means of a prifm.

The formation of focial laws, with reafon, ought to appear one of our moft admirable conceptions; but this fyftem is not fo united in all its parts, that a ftriking diforder would always be the neceffary effect of fome irregular movement: thus the man, who violates the laws, does not quickly difcover the relation of his actions with the intereft of fociety; but at the inftant enjoys, or thinks to joy, the fruit of his ufurpations.

Should

Should a theatre be on fire, it is certainly the intereſt of the aſſembly that every one go out with order; but if the people, moſt diſtant from the entrance, believed they ſhould be able to eſcape ſooner from the danger, by forcing their way through the crowd which ſurrounds them, they would aſſuredly determine on this violence, unleſs a coercive power prevented them; yet the common utility of reſtricting ourſelves to order in ſuch circumſtances, would appear an idea more ſimple, and more diſtinct, than is the univerſal importance of maintaining civil order in ſociety.

The only natural defence of this order, is government; its function obliges it ever to conſider the whole; but the need which it has of power to carry its decrees into execution, proves evidently, that it is the adverſary of many, even when acting in the name of all.

We are then under a great illuſion, if we hope to be able to found morality on the

con-

connection of private intereft with that of
the public; and if we imagine, that the
empire of focial laws can be feparated from
the fupport of religion. The authority of
thefe laws has nothing decifive for thofe
who have not affifted to eftablifh them; and
were we to give to the hereditary diftinctions
of property an origin the moft remote, it is
no lefs true, on this account, that the poor
fucceeding inhabitants of the earth, ftruck
with the unequal divifion of its rich do-
mains, and not perceiving the limits and
lines of feparation traced by nature, would
have fome right to fay; thefe compacts, thefe
partitions, this diverfity of lots, which procures to fome abundance and repofe; to
others, poverty and labour; all this legiflation, in fhort, is only advantageous to a
fmall number of privileged men; and we
will not fubfcribe to it, unlefs compelled
by the fear of perfonal danger. What are
then, they would add, thefe ideas of right
and wrong, with which we are entertained?
What are thefe differtations on the neceffity
of adopting fome order in fociety, and of
obferving

observing rules? Our mind bends not to those principles, which, general in theory, become particular in practice. We find some satisfaction and compensation, when the idea of virtue, of submiffion, and of sacrifice, are united to religious sentiments; when we believe we shall render an account of our actions to a Supreme Being, whose laws and will we adore, and from whom we have received every thing, and whose approbation presents itself to our eyes, as a motive of emulation, and an object of recompense: but if the contracted bounds of life limit the narrow circle in which all our interest ought to confine itself, where all our speculations and our hopes terminate, what respect owe we then to those whom nature has formed our equals? To those men sprung from lifeless clay, to return to it again with us, and to be loft for ever in the same duft? They have only invented these laws of justice, to be more tranquil usurpers. Let them descend from their exalted rank, that they may be put on our level, or, at leaft, present us with a parti-

tion

tion lefs unequal, and we fhall then be able to conceive, that the obfervance of the laws of right is of importance to us; till then, we fhall have juft motives for being the enemies of civil order, which we find fo difadvantageous; and we do not comprehend how, in the midft of fo many gratifications which excite our envy, it is, in the name of our own intereft, that we ought to renounce them.

Such is the fecret language which men, overwhelmed with the diftrefs of their fituation, would not fail to ufe; or thofe who, merely in a ftate of habitual inferiority, found themfelves continually hurt by the fplendid fight of luxury and magnificence.

It would not be an eafy tafk to combat thefe fentiments, by endeavouring to paint forcibly the vanity of pleafure in general, and the illufion of moft of thofe objects which captivate our ambition, and the apathy which follows in their train. Thefe reflections, without doubt, have their weight and

and efficacy; but if we attentively confider the fubject, every thing that deferves the name of confolation in this world, cannot be addreffed with any advantage; but to minds prepared for mild fentiments, by an idea of religion and of piety, more or lefs diftinct; we cannot, in the fame manner, relieve the barren and ferocious defpondency of an unhappy and envious man, who has thrown far behind him all hope. Concentred in the bare interefts of a life, which is for him eternity, and the univerfe itfelf; it is the paffion of the moment which enflaves him, and nothing can difengage him from it; he has not the means to catch any vague idea, nor of being content; and as even reafon has need, every inftant, of the aid of the imagination, he cannot be encouraged, either by the difcourfe of his friends, or his own reflections.

Befides, if we can maintain, in general, that the allotments of happinefs and mifery are more equal than we imagine; if we can reafonably advance, that labour is pre-

ferable

ferable to idlenefs; if we can fay, with truth, that embarraffments and inquietudes often accompany wealth, and that contentment of mind appears to be the portion of the middle ftate of life; we ought to acknowledge, at the fame time, that thefe axioms are only perfectly juft in the eyes of the moralift, who confiders man in a comprehenfive point of view, and who makes his calculation upon a whole life : but, in the recurrence of our daily defires and hopes, it is impoffible to excite to labour by the expectation of fortune, and detract, at the fame time, this fortune, in decrying the pleafures and conveniences that it procures. Thefe fubtle ideas, without excepting thofe which may be defended, can never be applicable to real circumftances ;and if we fometimes ufe with fuccefs fuch kind of reflections to alleviate unavailing forrow and regret, it is when we have only fhadows to cope with.

In fhort, when we have reduced to precept, all the well known reflections, on the

apparent,

apparent, but delufive advantages of rank and fortune, we cannot prevent uncultivated minds from being continually ftruck with the extreme inequality of the different contracts which the rich make with the poor; it might be faid, in thofe moments, that one . portion of mankind was formed only for the convenience of another; the poor man facrifices his time and his ftrength to multiply round the rich gratifications of every kind; and he, when he gives in exchange the moft fcanty fubfiftence, does not deprive himfelf of any thing; fince the extent of his phyfical wants is bounded by the laws of nature: equality then is only re-eftablifhed by the laffitude and apathy which the enjoyment even of pleafure produces. But thefe difgufts compofe the back ground in the picture of life; the people perceive them not; and as they have only been acquainted with want, they cannot form any idea of the langour attendant on fatiety.

Will

Will any one imprudently fay, that if the diftinctions of property are an obftacle to the eftablifhment of a political fyftem of morality, 'we ought, therefore, to labour to deftroy them? But if in paft ages, when the different degrees of talents and knowledge were not fo unequal, men were not able to preferve a community of poffeffions, can you imagine, that thefe primitive relations could be re-eftablifhed at a time when the fuperiority of rank and power is enforced by the immoveable ftrength of difciplined armies?

Befides, when even in the compofition of an ideal world, we fhould have introduced the moft exact divifion of the various poffeffions efteemed by men, it would ftill be neceffary, to preferve a fyftem of real equality, that every one fhould execute faithfully the duties impofed on him by univerfal morality; fince this is incumbent on every individual, for the facrifice that all the members of fociety have made; which fociety ought to recompenfe every
citizen

citizen in particular, for the reftriction to which he fubmits himfelf.

It is effential to obferve ftill further, that it is not only perfonal intereft, when clearly underftood, which ought to be annexed to the idea of public order; it is the fame intereft when led aftray by the paffions, then a mere guide is no longer fufficient; a yoke muft be impofed; a check always acting, which muft be ufed abfolutely. Nothing can be more chimerical than to pretend to reftrain a man, hurried on by an impetuous imagination, by endeavouring to recal to his remembrance fome principles and inftructions, which, in the terms of an academic thefis *, ought to be the *refult of analyfis, of methodizing, of the art of dividing, of developing, and circumfcribing ideas.*

* Thefis propofed by the French Academy, with a prize, for the beft Catechifm of Morals, the inftructions of which were to be founded on the principles of natural right only.

D 4   It

It would be, at prefent, a hardy enterprize, to attempt to conduct men by reafon
alone, fince the firft thing that reafon difcovers is its own weaknefs; but when we
want to reft on maxims which admit of
controverfy; when we wifh to oppofe to
the ftrong motive of perfonal intereft, a
moral confideration which cannot act but
with the concurrence of profound reflection; we recollect the doctrine of the firft
œconomifts, who, in eftablifhing the ex-
travagant principles refpecting an exclufive
right of exporting or monopolizing grain,
put off the care of preventing popular
commotions till they fhould happen.

It appears to me, that falfe reafoning,
on the union of private with public intereft, arifes from applying to the prefent
ftate of fociety, the principles which have
ferved as the bafe for their formation; this
very natural confufion is one grand fource
of error. Let us try to render clear a propofition, which, at firft, appears difficult
to comprehend; and in this light we will
fuppofe,

suppofe, for a moment the future generation affembled in idea, in an imaginary
world, and ignorant before they inhabit the,
earth, who thofe individuals are that fhall
be born of parents loaded with the gifts of
fortune, and thofe who are befet with mifery from their cradle. They are in-
ftructed in the principles of civil rights,
and the convenience of the laws of order,
has been reprefented to them, and a fketch
is drawn of the diforder, which would be
the inevitable confequence of a continual
variation in the divifion of property; then
all thofe who are to compofe the new
generation, equally uncertain of the lot that
the chance of birth referves for them, fubfcribe unanimoufly to thofe events which
await them; and at the very moment in
which the relations of fociety exift only in
fpeculation, it might be truly faid, that the
perfonal intereft is loft in the public; but
this identity ceafes, when each, arrived on
the earth, has taken poffeffion of his lot;
it is then no longer poffible, that the various
perfonal interefts fhould concur to the
main-

maintenance of thefe prodigious gradations of rank and fortune, which are derived from the chance of birth; and thofe to whom cares and wants have fallen, will not be refigned to the inferiority of their condition, but by a grand religious principle alone, which can make them perceive an eternal juftice, and place them in imagination before time, and before the laws.

There is nothing fo eafy, as the eftablifhment of conventions, and making rules to be obferved, till the moment of the drawing of a lottery; every one then, at the fame point of view, finds all good, all juft, and well contrived, and peace reigns by common agreement; but as foon as the blanks and prizes are known, the mind changes, the temper grows four; and without the check of authority, it would become unmanageable, envious, quarrelfome, and fometimes unjuft and violent.

We

We fee, however, the confequence to be drawn from the preceding reflections; that political focieties in contemplation, and in reality, prefent to our obfervation two different periods; and as thefe periods are not feparated by any apparent limits, they are almoft always confounded in the mind of the political moralift. He who believes in the union of private intereft with that of the public, and who celebrates this harmony, has only confidered fociety in its general and primitive plan; he who thinks, on the contrary, that the whole is wrong and difcordant, becaufe there is a great difference of power and fortune, has confidered it only under its actual viciffitudes. Both thefe miftakes have received a fanction from celebrated writers. The man hurried away by a lively imagination, and ftrongly impreffed by prefent objects, has been ftruck by the inequality of conditions; and the philofopher, who, tranfported by his abstractions beyond the circle of human fociety, has only perceived thofe relations and principles which led men to form the firft

inftitution

inftitution of civil law's. Thus, every where
we fee, that moft difputes relate to mere
difference of pofitions, and to the various
points of view in which the fame fubject is
confidered; there are fo many ftations in
the moral world, that, according to that
which we choofe, the picture changes entirely.

Hitherto we have endeavoured to underftand the effect which we might expect
from a fyftem of morality, by applying this
kind of inftruction only to private intereft,
when moft clearly afcertained. It remains
now to fhow, that every fpecies of education, which demands time and reflection,
cannot belong, in any manner, to the clafs
of men moft numerous; and to be fenfible
of this truth, it is fufficient to turn our attention on the focial ftate of thofe who are
deftitute of property, and talents which
might fupply its place; obliged to have recourfe to hard labour, where nothing is required but to employ their bodily ftrength,
their concurrence, and the power of riches
reduce

-reduce the wages of this numerous class to what is abfolutely neceffary; they cannot without difficulty fupport their children, and they may well be impatient of ·qualifying them for ufeful occupations to· relieve themfelves; and this prevents their being fent to public fchools, except during their infancy: thus, ignorance and poverty are in the midft of our focieties, and the hereditary lot of the greater part of the citizens; there is only to be found an alleviation of this general law, in thofe countries where the conftitution of the government encourages the high price of, labour, and gives the poor fome means of refifting the defpotifm of fortune. However, if fuch is the inevitable effect of our civil and political legiflation, how fhall we be able to bind men without diftinction, to the maintenance of public order, by any inftruction, I do not fay complicated, but to which the exercife of long reafoning forms only a neceffary introduction? It would not be fufficient to endow inftitutions, it would be ftill more neceffary to pay the fcholars for their time; since, fince, for the lower clafs, time is, even very early in life, their only means of fub- fiftence.

Neverthelefs, morality is not, like other human fciences, a knowledge, that we may be at liberty to acquire at our leifure; the quickeft inftruction is ftill too flow, fince man has a natural power of doing evil before his mind is in a ftate to apply to reflection, and connect the moft fimple ideas.

It is not then a political catechifm which would be proper for the inftruction of the people; it is not a courfe of precepts founded on the union of public and private intereft, which can fuit with the • meafure of their underftanding; when a doctrine of that kind would appear as juft as it feems to me liable to be difputed, they will never be able to render the principles of it diftinct enough, to apply them to the purpofes of inftructing thofe whofe education continues for fo fhort a time. Morality, founded on religion, by its active influence,

fluence, is precifely adapted to the particular
fituation of the greater number of men;
and this agreement is fo perfect, that it feems
one of the remarkable features of univerfal
harmony. Religion alone has power to
perfuade with celerity, becaufe it excites
paffion, whilft it informs the underftanding, becaufe it alone has 'the means of
rendering obvious what it recommends;
becaufe it fpeaks in the name of God, and
it is eafy to infpire refpect for him, whofe
power is every where evident to the eyes of
the fimple and fkilful, to the eyes of children, and men advanced to maturity.

In order to attack this truth, let it not
be faid, that the idea of a God is of all
others the moft incomprehenfible; and if
it is poffible to derive ufeful inftruction
from fo metaphyfical a principle, we ought
to expect more good from precepts which
depend on the common relations of life.
Such an objection is a mere fubtilty; the
diftinct knowledge of the effence of a God,
the creator of the world, is, undoubtedly
above

above the comprehension of men of every age, and all faculties; but it is not the same with the vague idea of a heavenly power, who punishes and who rewards; parental authority, and the helplessness of infancy, prepare us early for ideas of obedience and command; and the world is such a stupendous wonder, a theatre of such continual prodigies, that it is easy to annex, at an early period, $hope$ and fear to the $idea$ of a Supreme Being. Thus, the infinity of a God, creator and director of the universe, is so far from having power to divert our respect and adoration, that even the clouds with which he invelopes himself, lend a new force to religious sentiments. A man often remains uninterested amidst the discoveries of his reason; but it is always easy to move him, whenever we address ourselves to his imagination; for this faculty of our mind excites us continually to action, by presenting to our eyes a great space, and by keeping us always at a certain distance from the object we have in view. Man is so disposed to wonder at a power, of which

he

he is ignorant of the fprings; this fentiment is fo natural to him, that what we ought to guard againft the moft in his education, is the inconfiderate infinuation of various terrors, of which he is fufceptible. Thus, not only the true idea of the exiftence of an All-powerful God, but mere credulous faith in fuperftitious opinions, will always have more power over the common clafs of men, than abftract precepts, or general confiderations. I know not even, if it might not be faid, with truth, that the future of this fhort life, when we contemplate it, is further from us than the diftant perfpective offered to the mind by religion; becaufe our imagination is lefs reftrained, and the minuteft defcription of reafon can never equal in power, the lively and impulfive ardour of the affections of our fouls.

I refume the feries of my reflections, and fet down here an important obfervation: which is, that the more the increafe of taxes keeps the people in defpondency and mifery, the

E   more

more indifpenfable is it to give them a religious education; for it is in the irritation of
wretchednefs, that we all have need of a
powerful reftraint and of daily confolations.
The fucceffive abufe of ftrength and authority, in overturning all the relations which
originally exifted between men, have raifed,
in the midft of them, an edifice fo artificial,
and in which there reigns fo much difproportion, that the idea of a God is become
more neceffary than ever, to ferve as a le-
veller of this confufed affemblage of difpari-
ties; and if we can ever imagine, that a people fhould exift, fubject only to the laws of
a political morality, we fhould reprefent,
without doubt, a rifing nation, which,
would be reftrained by the vigour of patriotifm in its prime; a nation which would
occupy a country where riches had not had
time to accumulate; where the diftance of
the habitations from each other contributed
to the maintenance of domeftic manners;
where agriculture, that fimple and peaceful
occupation, would be the favourite employment; where the work of the hands
would

would obtain a recompenſe proportioned to the ſcarcity of the workmen, and the exten‑ ſive uſefulneſs of the labour; we ſhould re‑ preſent, in ſhort, a nation where the laws and the form of government would favour, during a long time, equality of rank and property. But in our ancient kingdoms in Europe, where the growth of riches conti‑ nually augments the difference of fortunes and the diſtance of conditions; — in our old political bodies, where we are crowded together, and where miſery and magnificence are ever mingled, it muſt be a morality, fortified by religion, that ſhall reſtrain theſe numerous ſpectators of ſo many poſſeſſions and objects of envy, and who, placed ſo near every thing which they call happineſs, can yet never aſpire to it.

It may be aſked, perhaps, in conſequence of theſe reflections, whether religion, which ſtrengthens every tie, and fortifies every obli‑ gation, is not favourable to tyranny? Such a concluſion would be unreaſonable; but religion, which affords comfort under every

E 2 afflíction,

affliction, would necessarily sooth also the
ills which arise from despotism; however,
it is neither the origin, nor the support of
it : religion, well understood, would not
lend its support but to order and justice ;
and the instructions of political morality
proposes to itself the same end.   Thus, in
both plans of education, the rights of the
sovereign, as well as those of the citizens,
constitute simply one of the elementary
parts of the general system of our duties.

I shall only observe, that the insufficiency
of political morality would appear still more
obvious, in a country where the nation, subject to the authority of an absolute prince,
would have no share in the government ; for
personal interest no longer having an habitual
communication with the general interest,
there would be just ground to fear, that in
wishing to hold out the union of these two
interests as the essential motive of virtue, the
greater number would retain only this
idea, that personality was admitted for
the first principle ; and consequently every
one

one ought to referve to himfelf the right of judging of the times and circumftances when felf-love and patriotifm are to be feparated, or united. And how many errors would not this produce? Public good, like all abftract ideas, has not a precife definition; it is for the greater part of mankind a fea without bounds, and it requires ·not much addrefs or fhrewdnefs to confound all our analogies. We may know how we would form, according to our tafte, the alliance of all the moral ideas, in confidering with what facility men know how to reconcile with one quality the habitual infirmities of their character; he who wounds without difcretion, prides himfelf in his franknefs and courage; he who is cowardly and timid in his fentiments and in his words, boafts of his caution and circumfpection; and by a new refinement of which I have feen fingular examples, he who afks of the fovereign pecuniary favours, endeavours to perfuade him that he is impelled to this folicitation, only by a noble love of honourable diftinction; every one is ingenious in fixing

E 3   the

the point of union which connects his paffions with fome virtue : would they then be
lefs expert at finding fome conformity between their own intereft and that of the
public ?

I cannot, I avow, without difguft, and
even horror, conceive the abfurd notion of
a political fociety, deftitute of that governing motive afforded by religion, and reftrained
only by a pretended connexion of their private
intereft with the general.   What circumfcribed judges ! What a multiplicity of opinions, fentiments, and wills ! All would be
in confufion, if we left to men the liberty
of drawing their own conclufions : they
muft abfolutely have a fimple idea to regulate their conduct, efpecially when the application of this principle may be infinitely
diverfified. God in delivering his laws on
Mount Sinai, had need but to fay, *Thou
fhalt not fteal*; and with the awful idea of
that God, whom every thing recals to our
minds, whom every thing impreffes on the
human heart, this fhort commandment
preferves,

preferves, at all times, a fufficient authority; but when political philofophy fays,
Thou fhalt not fteal, it would be neceffary
to add to this precept a train of reafoning,
on the laws of right, on the inequality of
conditions, and on the various focial relations;
in order to perfuade us that it comprehends
every motive, that it anfwers all objections,
and refifts all attacks. It is neceffary, further,
that by the leffons of this philofophy the
moft uncultivated minds fhould be quali-
fied to follow the different ramifications
which unite, difunite, and reunite afrefh
the perfonal to the public intereft: what
an enterprife! It is, perhaps, like wifhing
to employ a courfe of anatomy, in order to
direct a child in the choice of fuch ali-
ments as are proper for it, inftead of beginning to conduct it by the counfels and
the authority of its mother.

The fame remarks are applicable to all
the virtues, of which the obfervance is effential to public-order: what method would

E 4   plain

plain reasoning take to ·persuade a single man, that he ought not to deprive a husband of the affections of his wife? Where would you assign him a distinct recompense for the sacrifice of his passion? What windings should we not be obliged to run over, to demonstrate to an ambitious man, that he ought not, in secret, to calumniate his rival; to the solitary miser, armed with indifference, that he ought not to remove himself from every occasion of doing good; to a disposition ardent and revengeful, that he ought not to obey those urgent impulses which hurry him away; to a man in want, that he ought not to have recourse to falsehood to procure attention, or to deceive in any other manner? And how many other positions would offer the same difficulties, and still greater? ·Abstract ideas, the best arranged, can never conquer us but by long arguments, since the peculiar nature of these ideas is to disengage our reasoning from the feelings, and consequently from striking and sudden impressions; besides, political morality, like every

thing

thing which the mind only produces, would be always for us merely an opinion; an opinion from which we fhould have a right to appeal, at any time, to the tribunal of our reafon. The leffons of men are nothing but reprefentations of their judgment; and the fentiments of fome draw not the will of others. There is not any principle of morality, which, under forms abfolutely human, would not be fufceptible of exceptions, or of fome modification; and there is nothing fo compounded as the idea of the connexion of virtue with happinefs: in fhort, while our underftanding has a difficulty in comprehending and clearly diftinguifhing that union, the objects of our paffions are every where apparent, and all our fenfes are preengaged by them. The mifer beholds gold and filver; the ambitious man, thofe honours which are conferred on others; the debauchee, the objects of his luxury; virtue has nothing left but reafoning; and is then in want of being fuftained by religious

fentiments

fentiments, and by the enlivening hopes which accompany them.

Thus, in a government where you would wifh to fubftitute political morality for a religious education, it would become, perhaps, indifpenfible to guard men from receiving any ideas calculated to exalt their minds; it would be neceffary to divert them from the different competitions which excite felf-love and ambition; they muft withdraw themfelves from the habitual fociety of women; and it would be ftill more incumbent on them to abolifh the ufe of money, that attracting and confufed image of all kinds of gratifications: in fhort, in taking from men their religious hopes, and depriving them thus of the encouragements to virtue which the imagination gives birth to, every exertion muft be tried to prevent this unruly imagination from feconding vice, and all the paffions contrary to public order: it was becaufe Telemachus was accompanied by a Divinity, that he could, without danger, vifit the fumptuous court

of

of Sefoſtris, and the enchanting abodes of Eucharis and Calypſo.

It is indeed an age the moſt pleaſant, as well as the ſafeſt of our life, which we cannot paſs without a guide; we muſt then, in order to paſs with ſecurity through the tempeſtuous days of youth, have principles which command us, and not reflections to counſel us; theſe have not any power but in proportion to the vigour of the mind, and the mind is only formed by experience and a long conflict of opinions.

Religious inſtructions have the peculiar advantage of ſeizing the imagination, and of intereſting our ſenſibility, thoſe two brilliant faculties of our early years : thus, then even ſuppoſing that we could eſtabliſh a courſe of political morality, ſufficiently propped by reaſoning, for defending from vice men enlightened by maturity, I ſhould ſtill ſay, that a ſimilar philoſophy would not be ſuitable to youth, and that this armour is too heavy for them.

In

In ſhort, the leſſons of human wiſdom, which cannot govern us during the ardour of our paſſions, are equally inſufficient, when our ſtrength being broken by diſeaſe, we are no longer in a ſtate to comprehend a variety of relations; inſtead of which, ſuch is the pleaſing emotions that accompany, the language of religion, that in the ſucceſſive decline of our faculties, this language ſtill keeps pace with them.

Neverthelefs, if we were ever to be perſuaded, that there was on earth a more certain encouragement to virtue than religion, its powers would be immediately weakened; it would not be half ſo intereſting, nor could reign when divided; if its ſentiments did not overflow, as, we may ſay, the human heart, all its influence would vaniſh.

Religious inſtruction, in aſſembling all the means proper to excite men to, virtue, neglects not, it is true, to point out the relations, which exiſt between the obſervance of the laws of morality and the happineſs of life;

life; but it is as an acceffary motive, that thefe confiderations are prefented; and it is not neceffary to fupport them by the fame proofs as a fundamental principle requires. Alfo, when people are taught early that vices and crimes lead to mifery on earth, thefe doctrines make not a lafting impreffion on them, but in proportion as we fucceed at the fame time, in convincing them of the conftant influence of a Providence over all the events of this world.

One important reafon ftill exempts religious profeffors, from attaching themfelves to demonftrate, that the principal advantages which excite the envy of men, are an abfolute confequence of the obfervance of the laws of order: -it is, that facrifices, fupported by an idea of duty, are changed into real fatisfactions; and the fentiments, which the virtuous enjoy from piety, compofe an effential part of their happinefs. But what confolation can a man have by way of return; what fecret approbation can we grant him, when

when we know not any other authority than that of political morality, and when virtue is nothing but an oppofition between private and public intereft?

Religion certainly propofes to man his own happinefs, as an object and ultimate end; but as this happinefs is placed at a diftance, religion conducts us to it by wholefome reftrictions and temporary facrifices; it regards only the fublimeft part of us, that which difunites us from the prefent moment, in order to connect us with futurity; it offers us hopes, which withdraw us from worldly intereft, fo far as is neceflary to prevent us from being immoderately devoted to the diforderly impreffions of our fenfes, and the tyranny of our paffions. Irreligion, on the contrary, whofe leffons teach us, that we are only mafters of the prefent moment, concentres us more and more within ourfelves, and there is nothing beautiful or good in this condition; for grandeur, of every kind, relates to the extent of thofe relations which we compre-

comprehend; and, in a like acceptation, our fentiments fubmit to the fame laws.

Thofe who reprefent the obligations of religion as indifferent, affure us, that we may repofe fafely the maintenance of morality on fome general fentiments, which we have adopted; but do not confider that thefe fentiments derive their origin, and almoft all their force, from that fpirit of religion which they wifh to weaken. Yes, even humanity, this emotion of a noble foul, is animated and fortified by the idea of a Supreme Being; the alliance between men holds but feebly from the conformity of their organization; nor can it be attributed to the fimilitude of their paffions, that continual fource of fo much hatred; it depends effentially on our connexion with the fame author, the fame fuperintendant, the fame judge; it is founded on the equality of our right to the fame hopes, and on that train of duties inculcated by education, and rendered refpectable by the habitual dominion of reli-

gious

gious opinions. Alas! it is a melancholy
avowal, that men have fo many infirmities,
fo much injuftice, felfifhnefs, and ingratitude, at leaft, in the eyes of thofe who
have obferved them collectively, that we
never can keep them in harmony by the mere
leffons of wifdom : it is not always becaufe they are amiable that we love them;
it is fometimes, and very often indeed, becaufe
we ought to love them, that we find them
amiable. Yes, goodnefs and forbearance, thefe
qualities the moft fimple, ftill require to be
compared, from time to time, with an idea
general and predominate, the band of all our
virtues. The paffions of others wound us
in fo many ways, and there is often fo
much depth and energy in our felf-love;
that we have need of fome fuccour to be
conftantly generous in our fentiments, and
to be really interefted for all our fellow-creatures, in the midft of whom we are placed.

In fhort, not to diffemble, if a man once
came to confider himfelf as a being that is
the child of chance, or of blind neceffity,
and tending only to the duft from whence

4   he

he fprung, and to which he muft return,
he would defpife himfelf; and far from
feeking to rife to noble and virtuous reflections, he would confider this fpecies of
ambition as a fantaftic idea, which confumes
in a vain and illufory manner, a part of thofe
fleeting minutes which he has to pafs on
earth; and all his attention being fixed on
the fhortnefs of life, and on the eternal
filence which muft clofe the fcene, he would
only think *how to devour this reign of a
moment.*

How dangerous then would it be, on
this fuppofition, to fhow to men the extremity of the chain which unites them
together! It is in worldly affairs this
knowledge of having received the laft favour, which renders them ungrateful towards thofe from whom they no longer expect any thing; and the fame fentiment
would weaken the power of morality if our
leafe was manifeftly only for this world. It
is then religion which ought to ftrengthen
thofe ties, and defend the entire fyftem of
our duty againft the ftratagems of reafoning

and

and the artifices of our minds; it is neceffary, in order to oblige all men, to confider
with refpect the laws of morality, to teach
them early that the focial virtues are an
homage rendered to the perfections and to
the beneficent intentions of the Sovereign
Author of Nature, of that Infinite Being
who is pleafed with the prefervation of order, and the private facrifices which the ac-
complifhment of this grand defign requires.
And when I fee modern philofophers tracing, with an able hand, the general plan of
our duties; when I fee them fix with judgment the reciprocal obligations of citizens,
and giving, at laft, for the bafis to this legiflation, perfonal intereft and the love of
praife: I recollect the fyftem of thofe In-
dian philofophers, who, after having ftudied
the revolutions of the heavenly bodies, being
perplexed to determine the power which
fuftained the vaulted firmament, thought
they had freed it from difficulty, by placing
the univerfe on the back of an elephant; and
this elephant on a tortoife. We fhall imitate thefe philofophers, and, like them, fhall
never proceed but by degradation, whenever,

ever, by endeavouring to form a chain of duties and moral principles, we do not place the laſt link above worldly conſiderations, and beyond the limits of our ſocial conventions.

F 2 CHAP.

C H A P. II.

The same Subject continued. A Parallel between the Influence of Religious Principles, and of Laws and Opinions.

AFTER having examined, as I have juft done, in the preceding chapter, if it were poffible to found morality on the connexion of private with public intereft, it remains for me to confider, if the punifhments inflicted by the fovereign, if the fceptre, which public opinion fways, have fufficient power to reftrain men, and bind them to the obfervance of their duty.

It is neceffary to proceed by common ideas, in order to advance one degree in the refearch of truth : thus I ought at firft, in this place, to recollect, that the penal laws cannot be applied but to offences known and proved; this confideration contracts their power within a very narrow circle;

however,

however, ‘crimes fecretly committed, are
not the only ones which are beyond the
cognizance of laws; we muft place in this
rank every reprehenfible action, which, for
want of a diftinct character, can never be
pointed out; the number of them is prodigious: the rigour of parents, ingratitude
of children, the inhumanity of abandoning
their nurfes, treachery in friendfhip, the
violation of domeftic comfort, difunion
fown in the bofoms of families, levity of
principles in every focial connexion, perfi-
dious counfels, artful and flanderous infi-
nuations, rigorous exercife of authority,
favour and partiality of judges, their inat-
tention, their idlenefs and feverity, endeavours to obtain places of importance,
with a confcioufnefs of incapacity, corrupt flatteries addreffed to fovereigns or
minifters, ftatefmen indifferent to public
good, their vile and pernicious jealoufies,
and their political diffenfions, excited in
order to render themfelves neceffary, wars
inftigated by ambition, intolerance under
the cover of zeal; in fhort, many other fa-

F 3   tal

tal evils which the laws cannot either follow or defcribe, and which often do much mifchief, before they give any opportunity for public cenfure. We ought not even to defire that this cenfure pafs certain bounds, becaufe authority, applied to obfcure faults, or thofe fufceptible of various interpretations, eafily degenerates into tyranny; and as there is nothing fo tranfitory as thought, nothing fo fecret as our fentiments; none but an invifible power, whofe authority feems to participate of the divine, has a right to enter into the fecrets of our hearts.

It is then only, at the tribunal of his own confcience, that a man can be interrogated about a number of actions and intentions which efcape the infpection of government. Let us beware of overturning the authority of a judge fo active and enlightened; let us beware of weakening it voluntarily, and let us not be fo imprudent as to repofe only on focial difcipline. I will even venture to fay, that the power of confcience

confcience is perhaps ftill more neceffary in the age we live in, than in any of the preceding; though fociety no longer prefents us with a view of thofe vices and crimes which fhock us by their deformity; yet licencioufnefs of morals, and refinement of manners, have almoft imperceptibly blended good and evil, vice and decency, falfehood and truth, felfifhnefs and magnanimity; it is more important then ever, to oppofe to this fecret depravity, an interior authority, which pries into the myfterioüs windings of difguife, and whofe action may be as penetrating as our diffimulation feems artful and well contrived.

It is, undoubtedly, becaufe a fimilar authority appears abfolutely neceffary to the maintenance of public order, that feveral philofophic writers have endeavoured to introduce it as a principle of atheifm. In fuch a fyftem the whole is fictitious; they fpeak of our blufhing at the recollection of our follies, of dreading our own fecret reproaches, and of being afraid of the con-

demnation,

demnation, which, in the calm of reflection, we shall pronounce against ourselves; but these sentiments, which have so much force with the idea of a God, they know not what to unite them with, when they would give only for a guide the most active personal interest, and when all the grand communications, established, between men by religious opinions, are absolutely broken; conscience is then an expression void of meaning, a useless word in the language. We may still feel remorse, that is to say, regret at being deceived in the pursuits of ambition, in promoting our interest, in the choice of means which we employ to obtain the respect and praise of others; in short, in the various calculations of our worldly advantage: but such remorse is only an exaltation of our self-love; we deify, in some measure, our judgment and understanding, and we make at last all our actions appear before these false idols, to reproach us with our errors and weaknesses; we thus voluntarily become our own tormentors; but when this persecution is too importunate, we have it in our

power

power to command our tyrants .to ufe more indulgence towards us. It is not the fame with the reproaches of confcience; the fentiments which produce them have nothing compounded or artificial in them, we cannot . corrupt our judge, nor enter into a compromife with him; that which feduces men never deceives him, and amidft the giddinefs of profperity, in the intoxication of the greateft fuccefs, his looks are inevitably fixed on us; and we cannot but with terror enjoy the applaufe and the triumphs which we have not merited.

We read in feveral modern books, that with good laws we fhould always have morality fufficient; but I cannot adopt this opinion. Man is a being fo compounded, and his relations with his fpecies are fo various and fo fine, that to regulate his mind, and direct his conduct, he has need of a multitude of fentiments, on which the commands of the fovereign have not any hold; they are all fimple and declared duties, which the legiflators have reduced to precepts, and this

rough

rough building, termed civil laws, leaves vacancies throughout. The laws require merely a blind obedience; and as they enjoin and defend only actions, are abfolutely in-different to the private fentiments of men; the moral edifice which they raife is in fe-veral parts a mere exterior form, and it is at the roof, if I may fay fo, that they have begun. Religion proceeds in a manner dia-metrically oppofite; it is in the heart, it is in the receffes of confcience, that it lays its firft bafe; it appears to be acquainted with the grand fecrets of nature; it fows in the earth a grain, and this grain is nourifhed, and transformed into numerous branches, which, without any effort, fpring up, and extend themfelves to all dimenfions and in every kind of form.

I will fuppofe, neverthelefs, that we be-lieved it fufficient for the maintenance of public order, to reduce morality to the fpirit of civil laws, it would ftill be out of the power of men to draw from this affimilation familiar inftructions proper to form a code.

of

of education; for thefe laws, fimple in their commands, are not fo in their principles. We perceive not immediately why revenge, the moft juft, is prohibited; why we have not the power to do ourfelves juftice by the fame means a ravifher would ufe; why we have not a right to refift with violence the tyrannic oppreffor; in fhort, why certain actions, fome indifferent in themfelves, and fome hurtful to others, are condemned in a general and uniform manner: a kind of combination is neceffary to difcover, that the legiflator himfelf is wandering from natural ideas, in order to prevent every perfon from being a judge in his own caufe, and to avoid that, thofe exceptions and diftinctions, of which every circumftance is fufceptible, might never be determined by the judgment of individuals. In the fame manner, from thofe indirect motives, the laws treat with more rigour an offence difficult to define, than a diforder more reprehenfible in itfelf; but of which the exceffes might be eafily perceived: and they obferve ftill the fame rule with refpect

to

to crimes which are furrounded by greater allurements, though this feduction is even a motive for indulgence in the eyes of fimple juftice; in fhort, the laws, in adopting a more determinate method, to conftrain debtors to the difcharge of their obligations, prove that they are not compaffionate to unforefeen misfortunes, nor actuated by other motives of equity which merit an equal intereft; all their attention is fixed on the relation of engagements with the political refources, which arife from commerce and its tranfactions. There exifts thus a multitude of prohibitions of punifhments, or gradations in the penalties, which have not any connexion but with the general views of the legifla-, tion, and agree not with the circumfcribed good fenfe, which determines the judgment of individuals. It is then often, by confiderations very extenfive and complicated, that an action is criminal or reprehenfible in the eyes of the law: thus, we know not how to erect, on this bafe alone, a fyf-tem of morality; of which every one can have a clear perception; and fince the le-

giflator

giflator carefully avoids fubmitting any thing
to private examination, becaufe he facrifices
often to this principle natural juftice, how
then can he wifh, at the fame time, to
give us for a rule of conduct a political
morality, which is all founded on reafoning?

It is of confequence ftill to obferve, that
to the eyes of the greater number of men,
the fenfe of the laws, and the decrees
formed by thofe who interpret them, ought
neceffarily to be identified and blended, and
form only one point of view; and as the
judges are frequently expofed to error, the
true fpirit of legiflation remains often in
obfcurity, and we with difficulty difcern it.

It is, perhaps, becaufe laws are the work
of our underftanding, that we are difpofed
to grant them a univerfal dominion: but I
will avow, I am far from thinking that
they can ever be fubftituted inftead of the
falutary influence of religion, and that I
believe them infufficient even to regulate
the

the things immediately under their jurif-
diction ; thus I would requeft you to reflect, if the unfortunate errors with which
we reproach criminal tribunals, have not
their fource in the faults committed by fovereign authority ; when it has referred all
the duties of the judges to the injunctions
of the law, and when it has refufed to confide any longer in the confcience and private
fentiments of the magiftrates.

Let us render this obfervation more clear
by a fingle example chofen from a number. We demand at prefent, that the legiflator explain himfelf afrefh on the grand
queftion, what witneffes are neceffary? but.
will he not always run the rifk of being
deceived, whether he abfolutely rejects a
probable evidence, or whether he makes
the fate of a criminal depend upon it? How
will he determine, that the teftimony of
an honeft man, identifying the perfon of an
affaffin, in his own caufe, fhould not be
reckoned any thing by the judge; and how
can he pretend alfo, that a teftimony of

4   this

this nature is sufficient to determine a condemnation, when he who gives the evidence appears suspicious, either from the motives, which we must suppose actuate him, or from the improbability of his assertion? Reason is then placed between two extremes; but intermediate ideas not being consonant with the absolute language of law, we ought, in such circumstances, to leave much to the wisdom and integrity of the magistrates; and so far from serving innocence by acting otherwise, we visibly endanger it;* because judges habituate themselves to render the laws responsible for every thing, and respectfully submit to the letter, instead of obeying the spirit, which is the earnest desire of obtaining truth. What then, some will say, would you wish that there should be no positive instructions, neither to serve for a guide in the examination of crimes, nor to determine the character by which these crimes may be distinguished? This was never in my mind; but I could wish,

that

that in an affair of such serious importance, they would unite to the judgment
which proceeded from the prudence of the
legiflator, that which may be brought by
the wifdom of the judges; I could wifh,
that the criminal legiflation prefcribed to
the magiftrates, not all that they are obliged
to do, but all from which they are not
exempt ; not all that is fufficient to
determine their opinion, but all which
ought to be the indifpenfable condition
of a capital punifhment. Guided by fuch
a fpirit, the commands given by the
law, would be a fafeguard againft the ignorance, or poffible prevarication of the
judges; but as any general rule, any immutable principle, is not applicable to an
infinite diverfity of circumftances, I would
give to innocence a new defender, interefting in a more immediate manner the morality of the judges to fearch for and examine the truth, and to recal continually
all the extent of their obligations; I could
wifh, that previous to their paffing a
fentence of condemnation, raifing one of
their

their hands towards heaven, they pronounced with earneftnefs thefe words: " I atteft, that the man accufed before us, appears to me guilty, according to the law, and according to my own private judgment." It is not fufficient, that we command a judge to examine with probity, if the proofs of an offence, are conformable to thofe required by the ftatute; it is neceffary to inform a magiftrate, that he ought to enquire into the truth by all the means that fcrupulous anxiety can fuggeft; he fhould know, that, called to decide on the life and the honour of men, his underftanding and his heart, ought to be enlifted in the caufe of humanity, and that there are not any limits oppofed to bound his duty; then, without failing in any of the enquiries ordained by the laws, he would force himfelf to go ftill further, that no evidence proper to make an impreffion on a reafonable man might be rejected, at the fame time, that none might have fo decifive a force, that the examination of circumftances

G   would

would ever appear uſeleſs; the judges then would make uſe of that ſagacity, which ſeems to diſcern inſtinctively; they would not then diſdain to read even the looks of the accuſer and the accuſed, and they would not believe it a matter of in-difference to obſerve with attention, all thoſe emotions of nature, where ſometimes truth is painted with ſo much energy; then, in ſhort, innocence would be under the protection of ſomething as pure as it-ſelf, the ſcrupulous conſcience of a judge.

We have never, perhaps, ſufficiently con-ſidered how much a methodical order, when we confine ourſelves too ſervilely to it, contracts the bounds of the mind; it becomes then like a foot-path traced be-tween two banks, which prevents our diſ-covering what is not in a ſtrait line. The ſtrict obſervance of method diverts us alſo from conſulting that light, ſometimes ſo lively, of which the ſoul only is the focus; for in ſubjecting us to a poſitive courſe of things always regular, and in making us

find

find pleafure in a determined path; which offers continual repofe to our thoughts, it incapacitates for thinking that delicate perception of natural fentiments, which has nothing fixed or circumfcribed, but whofe free flight often makes us approach to truth, as by a kind of inftinct or infpiration,

I fhould ftray too far from my fubject, if I extended thefe reflections, and I haften to connect them with the fubject of this chapter, in repeating again, that if the laws are infufficient, even in thofe decifions fubmitted to their authority, and if the they have abfolute need of the aid of religion, whenever they impofe on their private expounders duties a little complicated; they would be ftill lefs able to fupply the habitual and daily influence of that motive, the moft powerful of all, and the only one at the fame time, of which the action will be fufficiently penetrating to follow us in the mazes of our conduct, and in the labyrinth of our thoughts.

G 2　　　　　I ought

I ought now to direct your attention towards other confiderations. All that is required by public order, all that is of importance to fociety, fome will fay, is, that criminals may not efcape the fword of juftice, and that an attentive fuperintendance difcover them under the cloud where they feek to conceal themfelves. I will not here recal the various obftacles, which are oppofed to the plenitude of this vigilance; every one may perceive them, or form an idea of them; but I haften to obferve, that in confidering fociety in it's actual ftate, we ought not to forget, that religious fentiments have greatly diminifhed the tafk of government; a fcene quite new would open, if we had for our guide only political morality; it would not then be a few men without principles, who would trouble the public order, more able actors would mix in the throng, fome conducted by mature reflection, and others, carried away by feducing appearances, would be inceffantly at war with all thofe, whofe fortune excited their jealoufy; and then

only

only we fhould know how many opportunities there are of doing evil, and injur-
ing others. It would alfo happen, that
all thefe enemies of public order not being
difconcerted by the reproaches of their confcience, would become every day more expert in the art of avoiding the obfervation
of juftice; and the dangers to which the
imprudent expofed themfelves, would not
difcourage the ingenious,

It is then, if I may be permitted fo
to exprefs myfelf, becaufe the laws find
men in a healthy ftate, prepared by religious inftruction, that they can reftrain
them; but if a fyftem of education merely
political was ever to prevail, new precautions
and new chains would become abfolutely
neceffary, and after having freed us from
the mild ties of religion, the projectors of
fuch a fyftem would increafe our civil
flavery, would bend our necks under the
hardeft of all yokes, that which is impofed
by our fellow-creatures,

Religion,

Religion, whofe influence they wifh us
to reject, is better appropriated than they
think, to the mixtue of pride and weaknefs, which conftitutes our nature, and for
us, fuch as we are; its action is far prefer-
able to that of the penal laws; it is not,
before his equals, armed with the rod of
vengance, that the culprit is made to appear; it is not to their ignorance, or to
their inexorable juftice, that he is abandoned; it is at the tribunal of his own
confcience, that religion informs againft
him; before a God, fovereïgn of the world,
that it humbles, and in the name of a tender and merciful Father that it comforts
him. Alas! while you at once take from
us both our confolation and our true dignity, you wifh to refer every thing to private intereft and public punifhment; but permit me to liften to thofe commands which
come from on high; leave me to divert my
attention from the menacing fceptre which
the potentates of the earth weild in their
hand; leave me to account with Him, before
whom they fhrink into nothing; leave me, in
                                    fhort,

fhort, to addrefs myfelf to him who pardons, and who, at the moment I have offended, permits me ftill to love him, and rely on his grace!—Alas! without the idea of a God,—without this connexion with a Supreme Being, author of all nature, we fhould only liften to the vile counfels of felfifh prudence, we fhould only have to flatter and adore the rulers of nations, and all thofe who in an abfolute monarchy, are the numerous reprefentatives of the authority of the prince; yes, talents, fentiments, ought to bend before thefe diftributors of fo much good and evil, if nothing exifts beyond worldly intereft; and when once every one cringes, there is no more dignity in the character, men become incapable of any great action, and unequal to any moral excellence.

Religious opinions have the double merit of maintaining us in the obedience due to the laws and the foveriegn, and of nourifhing in our hearts a fentiment which fuftains our courage, and which reminds men of

G 4   their

their true grandeur; teaches fubmiffion without meannefs, and prevents, above all, cowardly humiliations before tranfitory idols, in fhowing at a diftance the laft period, when all muft return to an equality before the Mafter of the World.

The idea of a God, at the fame diftance from all men, ferves alfo to confole us for that fhocking fuperiority of rank and fortune under the oppreffion of which we live; it is neceffary to tranfport ourfelves to the heights religion difcovers, to confider with a kind of calmnefs and indifference the frivolous pretentions of fome, and the confident haughtinefs of others; and fuch objects of regret, or of envy, which appeared a Coloffus to our imagination, are changed into a grain of fand, when we contraft them with the grand profpects which fuch fublime meditations difplay to our view.

They are then blind, or indifferent to our intereft, who wifh to fubftitute, inftead

ftead of religious inftructions, political and worldly maxims; and in like manner, thofe are inflexible and unfeeling, who believe they fhall be able to conduct men only by terror; and who, in contefting the falutary influence of religious opinions, expect lefs from them than the axe of the lictors, and the apparatus of execution. What is then this wretched fyftem? For fuppofing even that the different means of fecuring public tranquillity were equal in their effect, fhould we not prefer religious principles, which prevent crimes, to the ftrict laws which punifh them? I underftand not befides, how, with the fame hand that they repel religious fentiments, they wifh to raife every where feaffolds, and multiply, without fcruple, thofe frightful theatres of feverity; for if men, hurried onwards to crimes, were only governed by blind neceffity, alas! what do they deferve? And if we ftill determine to deftroy them as examples, we fhould affift at their execution, as at that of beings devoted for the good of fociety, as Iphigenia was facrificed at Aulis for the falvation of Greece.

Religion

Religion is, in another refpect, fuperior
to the laws, which are ever armed for
vengeance; inftead of that, religion, even
when threatening, nourifhes alfo the hopes
of pardon and felicity; and I believe, contrary to the generally received opinion,
that man, by his nature, is more conftantly animated by hope, than reftrained
by fear; the former of thefe fentiments
compofe the tenor of our life, whilft the
latter is the effect of an extraordinary
circumftance, or particular fituation; in
fhort, courage, or want of confideration,
turns our attention from danger, whilft ideas
of happinefs are perpetually prefent, and
blended, if I may ufe the expreffion, with
our whole exiftence.

I perceive, however, that fome may fay
to me, it is not only of civil and penal laws
that we mean to fpeak, when we maintain
that good public inftitutions would be an efficacious fubftitute for the influence of religion; it would be neceffary to introduce
laws of education, proper to modify, be-
forehand,

forehand, the mind and form the character.
But they have not explained, and I am ignorant that there are such laws, which they
wish to distinguish from the general doctrines we are acquainted with; doctrines
susceptible, undoubtedly, of different degrees
of perfection, which, before instructing us
not only in the virtues simple and real, but
in all those mixed and conventional, have
necessarily a vague character, and could not
separate themselves from the support that
they borrow from the fixed and precise ideas
of religion. They may cite the example of
Sparta, where the state undertook the education of the citizens, and formed by laws
the extraordinary manners which history
has delineated; but that government, aided
in this enterprize by all the influence of
paternal authority, nevertheless proposed but
two great great objects, the encouragement
of martial qualities, and the maintenance of
liberty: morality was not made interesting,
though among us it requires so much application; and it was rendered less necessary,
as every institution tended to introduce a

perfect

perfect equality of rank and fortune, and oppofed all kind of communication with foreigners. In fhort, it was, after all, a religious opinion which fubjected the Spartans to the authority of their legiflator; and without their confidence in the oracle of Delphos, Lycurgus had only been a celebrated philofopher.

We are ftill further, at prefent, from the difpofition and fituation which would allow laws of education to govern us, fupported only by a political fpirit; in order to make the trial, we muft be divided into little affociations; and by fome means, not yet difcovered, be able to oppofe invincible obftacles to the enlargement of them, and to preferve us from the defires and voluptuoufnefs which are the inevitable confequence of an augmentation of wealth, and the progrefs of the arts and fciences : in fhort, and it is a fingular remark, at a period when man is become a being the moft compounded, on account of thefe focial modifications, he has need, more than ever, of a principle which will

will penetrate to the very source of his numerous affections; consequently it would be ne-
.cessary suddenly to carry him back to his primitive simplicity, to make him agree, in some
measure, with the limited extent of an education purely civil. Let me add, that a
like education could not be adapted to the commonalty, as in Sparta; they must be separated from the citizens, and kept in servitude : an observation which leads me to a
very important reflection; it is, that in a country where slavery would be introduced, where the most numerous class would be governed by the continual fear of the severest chastisement, they would be able to confide more in the mere ascendancy of political morality; for this morality only having to keep in order the part of society represented by those who have property, the task would not be difficult; but among us, where happily all men, without any distinction, are subject to the yoke of the law, an authority so extensive, must necessarily be strengthened and seconded by the universal influence of religious opinions.

I shall

I fhall conclude this part of my fubject by one reflection more; fuppofing, even in the fovereign authority, an exertion fuffi- ciently general to prevent or reprefs evil, religion would ftill have this great advan- tage, that it inculcates the beneficent vir- tues, which the laws cannot reach; and yet, in the actual ftate of fociety, it is become im- poffible to omit thofe virtues. It is not fuf- ficient to be juft, when the laws of pro- perty reduce to bare neceffaries the moft numerous clafs of men, whofe weak re- fources the moft trivial accident difconcerts; and I hefitate not to fay, that fuch is the extreme inequality eftablifhed by thefe laws, that we ought at prefent to confider the • fpirit of beneficence and forbearance, as conftituting a part of focial order; as in all places and times, it foftens by its affiftance the excefs of wretchednefs, and by an in- numerable multitude of fprings fpreads it- felf as the vital juice, through forlorn be- ings, whom mifery had almoft exhaufted. But if this fpirit, properly intermediate be- tween the rigour of civil rights, and the
original

original title of humanity, did not exist, or should ever be extinct, we should see all the subordinate ties relax imperceptibly; and a man, loaded with the favours of fortune, never presenting himself to the people under the form of a benefactor; they would more forcibly feel the great extent of his privileges, and would accustom themselves to discuss them: Men must then find a way of moderating the despotism of fortune, or render homage to religion, which, by the sublime idea of an exchange between the blessings of heaven and earth, obliges the rich to give what the laws cannot demand.

Religion then comes continually to assist the civil legislation, it speaks a language unknown to the laws, it warms that sensibility which ought to advance even before reason; it acts like light and interior warmth, as it both enlightens and animates; and what we have not sufficiently observed, is, that in society its moral sentiments are the imperceptible tie of a number

of

of parts, which feem to be held by their own agreement, and which would be fucceffively detached, if the chain which united them was ever to be broken: we fhall more clearly perceive this truth, in the examination we are going to make of the connexion of opinion with morality.

When we imagine we fhould be able to fubject men to the obfervance of public order; and infpire them with the love of virtue, by motives independent of religion, we propofe, undoubtedly, to put in action two powerful fprings; the defire of efteem and praife; and the fear of contempt and fhame. Thus, to follow my fubject in all its branches, I ought neceffarily to examine what is the degree of force of thefe different motives, and what is alfo their true application. I have already fpoken, in other works of mine, of the opinion of the world, and of its falutary effects; but the fubject I am now treating obliges me to confider it under a different point of view, and it is by

placing

placing myself behind the scene, that I shall be able to fulfil this task.

I remark, at first, that the opinion of the world exercises its influence in a very confined space, as it is particularly called in to judge men, whose rank and employments have some splendour in the world; the opinion of the public is an approbation or censure, exercised in the name of the general interest; thus it ought only to be applied to actions and to words, which either directly or indirectly affect this interest. The private conduct of him who discharges in society the most important functions, is indeed submitted to the judgment and superintendance of the public at large; and we ought not to wonder that it should, since in similar circumstances the principles of an individual appear an earnest, or presage of his public virtues; but all those, whose sole occupation is to spend their income, those who are entirely devoted to dissipation, and have not any connexion with the grand interests of

H   the

the community, become independent of the opinion of the world; or at leaft they do not experience its severity, till, by foolifh extravagance or inconfiderate pretenfions, they draw the attention of the public on their conduct. In fhort, a great number of men, who, by the obfcurity of their condition and moderate fortune, find themfelves loft in a crowd, will never dread a power that fingles out of the ranks its heroes and victims: thus people, concealed under humble roofs fcattered in the country, are as indifferent to the opinion of the world, as are to the rays of the fun, thofe unhappy tribes who labour at the bottom of mines, and pafs their whole lives in a dark fubter-raneous cavern.

We cannot then form any kind of comparifon between the peculiar afcendency of reputation, and the general influence of religious morality.

Fame only recompenfes rare actions; and would have nothing to beftow on a nation

of

of heroes. Religion. tends continually to render virtue common; but the univerfal fuccefs of its inftructions would take away nothing from the value of its benefits.

In order to receive the rewards which fame beftows, men muft appear with fplendour on the ftage of life. Religion, on the contrary, extends its moft diftinguifhed favours to thofe who defpife praife, and who do good in fecret.

The world almoft always requires, that talents and knowledge fhould accompany virtue; and it is thus that the love of praife becomes the feed and fpring of great actions. Religion never impofes this condition; its recompenfes belong to the ignorant as well as the learned, to the humble fpirit as well as to the exalted genius; and it is in animating equally all men, in exciting univerfal activity, that it effectually concurs to the maintenance of civil order.

The world, only judging of actions in their ftate of maturity, takes not any ac-

count

count 'of· efforts ; · and, as . men› do· not ſeize·the palm till the ·moment when. they approach the goal, ·it· is neceſſary, at the commencement of the career, that every one ſhould derive from his own force his courage and .perſeverance. Religion, on the con-trary, if I may ſay ſo, dwells with us from the . moment that 'we begin to think ; it welcomes our intentions, ſtrengthens our reſolutions, and ſupports us even in the hour of temptation ; it is, at all times, and in all ſituations, that we ·experience its influence, as ,we·are continually reminded of its re-wards. .

·Fame diſtributing only. favours, whoſe principal, value ariſes from compariſons and competitions, often draws on its favourites the envenomed.breath of ſlander, and then ſometimes they doubt about their real .value. Religion mingles no.bitterneſs with its re-ward; it,is in·obſcurity that it confers con-tent; and as it has treaſures for all the world; ·what is granted· to· ſome· never .im-poveriſhes others.

The

The world is often miftaken in its judgment, becaufe in the midft of fo vaft a circle it is often difficult to diftinguifh true merit and the fplendour which follows it, from the falfe colours of hypocricy. Religion extends its influence to the inmoft receffes of the heart, and places there an obferver, who has a clofer view of men than their actions afford, and whom they cannot either deceive or furprife.

In fhort, I will fay it, there are moments when the opinion of the world lofes its force, and becomes enervated or governed by a fervile fpirit, it fearches to find faults in the oppreffed, and attributes grand intentions to powerful men, that it may, without fhame, abandon one, and celebrate the other. Ah! it is in fuch moments we return with delight to the precepts of religion, to thofe independant principles, which, while they illuftrate every thing deferving of efteem or contempt, enable us to follow the dictates of our heart, and fpeak, according to our confcience!

H 3   Thus,

Thus, the opinion of the world, whose influence I have seen increase, which unites so many motives to excite men to distinguished actions, and to exalt them even to the great virtues, still ought never to be compared with the universal, invariable influence of religion, and with those sentiments which its precepts inspire men of all ages, of all conditions, and every degree of understanding.

Would it be straying from my subject, to remark here the illusion we are under, if we expect any important utility to arise from those marks of distinction lately introduced into France, under the name of public rewards for virtue? Those trivial favours of opinion can never be decreed but to a few dispersed actions; and it might be apprehended, that if we rendered such institutions permanent and general, they might turn the attention of the people at large from the grand recompense, which ought to be the spring and encouragement of all that is great and virtuous. Experienced

rienced hunters, .at the moment when all the pack is ftill purfuing the moft noble ranger ·of the foreft, would not permit them to turn, to run after·a prey which darted out of a lurking hole or thicket.

·The· eftablifhments on which I here fix my attention, have, 'perhaps, alfo' the inconvenience of roufing a fentiment of furprife at the. appearance of a good action,, and announcing thus too diftinctly, that. they believe them rare, and above the com-·· mon exertions of humanity; and if we extended ftill further thefe inftitutions, they would only introduce a fpirit of parade, always ready to languifh, when applaufe was diftant ; and it would be a great misfortune, if fuch a fpirit ever took · place of fimple and. modeft integrity, which ·receives· from itfelf ·its motives and reward : virtue and vanity make a bad mixture ; men are. then accuftomed only to act to be feen, and thefe oportunities, at prefent ·not very numerous, they wifh to choofe.   There is befides a clafs of men fo ill treated by for-

H 4   tune,

tune, "that we fhould commit" a great mif-
take in habituating them to connect conti-.
nually ·. calculations · of · probable rewards
from men, with the practice of ·their-duty; ·
they would too often be deceived.

· It is then, we cannot too often repeat it, it
is refpect for morality,. which it is neceffary :
to maintain, - by ftrengthening religious ·
principles, its moft folid foundation; all ·
other extraordinary helps derive their force
from novelty ; and at the period when fo-.
ciety would have the greateft need of 'their ·
fuccour, it would, perhaps, have arrived at·
its greateft depravity.

Thus far at prefent, I have confidered ·
the influence of opinion, only in general ;
but men manifeft 'more in a private
manner; the idea that they have conceived of each other; and this fentiment, ·
which takes then the fimple name of efteem, is connected with a determinate
knowledge of the moral character' of 'thofe·
with whom we have an habitual correfpondence ;

dence; esteem under this view, has not the splendour of reputation; but as every-one can pretend to it in the circle where his birth and occupations have placed him, the hope of obtaining it ought to be reckoned among the grand motives which excite us to the observance of morality. However, if we supposed that this esteem was entirely-separated from religious sentiments, it would be like many other advantages, which every one would estimate by his own fancy; for whatever comes solely from men, can only have a price relative to our connexion with them: thus the esteem of one, or of several persons, would not indemnify for such a sacrifice; and often also this sentiment, on their part, would appear inferior to some other objects of ambition; in a word, from the moment every preference, every valuation was brought to a standard, each would insensibly have his own book of rates; and the justness of them would depend on the degree of judgment and foresight of every individual. But how can we imagine that perfection in morality would ever be secure,

when

when it depended on wavering and arbitrary comparifons, whofe foundation would be continually changed by the various circumftances and fituations of life? The motives which religion prefents are abfolutely different; it is not by confufed contrafts, that it directs men; it is a predominate intereft to which they are recalled; it is round a beacon, of which the brilliant flames are feen on all fides, that they are affembled; in fhort the rules which it prefcribes are not uncertain, and the advantages which it promifes do not admit of an equivalent.

Let us further obferve here, that felfifhnefs, after having compared the enjoyment of efteem with pleafures of a different kind, would not fail to reckon the chances which afford a hope of impofing on men; and in the midft of thefe perplexed calculations, the paffion of the moment would be almoft always victorious. Befides, we might afk, what is the efteem of others, to that numerous clafs which mifery makes folitary?

3

tary? And what is it but a sentiment, of, which the effect is never obvious, to those whose view is limited to the present day, or the next, because they only live by instantaneous resources? All the advantages annexed to reputation are promisory notes, of which it is necessary to be able to wait the distant expiration; reflection and knowledge only acquaint us with their value; and the ignorance of the greater part of a nation would render them unequal to this kind of combination.

If then, after having taken a view of the lowest, I observe those who compose the superior class, I will venture a reflection of a very different kind; that in a country where we have the hope of obtaining the most splendid marks of distinction, and where fame has power to raise heroes, great ministers, and men of genius in every profession, we do not find that the duties of private life are best known and the most respected. Men, uniting to celebrate with ardour great talents and actions, consider

with

with more indifference the morals and manners of individuals; they make an ideal
beauty, composed of every thing which
contributes to the celebrity of their country,
and the honour of their nation; but by ac-
cuftoming themfelves to refer every thing to
thefe interefts, they become extremely negli-
gent with refpect to common virtues; and
fometimes they even decide, that the rare qualities of the mind may abfolutely difpenfe with
them. . Befides, if fame can ferve to reward
the moft affiduous labour and painful felf-
denial, it is far from being neceffary, that
moderate fentiments of efteem fhould indemnify thofe who obtain them for the facrifice of their paffions; it does not follow,
that this fentiment fhould give them
ftrength to refift the multiplied feductions
that the hopes of ambition and the chances
of fortune prefent to our view; and this
confideration acquires more force in a kingdom, where, among the diftinctions of
which the favour of the prince is the origin,
there are fome which attract fo much homage, that they refemble fame itfelf.

In

In fhort, and what I am going to fay comprehends, in a general manner, the various queftions which I have juft treated: the efteem of men, even when this fentiment feems the moft foreign to religion, receives, neverthelefs, from it its principal ftrength, and even origin; it is a reflection of great importance, and of which I will endeavour to demonftrate the truth.

We ought, at firft, to afk what is the original principle of fociety, which gives weight to the various expreffions of the fentiment of efteem: we fhall find, undoubtedly, that it is a diftinct idea of the duties of men, a notion of good morals, as general as firm. Now the duties of life cannot be fulfilled without the affiftance of religion, fince the connexion of private and public intereft, the only foundation of the virtues of our framing, is, as we have demonftrated an imperfect fyftem, and fufceptible of a multitude of exceptions, or arbitrary interpretations. It is neceffary then that our focial obligations fhould be fixed in an authentic manner,

manner, if we wish that our judgment and
the sentiments which we adopt should be
a real indication of the relation the conduct of men has with moral perfection;
but, if this perfection was only determined
by human conventions, if it was despoiled
of the majesty which religion invests it
with, reputation, and sentiments of esteem,
which are the pledge and stamp of good
morals, would insensibly lose their value;
we should then recollect that coin, which
some vainly wished to preserve the current
value of in commerce, after having mate-
rially altered either the weight or the standard; and, in effect, to follow the simile a
moment longer, how could we alter the
essence of morality more, and lessen the respect which is due to it, than by separating
it from the sublime motives which religion
presents, to unite it only to political considerations.

One objection I ought to obviate: it may
be said, perhaps, that the influence of honour in the army, seems to be a proof
that

that reputation, without the aid of any other impulfe, would have fufficient influence to direct the mind to the end which we propofe to ourfelves. This objection does not appear to me decifive : honour in armies preferves a great afcendency, becaufe amongft men thus affembled, it is impoffible to efcape fhame, and the punifhment incurred by cowardice ; it is in war that the power of authority and that of fame unite all their forces, becaufe that they exercife their influence on men engaged in one action, actuated by the fame fpirit, by that fingular fubordination, termed difcipline. Thus, when in the commencement of the Roman republic, the army participated more of the air of the city, and was not yet familiarized to the military yoke, it was then only through the fanction of an oath, fupported by religious fentiments, that the general contrived to prevent the inconftancy and defection of thofe who followed him to the camp. Whatever then may be at prefent, the power of honour in armies, whatever at prefent may be its influence in the field

of

of battle, where the actors, spectators, and judges, are on the same stage, and have nothing else to do but to practise, remark, and praise a particular virtue, we should not be able to draw any deduction from it, applicable to the social relations, whose extent is immense, and to whose diversity there is no bound. Besides, military honour is very far from being foreign to the general principles of morality, and consequently to religious opinions, the most solid support of those principles; for sentiments which contain, in some manner, the idea of a noble sacrifice, would lose great part of their force, if the great basis of our duty was ever shaken.

A perfect model is necessary to fix the admiration of men; and it is only by an intercourse more or less constant with that first model, that several opinions which seem, in appearance, to arise merely from convenience have consistency.

However,

However, there has refulted from our warlike cuftoms an opinion purely focial, which is very powerful : it is that of the point of honour, when we confider it in its fingular and fimple acceptation, when a man is ready to facrifice his life to guard himfelf from the flighteft humiliation. This opinion, it is true, only dictates its rules among equals, and the exercife of its authority extends to an inconfiderable part of a nation, which, wholly given up to worldly concerns, are occupied entirely with comparifons and diftinctions ; it is one of the ancient appendages of military honour, and in uniting all its force towards a fingle idea it is become a fimple principle, which has been blindly tranfmitted and as blindly refpected.

It is by the effect of a fimilar habit that favages affix all their glory to a contempt of bodily pain, and to demonftrations of gaiety, in the midft of the moft cruel torments. Can we doubt, that their fupernatural exultation would not be weakened, at the very inftant they were acquainted with our moft

I   common

common ideas of virtue? likewife our notions of honour, which, in its exaggerated
ftate, refembles their death fongs, would
not refift metaphyfical arguments, if ever
metaphyfics became our fole guide in morality; for after having analyzed the motives of our moft important obligations,
we fhould analyze alfo our fine-fpun fentiment, which makes us regardlefs of danger.
Yes, if refpect for religion was abfolutely
deftroyed; if this fimple opinion, which
carries with it fo many obligations, and
ferves to defend fo many duties, had no
other fupport, the idea of honour would
foon be weakened; and our perfonal intereft, infenfibly difengaged from all the ties
of the imagination, would take a character
fo rude, and fo determined, that our habitual impreffions, and our relation with
others, would be abfolutely changed.

Permit me then to make another reflection: it will be always eafy to fubject men
to a governing opinion, when they themfelves, and thofe who govern them, unite
all

al their efforts to attain the fame end ; but, if this governing opinion is not, like religion, the general principle of our conduct; if it cannot give us laws in the different fituations of life, it would ferve only to throw us out of an equilibrium, or at leaft its utility would be partial and momentary. Neverthelefs, if, with a defign of remedying this inconvenience, we fearched to multiply thefe opinions, they would weaken each other ; for every time we wifh ftrongly to reftrain the imagination, it is neceffary that a fingle idea, a fingle authority, a fingle object of intereft, fhould engage the attention of men. Perfection, in this refpect, is the choice of a fingle principle, whofe confequence extends to all ; and fuch is the particular merit of religious opinions.

We can then, in the name of reafon, of policy, and philofophy, demand fome refpect for them; and I ought to repeat, fince it is time for me to refume my fubject, that efteem or contempt, honour or fhame, are fo far from being able to fupply the place of

I 2

the

the active influence of religion, that its fentiments confirm the opinion of the world,
and, more or lefs, obvioufly direct it. It
follows, that we fhould foon reafon fhrewdly,
on the value which we ought to fet on the efteem of the world, if the expreffion of its approbation was not united in our contemplation
to fomething more noble than the judgment
of mankind, and if an awful refpect for
virtue was not imbibed by means of a religious education. We fhould foon experience that, in wifhing to found every thing
on the calculations of worldly wifdom, thefe
fame calculations would deftroy all; and
morality having at once loft its grand fupport, we fhould try in vain to prop it by a
fcaffold of laws, and the vain efforts of an
opinion without a guide. Hypocrify and
diffimulation would become immediately a
neceffary fcience, a legitimate defence, which
would weary the attention of every infpec-
tor; and teftimonies of efteem appearing
only an ingenious encouragement granted to
the facrifices of felfifhnefs, the applaufe decreed

creed to a generous mode of conduct would be infenfibly difcredited by thofe who gave and by thofe who received them, and would end, perhaps, in becoming a fecret object of derifion, as mere play from one to another.

Every thing is replaced and firmly efta-blifhed by religion; it furrounds, I may fay, the whole fyftem of morality, refem-bling that univerfal and myfterious force of phyfical nature, which retains the planets in their orbits, and fubjects them to a re-gular revolution; and which, in the midft of the general order it maintains, efcapes the obfervation of men, and appears to their feeble fight unconfcious of its own work.

I 3 CHAP.

C H A P. III.

*An Objection drawn from our natural Dif-
positions to Goodness.*

MEN, according to the opinion of some, have received from nature a secret tendency towards every thing just, good, and virtuous; and from this happy inclination, the task of the moralist is confined to prevent the altera- tion of our original constitution; an easy task, add they, and which may be fulfilled without any extraordinary effort, and with- out having recourse to religion.

We ought, at first, to observe, that the existence of this excellent innate goodness has been a long time a subject of debate, as every assertion always will be, of which we cannot demonstrate the truth, either by argument or experience. We shall never be able to perceive distinctly the natural

4   dispo-

difpofitions of men, fince, to our view, they are never feparated from the improvement, or the modification, which they owe to education and habit. One or two examples they produce of children arrived at maturity found in a foreft; but we are ignorant at what precife age they were abandoned by their parents, and what might have been their difpofitions, if, brought back to fociety, they had not been guided by inftruction, or reftrained by fear and fubordination. It is not very probable, that man derived from his original nature all the difpofitions which lead to goodnefs; fuch a thought agrees not with his pride or dignity, fince the intellectual faculties with which he is endowed, the power he has of gradually tending to perfection, announce to him that he ought to fulfil his career with the affiftance of reafon, and that, very different from thofe beings governed by an invariable inftinct, he fhould elevate himfelf as much above them, by cultivating the abilities entrufted to him, as by the

grandeur

granduer of the destiny to which he is permitted to aspire.

Reason, however, our faithful guide,
would be insufficient to attach us to sentiments of order, justice, and beneficence, if
it was not seconded by a nature proper
to receive the impression of every noble
sentiment; but such reflections, far from
favouring any system of independence or
impiety, receive from religious opinions
their principal force. What is, in effect,
in this respect the course of our thoughts?
We attribute, at first, to a Supreme and
Universal Being all the perfections which
seem to constitute his essence; and from
this principle we are led to presume, that
we, his intelligent creatures, and his most
noble work, participate, in some manner,
of the Divine spirit, of which we are an
emanation : but, if we could ever be persuaded, that our confidence in the idea of a
God is a deceitful illusion, we should not
have any reason to believe that the mere
child of nature, blind and without a guide,
would

would be difpofed to good, rather than'evil.
We muft derive our opinion of innate
goodnefs from a fecret fentiment, and from
a pefect conviction of the exiftence of a
power which keeps every thing in order,
the model of all perfection: but, as we
obtain equally from this power, the faculties which render us capable of acquiring
knowledge, of improving by experience,
of extending our views into futurity, and
elevating our thoughts to God; we fhould
not know how to diftinguifh thefe laft ex-
pedients of ability and virtue from thofe
which belong to our firft inftinct; and we
have no intereft in doing it.

That which we perceive moft clearly is,
that there is a correfpondence, a harmony
between all the parts of our moral nature;
and therefore we cannot deny the exiftence
of our natural inclination towards goodnefs,
nor confider this inclination as a difpofition
which has not need of any religious fentiment to acquire ftrength, and become a rational conductor through the rough road
of

of life. The production of falutary fruits requires, before all things, a favourable foil;
but this advantage would be ufelefs without
feed and the labour of the hufbandman, and
the fertilizing warmth of the fun: the
Author of Nature has thought fit that a
great number of caufes fhould concur continually to renovate the productions of the
earth; and the fame intention, the fame
plan, feems to have determined the principle and the developement of all the gifts of
the mind: it is neceffary, in order to attach intelligent beings to the love of virtue,
and refpect for morality, that not only happy
natural difpofitions, but ftill more, a judicious
education, good laws, and, above all, a continual intercourfe with the Supreme Being,
from which alone can arife firm refolutions,
and every ardent thought, fhould concur;
but men ambitious of fubmitting a great
number of relations to their weak comprehenfion, would wifh to confine them to a
few caufes. We fhall difcover, every moment, the truth of this obfervation; actuated by a fimilar motive, many wifh to
attribute

attribute every thing to education; whilft others pretend, that our natural difpofitions are the only fource of our actions and intentions, of our vices and virtues. Perhaps, in fact, there is, in the univerfe, but one expedient and fpring, one prolific idea, the root of every other: yet, as it is at the origin of this idea, and not in its innumerable developements, that its unity can be perceived, the firft grand difpofer of nature only ought to be in poffeffion of the fecret; and we, who fee, of the immenfe mechanifm of the world, but a few wheels, become almoft ridiculous, when we make choice fometimes of one, and fometimes of another, to refer to it exclufively, the caufe of motion, and the fimpleft properties of the different parts of the natural or moral world.

C H A P.

C H A P. IV.

An Objection drawn from the good Conduct
of many irreligious Men.

YOU may think, perhaps, after having
read the preceding chapter, that I
have taken little room to treat a queftion on
which fo much has been written; but if it
be allowed that I have made fome approaches
to truth, I fhall not need any excufe. The
refearches after truth refemble thofe cir-
cles which we trace fometimes one round
another; the furtheft from the centre has
neceffarily the greateft extent.

I will then endeavour, with the fame
brevity, to examine the objection which is to
make the fubject of this chapter.

Society, fome fay, is at prefent filled with
perfons, who, to borrow the expreffion of
the times, are abfolutely difengaged from
every

every kind of prejudice, who believe not
even the exiftence of a Supreme Being; and·
yet, their conduct appears as regular as that
of the moft religious men.

Before replying to this objection I ought
to make an important obfervation. The
detractors of a religious fpirit habitually
confound, in their difcourfe, devotion and
piety; they attribute befides to devotion an
exaggerated fenfe, which its natural défini-
tion will not bear; and derive from this
mifconception a great advantage. Piety,
fimple in its fentiments and deportment,
commonly efcapes the heedlefs glance of a
man of the world; and the greater part of
thofe who fpeak of it, would have fome difficulty to delineate it well; devotion, on
the contrary, fuch as we are accuftomed to
reprefent, feems to attach fome value to appearances; it difplays itfelf, it makes a parade of the aufterity of its principles; and
often foured by the facrifices, or the conftraint, which it has impofed on itfelf as a
law, it contracts a rough and inflexible fpirit,

rit, which banifhes fentiment, amiable and indulgent: in fhort, devotion is fome-times mixed with hypocrify, and then it is only a defpicable affemblage of the moft contemptible vices. It is eafy to judge, from thefe two pictures, that judicious piety, rational and indulgent, forms the true cha-racteriftic of a religious fpirit, confidered in its purity. It is then with morality, infpired by a like fpirit, that it is neceffary to compare thofe men, who are guided only by the prin-ciples they frame to themfelves; and I be-lieve, that one of thefe two fyftems of mo-rality is far fuperior to the other; but we run a rifk of deceiving ourfelves in our ob-fervations, when we do not extend them beyond the narrow circle, known amongft us by the name of *fociety*. Men, in the cir-cumfcribed relations which arife from the communications of idlenefs and diffipation, require of each other, only qualities applica-ble to thefe kind of relations; their code of laws is very fhort, integrity in the com-merce of life, conftancy in friendfhip, or, at leaft, politenefs in our intercourfe, a kind of elevation

elevation in their difcourfe and manner.; in fbort, probity is the grand outline; and this is all that is required, in order to difplay ourfelves to the beft advantage in the midft of the active fcenes which furround us; where we fometimes form a confederacy proper to ferve as a fupport of the great virtues; but what they wifh for before every thing is, a grant of indulgence in favour of vices, which do not difturb the order or the peace of their pleafures, and which only render unhappy parents, hufbands, and creditors, vaffals and the commonalty. Far diftant, indeed, from a like tolerance, are thofe collective obligations which morality dictates, obligations, of which I made a concife fketch, when I compared them with thofe which are impofed by civil laws. It is then only, after having retraced ourfelves the entire fyftem of our duties, it is only after having compared them with the conventions foftened by fafhionable fociety, that we are in a ftate to judge, if the conduct of perfons, difengaged from every religious tie, ought to be given as an example; and if their

morality

morality can fuffice for all the circumftances of life.

But in admitting, for a moment, this.fup-pofition, we fhould not have a right to draw any deduction contrary to the truths, which I have endeavoured to eftablifh; for all thofe who free themfelves at a certain age, from the yoke of religion, have been at leaft pre-pared by it to refpect virtue. Principles inculcated early in life, have a great influence on the human heart, a long time even after our underftanding has rejected the reafon-ing which ferved as the bafis of thofe prin-ciples: the foul, formed when the reafon begins to dawn, to the love of order, and fuftained in this difpofition by the force of habit, never entirely lofes this principle. So that, whatever be the opinions adopt-ed when the judgment is formed, it is flowly, and by degrees, that thefe opinions act on the character and direct the conduct. Befides, while religion maintains amongft the greater number of men, a profound re-fpect for morality, thofe who reject thefe

fentiments

fentiments know, neverthelefs, that probity leads to efteem, and to the various advantages which depend on it. Of courfe, a virtuous atheift merely makes us recollect, that he lives where virtue is refpected ; and it is not the inefficacy, but, on the contrary, the indirect influence of religious opinions, which his conduct demonftrates to me. I think I fee, in a beautiful piece of mechanifm, a fmall part broken off from the chain, and which maintains its place, by the force ftill fubfifting of general equilibrium.

What! would you have need of religion to be an honeft man ? Here is an interrogative, with which they hope to embarrafs thofe who wifh to preferve to morality its beft fupport ; and the dread that fome have of not giving an honourable idea of their fentiments, induces them to reply with quicknefs, that certainly they fhould not need the check of religion, and that the dictates of their heart would always be fufficient to direct them. This anfwer is undoubtedly very refpectable; but for my part,

K I avow,

I avow, I fhould merely fay, that virtue has
fo many charms, when it has been a long
time practifed, that a truly fenfible man
would continue to be juft, even when every
religious fentiment was annihilated; but
that it is uncertain whether, with a political
education, his principles might have been
the fame: and I fhould add further, that
no one, perhaps, could be certain, that he
would have fufficient ftrength to refift a revolution of ideas fimilar to thofe that we
have juft fuppofed, were he to fall at the
fame time into a ftate of mifery and dejec-
tion, which would make him revolt at the
enjoyments and the triumphs of others. It
is always in a like fituation, that it is neceffary to place ourfelves, to judge properly of
certain queftions; for all thofe who enjoy
the favours of fortune, have, in confequence
of this fortunate condition, fewer objects of
envy, and are lefs fubject to temptations;
and in the midft of the different comforts,
which peaceably furround them, it is not
the principles of others of which they know
the want.

As

As for philofophical writers, if it were amongft them, that we are to fearch for the principal defenders of the new opinions, and if, at the fame time, their moral conduct was cited as an example, we fhould have to obferve, that a retired life, love of ftudy, and a conftant habit of reflection, ought to fpread a kind of calm over their fentiments; befides, delivered up to abftraction, or preoccupied by general ideas, they know not all the paffions, and they are feldom perfonally engaged in thofe ardent purfuits which ftimulate fociety. They cannot then determine, with certainty, what would have been the degree of their re-fifting force, if without any other defenfive arms than their principles, and no guide but convenience, they had to combat againft the allurements of fortune and ambition, which prefent themfelves in every ftep of our worldly career. They have alfo, like all the inventors and the propagators of a new fyftem, vanity, which engages them to multiply the number of their difciples : and how, in fact, could they be able to flatter

them-

themfelves with any fuccefs, if, in attack-
ing the moft refpectable opinions, they had
not endeavoured to prove that their doctrines were not in oppofition to morality.
Befides, it is very neceffary, after having
filently fapped the foundation of our dwelling, that they fupport for fome time the edifice, were it only while they have with us
a common habitation; were it only during
the interval when we fhould be able to
judge in their prefence, of the utility of
their inftructions: in fhort, very often,
perhaps, the dupes of their own heart, they
have been induced to believe that, becaufe
they were at the fame time irreligious by-
fyftem, and juft by character and habit, religion and virtue, have not a neceffary
union; and if it is true, that in the grand
interefts of life, the flighteft doubt has fome
influence on our actions, would it be poffible, that at the time when they would
feek to fhake religious opinions, even when
they are ridiculed in converfation, that they
would ftill endeavour, to preferve a fecret
connexion with them, by the propriety of
their

.their conduct? It is thus that, in the difputes of princes, or in the quarrels of minifters, the members of the fame family have fometimes the art of dividing themfelves, in order, at all events, that one of their friends fhould be in each party.

Thefe different reflections ought necef-farily to be taken into confideration, before we give ourfelves up to the, inferences that they would wifh to draw from the manners of irreligious men; but, to difcredit their arguments, it is fufficient to ob-ferve, that we cannot make any application of them to the moft numerous clafs of men: honeft atheifts have never exifted among the commonalty, religion compre-hends all their knowledge in morality; and if once they were to lofe this guide, their conduct would be abfolutely dependent on chance and circumftances.

It is ftill effential to obferve, that, ac-cording to the motives to which we can at-tribute the relaxation of moral principles,

K 3   there

there exifts a great difference between the various characters which attend vicious actions: a depraved man; though religious; does wrong by accident, through weaknefs; and according to the fucceffive tranfports of his paffions; but the wicked atheift has not a fixed time; opportunities do not furprife him, he fearches for them, or waits for them with impatience; he yields not through the contagion of imitation; but he takes pleafure in fetting an example; he is not a corrupt fruit, he is himfelf the tree of evil.

Another objection is raifed, but of a very different kind: they point out the contraft, frequently perceived, between the conduct and the religious fentiments of the greater part of men; an oppofition from whence they would wifh to conclude, that thefe fentiments are not a certain fafeguard; and they add, to fupport their argument; that in examining the belief of all thofe, whofe licentious life is terminated by an ignomious death; we perceive

ceive that the greater number is composed of people blindly subject to religious opinions.

Undoubtedly, these opinions form not, at all times, a complete resistance to the different starts of our passions; but it suffices, that they may be the most efficacious. There has been, and there ever will be, vicious men in the bosom of society, even where religion has the greatest influence; for it acts not on us like a mechanical force, by weights, levers, and springs, of which we can calculate exactly the power; it is not an arbitrary modification of our nature; but we are enlightened, guided, and animated, according to our dispositions and sensibility, and according to the degree of our own efforts in the numerous conflicts which we have to sustain; it would be then an evident piece of treachery, to attack religion, by drawing a picture of the vices and crimes, from which it has not been able to guard society, instead of fixing our attention on all the disorders which it checks or prevents.

K 4

They

They would be equally wrong, who re-prefent the general languor of religion, as a proof that it has, in our time, very little influence on morality; it would be neceffary rather to remark, how great muft have been that power, which even in the decline of its force is ftill fufficient to concur to the maintenance of public order; we fhould be authorized to fay, how valuable is the whole, when we receive fo much advantage from a part?

In fhort, the confequence that they would wifh to draw from the opinions, and from the faith of wretches finking under the fword of juftice, in an abufe of reafoning: men termed religious, forming the major part of the populace, we muft among them neceffarily meet the greater number of malefactors; in the fame manner that we are fure to find, in this clafs, more men of a particular age, ftature, or complexion; but, if they have a right to ufe fuch an argument to cenfure a religious education, they might, with the fame reafon, conteft

the

the falubrity of breaft milk, alledging, that many fick and dying perfons have received this nourifhment. We fhould never confound a common circumftance with a general caufe; thefe are two ideas abfolutely diftinct.

There are other objections which equally deferve to be difcuffed; but they will find a place, with more propriety, after the chapter where, I fhall examine, under different heads, the influence of religious opinions on our happinefs. You have feen, and you will perceive ftill more, in the progrefs of this work, that I do not endeavour to elude difficulties; for before I determined to defend, according to my abilities, a caufe which I could wifh to render dear to mankind, I carefully ftudied the means; and after having fortified myfelf againft the fyftems oppofite to my fentiments, I fear not to examine the motives which ferve to fupport them.

CHAP.

CHAP. V.

The Influence of Religious Principles on our Happiness.

AS we have fhown the clofe connexion of morality with religious opinions, we have already pointed out the principal relation of thefe opinions with public good, fince the repofe and interior tranquillity of fociety effentially depend on the mainten- ance of civil order, and the exact obfervance of the laws of juftice. But a great part of human happinefs does not arife from the community: thus, the benefits religion im- parts would be very imperfect, if they were not extended to our moft intimate fenti- ments, if they were not ufeful in thofe fe- cret conflicts of different affections which agitate our fouls, and which pre-occu- py our thoughts. Religion is very far from deferving this reproach ; that which raifes it indeed above every kind of

4

legiflation

legiflation is; that it influences equally public good and private happinefs. We ought
to examine this truth ; but to do it philo-
fophically, we muft neceffarily contemplate,
and pry into our nature; and examine, for a
moment, into the firft caufes of the enjoyments or the anxieties of our minds.

Men, when they have advanced a few
fteps in the world, and as foon as
their intellectual faculties begin to open,
extend their views, and live in the future ; fenfual pleafures and bodily pain only
detain them in the prefent ; 'but in the
long intervals which exift between the renewal of thefe fenfations, it is by anticipation and memory that they are happy or
miferable ; and recollection is only interefting, as it is perceived to keep up the connexion between the paft and future. Undoubtedly, the influence of the future, on
all our moral affections, efcapes often our
notice; to cite fome examples of this
truth, we believe, that only the prefent
moment produces happinefs, when we receive

ceive elogiums, obtain some mark of distinction, or are informed of an unexpected augmentation of our fortune; and still more,
when we are pleased with the sport of our
imagination, or the discoveries of our reason
in our closet or in conversation. These enjoyments, and many others similar, we call
present happiness; though there is not any
one of them which does not owe its value,
and even reality, to the single idea of futurity.
In fact, respect, applause, the triumphs of
self-love, the forerunners of fame, and even
fame itself, are the acquisitions which education and habit have rendered precious, in
exhibiting always beyond them some other
advantage, of which these first were only
the symbols. Often, indeed, the last object
of our ambition is but an enjoyment of opinion, the confused image of some possession
more real. Every where we see vague hopes
hurry away our imagination; we see the ex-
pected good, the immediate end of our meditation, or the obscure motive of the estimation we annex to the various satisfactions,
of which our present happiness is composed.
Thus,

Thus, indirectly, and almoft unknown to ourfelves, all is in perfpective in our moral exiftence; and it is by this reafoning that, always deluded, we are feldom perfectly de_. ceived. Subjected by long habit, it is in vain that we would wifh to feparate the imaginary advantages of opinion from the delufions of hope which furround them, and by which we have been feduced all our life.

There is but a fmall part of the moral fyftem, which we cannot make agree with this manner of explaining the principal caufe of our pleafures and of our pains. I am very far, however, from wifhing to make the fentiments, which unite men by the charm of friendfhip, depend on the fame principle; and which have fuch an effential influence on their happinefs. All is real in thefe affections, fince they are a fimple affociation of ourfelves to others, and them to us; in this view it may be confidered as, in fome meafure, prolonging our own exiftence; but this divifion, fo intimate, of. the

the good and evil of life, does not deſtroy
their eſſence. Friendſhip doubles our plea-
ſures and our comforts; and it is by the
cloſe alliance of two ſympathizing ſouls
that we are fortified againſt all events; but
it is always with the ſame paſſions that
it is neceſſary to combat; thus whether we
remain ſolitary, or live in others, the future preſerves its influence over us.

If ſuch is, however, our moral nature,
that the object of our wiſhes will always be
at ſome diſtance; if our thoughts, like the
courſe of the waves, are ever active, and
preſſing forward; if our preſent enjoyments
have a ſecret tie with the imaginary advantages of opinion, of which the laſt term is
ſtill a fleeting ſhadow; in ſhort, if all is
future in the fate of man; with what intereſt, with what love, with what reſpect,
ought we not to conſider this beautiful ſyſtem of hope, of which religious opinions
are the majeſtic foundation! What encouragement they preſent! What an end to all
other ends! What a grand and precious
idea,

idea, by its connexion with the moſt intimate and general ſentiment, the déſire of
prolonging our exiſtence! That which men
dread moſt, is the image of an eternal annihilation; the abſolute deſtruction of all
the faculties which compoſe their being, is
for them the downfall of the whole univerſe; and they are anxious to ſeek for a
refuge againſt this overwhelming thought.

Uudoubtedly, it is according to nature,
according to the degree of ſtrength of their
religious opinions, that men ſeize with
more or leſs confidence the hopes which
they give, and the recompenſe they pro-
miſe; but, doubt and obſcurity have a powerful action, while ſupreme happineſs is the
object; for even in the affairs of this life,
the grandeur of the prize offered to our
ambition excites ſtill more our ardour, than
the probability of ſucceſs. But where
ſhould we fix, where attach the ſlighteſt
hope, if even the idea of a God, this firſt
prop of religion, was ever deſtroyed; if,
from the infancy of men, we did not preſent

sent to their reflection, that worldly confiderations are as transient as themselves; and if, early in life, they were humbled in their own eyes; if men applied themselves to stifle the internal sentiments, which inform them of the spirituality of their souls? Discouraged in this manner, by the first principles of their education, slackened in all the movements which carry thier reflections into futurity, they would often take retrospective views: the past recalling an irreparable loss, would too much captivate their attention; and their minds, in the midst of time, would no more be in a necessary equilibrium to enjoy the present moment; in short, this moment, which is not, in reality, but an imperceptible fraction, would appear almost nothing to our eyes, if it were not united in our contemplations, to the unknown number of days and years which are before us. It is then, because that there is nothing limited in the ideas of happiness and duration, with which religious sentiments impress us, that our imagination is not forced to recoil on itself, when

it

it is infenfibly loft in the immenfity of futurity.

. When, in following the courfe of a noble river, a vaft horizon is prefented to our view, we turn not our obfervation on the fandy banks we are coafting: but if, changing our fituation, or twilight narrowing this horizon, our attention was turned on the barren flat, we are near; then only we fhould remark all its drynefs and fterility. It is the fame in the career of life: when the grand ideas of infinity elevate our thoughts and our hopes, we are lefs affected by the wearinefs and difficulties ftrewed in our path; but, if changing our principles, a gloomy philofophy were to obfcure our perfpective, our whole attention drawn back on the furrounding objects, we fhould then very diftinctly difcover the void and illufion of the fatisfactions of which our moral nature is fufceptible.

Let us recollect, then, all the happinefs which we owe to religious fentiments and

obvious

obvious reflections, which, in attracting us continually towards the future, seem willing to save from the present moment the purest part of ourselves; these are, without our perceiving it, the enchantments of the moral world; if it were possible that, by cold reasoning, we at length destroyed them, a sad melancholy would ally itself to most of our reflections; and it would seem as if a winding-sheet had taken place of that transparent veil, through which the prospects of life are embellished. Undoubtedly, there would be still some charm in the days of youth, when the pleasures of the senses press on us, and fill a considerable time; but when the passions are tempered by age, when our strength has been broken by years, or prematurely attacked by sickness; in short, when the time is arrived, when men are constrained to seek, in the principles of morality, the chief support of their happiness; what would become of them, if those hopes and opinions were dissipated, which afford solid comfort and encouragement; and if an imagination, thus active, were weakened,

3

weakened, which enlivens all the objects that anticipation can reach ?

Reflect, then, with attention, on the different confequences which would be the fatal train of the annihilation of religious opinions; it is not a fingle idea, a fingle view, that men would lofe; it would be, befides, the intereft and the charm of all their defires and ambition. There is nothing indifferent, when our actions and defigns can be in any refpect attached to a duty; there is nothing indifferent; when the exercife and the improvement of our faculties appear the commencement of an exiftence, whofe termination is unknown : but, when this period offers itfelf on all fides to our view, when we approach it every moment, what ftrong illufion would be fufficient to defend us from a fad defpondency ? Strictly circumfcribed in the fpace of life, its limits would be in fuch a manner prefent to our mind, to every fentiment and enterprife perhaps, that we fhould be tempted to examine, what it is which can merit, on our

L 2   part,

part, an affiduous refearch; what it is
which deferves clofe and painful application. Indeed, fame itfelf, which is called
immortal, would no more hurry us on in
the fame manner, if we had a fecret conviction, that it cannot grow, rife, fubfift,
but in fuch portions of fpace, and fuch
durations of time, as our imagination cannot conceive. It is neceffary, that the uncertain future be ftill our country, in order that we fhould be able to feel that un-
quiet love of a long celebrity, and thofe ardent
impulfes towards great things which is the
falutary effect of it.

We deceive ourfelves then, I think, when
we accufe religion of neceffarily rendering
the bufinefs and the pleafures of the world
uninterefting; its chief pleafures, on the
contrary, are derived from religion, from
thofe ideas of eternity, which it prefents to
our mind, which ferve to fuftain the enchantments of hope, and the fenfe of thofe
duties of which our moral nature is ingenioufly compofed,

Religious

Religious opinions are perfectly adapted to our nature, tò our weaknesses and per-fections; they come to our succour in our real difficulties, and in those which the abuse of our foresight creates. But in what is grand and elevated in our nature, it sympathizes most: for, if men are animated by noble thoughts; if they respect their intelligence, their chief ornament; if they are interested about the dignity of their nature, they will fly, with transport, to bow before religion, which ennobles their faculties, preserves their strength of mind, and which, through its sentiments, unites them to Him, whose power astonishes their understanding. It is then that, considering themselves as an emanation of the Infinite Being, the commencement of all things, they will not let themselves be drawn aside by a philosophy, whose sad lessons tend to persuade us, that reason, liberty, all this immaterial essence of ourselves, is the mere result of a fortuitous combination, and an harmony without intelligence.

We

We have never perhaps obferved, with fufficient attention, the different kinds of happinefs which would be deftroyed, or at leaft fenfibly weakened, if this difcouraging doctrine was ever propagated.

What would then become of the moft fublime of all fentiments, that of admiration, if, inftead of the grand view of the univerfe, far from reviving the idea of a Supreme Being, we retraced only a vaft exiftence, but without defign, caufe, or deftination; and if the aftonifhment of our minds was itfelf but one of the fpontaneous accidents of blind matter?

What would become of the pleafure which we find in the developement, exercife, and progrefs of our faculties, if this intelligence, of which we love to glory, was only the refult of chance, and if all our ideas were but a mere obedience to the eternal law of motion; if our liberty was but a fiction, and if we had not, if I may fay fo, any poffeffion of ourfelves?

What

‘ What would become then of that active spirit of curiosity, whose charm excites us to observe continually the wonders with which we are surrounded, and which inspires, at the same time, the desire of penetrating, in some measure, into the mystery of our existence, and the secret of our origin? Certainly it would little avail us to study the course of nature, if this science could only teach us to comprehend the afflicting particulars of our mechanical slavery: a prisoner cannot be pleased to draw the form of his fetters, or reckon the links of his chains.

But how beautiful is the world, when it is represented to us as the result of a single and grand thought, and when we find every where the stamp of an eternal intelligence; and how pleasing to live with the sentiments of astonishment and adoration deeply impressed on our hearts!

But what a subject of glory are the endowments of the mind, when we can consider them as a participation of a sublime

L 4   nature,

nature, of which God alone is the perfect model. . And how delightful then to yield to the ambition of elevating ourselves still more, by exercising our thoughts and improving all our faculties !

In short, how many charms has the obfervation of nature, when, at every new difcovery, we believe we advance a step towards an acquaintance with that exalted wifdom which has prefcribed laws to the univerfe, and maintains it in harmony ! It is then, and only then, that the ftudy is truly interefting, and the progrefs of knowledge becomes an increafe of happinefs. Yes, under the influence of opinions, arifing from the notions of materialifts, all is languifhing in our curiofity, all is mere inftinct in our admiration, all is fictitious in the fentiments which we have of ourfelves; but with the idea of a God, all is lively, all is reafonable and true: in fhort, this happy and prolific idea appears as neceffary to the moral nature of man, as heat is to plants and to all the vegétable world. You may think, perhaps, that

in

in examining the influence of religion on happinefs, I have dwelt on feveral confidera-tions, which are not of equal importance to all men; there are, indeed, fome more par-ticularly adapted to that part of fociety, whofe minds are improved by education; but I am very far from wifhing to divert a moment my attention from the numerous clafs of the inhabitants of the earth, whofe happinefs and mifery arifes from a fimple idea, proportioned to the extent of their in-terefts and reflections.

Thofe who feem to have a more preffing and conftant need of the affiftance of reli-gion, have been left by the misfortunes of their parents to the wide world, devoid of property, and deprived alfo of thofe re-fources which depend on education. This clafs of men, condemned to hard labour, are, as it were, confined in a rough and uni-formly barren path, where every day refem-bles the laft, where they have not any con-fufed expectations, or flattering illufion to divert them: they know that there is a wall

of

of feparation between them and fortune; and if they carried their views in life forward, they would only difcover the dreadful ftate any infirmity would reduce them to; and the deplorable fituation to which they might be expofed, by the cruel negleƈt which attends old age. With what tranfport, in this fituation, would they not catch at the comfortable hopes which religion prefents! With what fatisfaction would they not learn, that after this probationary ftate, where fo much difproportion overwhelmed them, there would come a time of equality! What would be their complaints, if they were to renounce a fentiment which ftill conforms itfelf, for their advantage, to a general idea, [the only one, in fhort, of which they can make ufe in all events and circumftances of life. It is God's will, they fay to themfelves, and this firft thought fupports their refignation: God will recompenfe you, God will return it to you, fay they to others, when they receive alms; and thefe words remind them, that the God of the rich and powerful is

alfo

alſo theirs; and that far from being indifferent to their fate, He deigns Himſelf to
diſcharge their obligations.

How many other popular expreſſions
continually recal the ſame ſentiment of confidence and conſolation. It is this continual
relation of the poor with the Deity which
raiſes them in their own eyes, and which
prevents their ſinking under the weight of
contempt with which they are oppreſſed,
and gives them ſometimes courage to reſiſt
the pride of earthly greatneſs. What grander
effect could be produced by an idea ſo ſimple? Thus, among the different things
which characteriſe religion, I remark, above
all, what ſeems more particularly the ſeal of
a divine hand; it is, that the moral advantages, of which religion is the ſource, re-
ſembling the grand bleſſings of nature, belong equally to all men; and as the ſun, in
the diſtribution of its rays, obſerves neither
rank nor fortune, in the ſame way thoſe
comforting ſentiments, which are connected
with the conception of a Supreme Being,
and

and the hopes united to it, become the property of the poor as well as the rich, of the
weak as well as the powerful, and can be
as fecurely enjoyed under the lowly roof of
a cottage, as in a fuperb palace. It is civil
laws which increafe, or give a fanction to
the inequality of poffeffions; and it is religion which fweetens the bitternefs of this
hard difproportion.

We could not avoid feeling a compaffion
as painful as well founded, if, in confidering attentively the fate of the greater number of men, we fuppofed them all at one
ftroke deprived of the only thought which
fupported their courage; they would no
more have a God to confide their forrows
with; they would no more attend his ordi-
nances to fearch for the fentiments of refignation and tranquillity; they would have no
motive for raifing their looks to heaven;
their eyes would be caft down, fixed for ever
on this abode of grief, of death, and eternal
filence. Then defpair would even ftifle
their groans, and all their reflections preying
on

on themfelves, would only ferve to corrode their hearts; then thofe tears which they have a fatisfaction in fhedding, and which are attracted by the tender perfuafion, that there exifts fome where commiferation and goodnefs, thefe confoling tears would no more moiften their eyes.

Who has not feen, fometimes, thofe veteran foldiers, who are proftrate here and there on the pavement of a fanctuary, erected in the midft of their auguft retreat? Their hair, which time has whitened; their forehead marked with honourable fcars; that tottering ftep, which age only could imprefs on them, all infpire at firft refpect; but by what fentiments are we not affected, when we fee them lift up and join with difficulty their weak hands, to invoke the God of the univerfe, of their heart and mind; when we fee them forget, in this interefting devotion, their prefent pains and paft griefs; when we fee them rife with a countenance more ferene, and exprefſive of the tranquillity and hope devotion has infufed through
their

their souls. Complain not in thofe moments, you who judge of the happinefs of this world only from its enjoyments; their looks are humbled, their body trembles, and death awaits their fteps; but this inevitable end, whofe image only terrifies us, they fee coming without alarm; they, through religion, have approached Him who is good, who can do every thing, whom none ever loved without receiving comfort. Come and contemplate this fight, you who defpife religion, you who term yourfelves fuperior; come and fee the real value of your pretended knowledge for promoting happinefs. Change the fate of men, and give them all, if you can, fome portion of the enjoyments of life, or refpect a fentiment which ferves them to repulfe the injuries of fortune; and fince even the policy of tyrants has never dared to deftroy it, fince their power would be infufficient to enable them to fucceed in the favage attempt, you, to whom nature has given fuperior endowments, be not more cruel, more inexorable than they; or if, by a pitilefs

tilefs doctrine, you wifh to deprive the old, the fick, and the indigent, of the only idea of happinefs which they can apply to, go from prifon to prifon, and to thofe dreary cells, where the wretched prifoners ftruggle with their chains, and fhut with your own hands, if you have the heart to do it, the only aperture through which any ray of light can reach them.

It is not, however, a fingle clafs of fociety which derives an habitual affiftance from religion, it is all thofe who have to complain of the abufe of authority, of public injuftice, and the different viciffitudes of their fate; it is the innocent man who is condemned, the virtuous man who is flandered, the man who has once acted inconfiftently, and been cenfured with too much rigour; all thofe, in fhort, who, convinced of the purity of their own confcience, feek for, above all, a fecret witnefs of their intentions, and an enlightened judge of their conduct.

A man

· A man of an exalted character, endowed with fenfibility of heart, experiences
alfo the neceffity of forming to himfelf an
image of an unknown Being, to which he
can unite all the ideas of perfection which
fill his imagination; it is to Him that he
refers thofe different fentiments, which are
ufelefs amidft the corruptions which furround him ; it is in God alone that he can
find an inexhauftible fubject of aftonifhment and adoration ; and with Him alone
can he renew and purify his fentiments,
when he is wearied with the fight of the
vices of the world, and the habitual return
of the fame paffions. In fhort, at every
inftant the happy idea of a God foftens and
embellifhes our path through life, and by it
we affociate ourfelves with delight to all the
beauties of nature; by it every thing animated enters into communication with us;
yes, ·the noife of the wind, the murmurs of
the water, the peaceable agitation of plants,
all ferves to fupport, or melt our fouls,
·provided that our thoughts can rife to a
univerfal caufe, provided we can difcover

every

every where the works of Him whom we love, provided we can diftinguifh the veftiges of His footfteps and the traces of His intentions; and, above all, if we can fuppofe, .that we ourfelves contribute to the difplay of His power, and the fplendour of His goodnefs.

But it is principally over the enjoyments of friendfhip that piety fpreads a new charm; bounds, limits, cannot agree with the fentiment which is as infinite as thought, it would not fubfift, at leaft would be troubled with continual anxiety; we fhould not confider without terror the revolution of years and the rapid courfe of time, if thofe benevolent opinions, which enlarge for us the future, did not come to our affiftance. Thus, when we find ourfelves feparated from the objects of our affection, lonely meditations bring them back to aid the general idea of happinefs, which, more or lefs, diftinctly terminates our view; then the tender melancholy, in which one is loft, is changed into pleafing emotions:

M   and

and you have, above all, need of thofe precious opinions, you, who, timid in a buft-
ling world, or difcouraged by difappointments, find yourfelf a folitary wanderer on
the earth, becaufe you partake not of the
paffions which agitate the greater part of
mankind! You want a friend, and you only
fee pecuniary affociations; you want a
comforter, and you only fee the ambitious,
ftrangers to all thofe who have not power
or a diftinguifhed reputation; a tender confident is at leaft neceffary, and the active
fcenes of fociety difperfes the affections and
diminifhes every intereft. In fhort, when
you have this friend, this confident, this
comforter; when you have acquired it by
the moft tender union; when you live in a
fon, a hufband, or a cherifhed wife, what
other idea, but that of a God, can come
to your relief, when the frightful image of a
feparation prefents itfelf to your thoughts?
It is, indeed, in fuch moments that we
embrace with tranfport all thofe [opinions
which tend to fofter the idea of continuity
and duration? How gladly then we lend an

ear

ear to those words of comfort which are so perfectly confonant with the defires and the wants of our foul! What affociation of ideas, fo frightful as that of the eternal an‐nihilation of life and love? How can we unite to that foft divifion of interefts and of fentiments, to that charm of our days; how can we unite to fo much of 'exiftence and happinefs, the internal perfuafion and habitual image of a death without hope, a deftruction without return? How can we offer only the idea of oblivion to thofe 'af‐fectionate minds, who have centred all their felf-love, all their ambition in the object of their efteem and tendernefs; and who, after having renounced themfelves, are, as it were, depofited entirely in the bofom of another, to fubfift there by the fame breath of life and the fame deftiny? In fhort, near the tomb, which, perhaps, they will one day bedew with their tears, how can they .pronounce the overwhelming words, for‐ever!—forever!—Oh! horrors of horrors, both for the mind and feelings! and if it be .neceffary that the contemplations of a

M 2   man

man of feeling approach a moment to the frightful confines, let a benevolent cloud at leaft cover the dark abyfs! Tears and forrow ftill afford fome comfort, when we give them to a beloved fhade, when we can mix with our griefs the name of a God, and when this name appears to you the cement of all nature: but if in the univerfe all was deaf to our voice; if no echoes were to repeat our plaints; if the fhades of eternal darknefs had hid from us the object of our love, and if they were advancing to drag us into the fame night; if he is the moft unhappy being, he who furvives, and cannot even hope, that what death has fevered will again be united; if, when his whole foul was filled with the recollection of a loved object, he could not fay, he is in fome place, his heart fo affectionate, his foul fo pure and heavenly waits for me, and calls me perhaps to be near that unknown Being, whom we have, with common confent, adored; and if, inftead of a thought fo dear, it was neceffary, without any doubt, to confider the earth as a fepulchre forever fhut ſhut—my heart dies within me—unable to contend with the dreadful images, the uni-verſe itſelf ſeems to diſſolve, and overwhelm us in its downfal. O ſource of ſo many hopes, ſublime idea of a God! abandon not the man who has ſenſibility; Thou art his courage, Thou art his futurity, Thou art his life; leave him not deſolate, and, above all, defend him from the aſcendency of a barren and fatal philoſophy, which would afflict his heart by pretending to com-fort it.

Well, I make another effort, and I ad-dreſs myſelf to you, who boaſt of being en-lightened by a freſh ray of wiſdom. I am loſt in the moſt profound grief; a father, a mother, who guided me by their counſels, and watched over me by their tenderneſs, theſe protecting parents have juſt been taken from me; a ſon, a daughter, both my com-fort and pride, have been cut off in the prime of youth; a faithful companion, whoſe words, ſentiments, and actions, were the ſupport of my life, has vaniſhed from

M 3

my

my arms;—a moment of ſtrength remains with me, I come to you, ye philoſophers; what have you to ſay?—" Seek for diſſipa-
" tion, turn your thoughts to ſome other
" object, an abyſs not to be fathomed ſe-
" parates thee for ever from the objects of
" thy tendernefs; and theſe recollections,
" which pierce thee through with ſo many
" ſorrows, they are only a form of vegeta-
" tion, the laſt play of organized matter."
Alas! have you ever loved, and can you pronounce tranquilly theſe cruel words! Baniſh far from me ſuch conſolations, I dread them more than my anguiſh. And thou, O daughter of heaven, lovely and mild religion, what wouldſt thou ſay? Hope, hope; " what God gave thee—He
" can again reſtore." What a difference between theſe two languages! One abaſes, the other exalts us! It is left to men to chooſe, amongſt their different guides, or rather to determine, whether they prefer darkneſs to light, death to life; whether they prefer blighting winds to refreſhing dews; the froſt of winter to the charms of

ſpring;

spring; and the infenfible ftone to the moft.
brilliant gifts of animated nature.

I will fay it: the world, without the
idea of a God, would be only a defert, embellifhed by a few delufions ;—yet man, dif-
enchanted by the light of reafon, would find
nothing throughout but fubjects of fadnefs.
I have feen them, the dreams of ambition,
the allurements of fame, and the vain fhews
of grandeur; and even when the illufion
was moft dazzling, my heart always retired
into itfelf, and was attracted to an idea more
grand, to a confolation more fubftantial; I
have experienced, that the idea of the exiftence of a Supreme Being threw a charm
over every circumftance of life; I have
found, that this fentiment alone was able to
infpire men with true dignity: for every
thing which is merely perfonal is of little
value, all that places fome an inch high
above others; it is neceffary, in order to
have any reafon to glory, that, at the fame
time we exalt ourfelves, we elevate human
nature; we muft refer it to that fublime in-

M 4   telligence,

telligence, which feems to have dignified it with fome of its attributes. We then hardly perceive thofe trivial diftinctions which are attached to tranfitory things, on which vanity exercifes her fway; it is then that we leave to this queen of the world her rattle and toys, and that we fearch elfewhere another portion; it is then alfo that virtue, exalted fentiments, and grand views, appear the only glory of which man ought to be jealous.

C H A P.

CHAP. VI.

The same Subject continued. The Influence of Virtue on Happiness.

IT is not sufficient to have demonstrated, that religion, so necessary to feeling minds, agrees perfectly with the moral nature of men; it is still necessary to observe, that the habitual exercise of virtue, enjoined as a duty in the name of God, is not in opposition with happiness; and after having considered a truth so important, I will prove, that it is not contrary to what has been said in the first chapter of this work, on the impossibility of making men attentive to public order, only by the motive of personal interest.

We cannot deny, that virtue often obliges us to conquer our appetites, and struggle with our passions; but if these conflicts, and the victory which attends them,

them, lead to more solid and durable satisfactions, than those which folly and vice
portrays the image of, they would misconceive the restrictions of morality, who perpetually united the idea of self-denial with
that of a sacrifice.

We cannot fix our attention on the various objects of desire which occupy the
thoughts of men, without seeing clearly,
that if they abandoned themselves, unrestrained, to all their wild propensities, they would
often stray far from the state of happiness
which forms the object of their wishes.
Any of the blessings, strewed here and there
in our path, cannot fill the void of life. Are
they the gratifications of the senses which
captivate us? Their duration is determined
by our weakness; and we cannot break loose
from the immutable limits opposed by nature. Are they the advantages dependent
on opinion that we look for, such as honour
and praise; or the exterior splendour, which
fortune gives? You will soon perceive, that
quickly after they are obtained the charm is
flown;

flown; they refemble Proteus in the fable, who only appeared a God at a diftance. Men then have more need than is fuppofed of an intereft independent of their fenfes and imagination; and this intereft we find in the duties morality inculcates and eftablifhes.

In all times, in all circumftances, we have a choice between good and evil: thus, virtue may be continually in a ftate of action, and we may find the application of it even in the moft apparently indifferent relations of life, becaufe virtue only has the privilege of connecting little things to a great object; and that it can only be encouraged by confcience, which, in accompanying all our actions and meditations, feems to augment our exiftence, and procure thofe fatisfactions which are not known to the crowd who do not act from principle.

Senfual pleafures, the defires of vanity, the longings of ambition, would foon extinguifh themfelves, if they were not fed by the continual activity of fociety, which produces

produces new fcenes, and difplays every mo‐
ment fome changes of decoration. Virtue,
fatisfied with its views, has not need of a
fucceffion of fimilar defires; its paths are
varied, but the end is ever the fame.

We cannot fearch for the enjoyments of
life in the imaginary advantages of opinion,
without allowing others to conftruct the
laws on which our happinefs is founded;
and of courfe difcord muft refult, which leaves
us a prey to every kind of emotion. Virtue
has not any affociates in her counfels, fhe
judges herfelf of all that is good; and in this
refpect a virtuous man is the moft indepen‐
dent of all beings, for it is from himfelf
alone that he receives commands, and ex‐
pects approbation. Yes, the obfcure man,
who does good in fecret, is more mafter of
his deftiny, than the being ever will be who
feems loaded with all the favours of fortune,
and has need, that fafhion and tranfient
gratifications come to determine his tafte,
and give laws to his vanity, to enable him
to enjoy them

The

The little paffions of the world, trying to render us happy, lead us on from one illufion to another, and the laft boundary always appears at a diftance. Virtue, very different, has its recompenfes within itfelf: it is not in events nor in uncertain fuccefs that it places contentment; it is even in our refo-lution, in the calmnefs which accompanies it, and the fecret fentiment which precedes it.

Recollection ever compofes the principal happinefs of virtue, whilft worldly vanity is tormented by the remembrance of what is gone for ever; and with regard to the paf-fions in general, the paft is but a gloomy fhadow, out of which proceed, from time to time, forrow and remorfe.

The intervals which occur between the ftarts of violent paffions, are almoft always filled by fadnefs and apathy; we all know, according to the laws of nature, that lively and ardent fenfations produce languor the moment the tumult is over. Virtue, in the enjoyment of thofe pleafures peculiar to itfelf,

3   knows

knows nothing of thofe irregular emotions, becaufe all its principles are firm, and it acts round its own centre; befides, it alfo invites us continually to fet a juft value on that happinefs which is moft proper for us; it dictates its firft laws in the bofom of domeftic life, and employs all its ftrength to fuftain, by the ties of duty, our moft rational and fimple affections.

Virtue, which is the offspring of religion, is of the greateft ufe in delivering men from the tormenting folicitude of doubt, by prefenting a general fyftem of conduct; and above all, by marking fixed points to direct them, by telling them what to love, choofe, and do. Thus, whilft men, carried away by their imagination, continually allow that they are deceived by phantoms, and lend the moft glowing colours to thofe which have juft efcaped them, virtue fets no value but on what it poffeffes, and knows not regret. It would feem, at the firft glance, that the defires and caprices of the imagination cannot agree with any kind of reftraint;

however,

however, it is not lefs true, that thefe trifling forerunners of our will have need of a
guide, and often of a mafter; our firft inclinations and fentiments are frequently uncertain, weak, and wavering; it is of confequence to our happinefs, that this trembling ftalk fhould be fixed and fupported;
and fuch is the fervice virtue renders to the
human mind.

We fee not any uniformity in the conduct
of thofe who are not influenced by motives
of duty; they have too many things to regulate, too many to decide about every inftant, when convenience is their only guide:
to fimplify the management of ourfelves, we
fhould fubmit to the government of a principle, which may be eafily applied to moft
of our deliberations.

In fhort, virtue has this great advantage,
that it finds its happinefs in a kind of refpect for the rights and claims of the different members of the community, and that
all its fentiments feem to unite themfelves

to

to the general harmony. The paffions, on the contrary, are almoft always hoftile; the vain man defires that others fhould grace his triumphs; the proud wifhes them to feel their inferiority; the ambitious, that they keep clear of his purfuit; the imperious, that they bend to him. It is the fame of the different competitions, which an exceffive love of praife, high reputation, or fortune, gives birth to; in the path they choofe every one would wifh to go alone, or advance before all the reft, and occupied about their own intereft, they clafh inconfiderately with thofe of others. Virtue, very different in following its courfe, fears neither rivals nor competitors; it does not joftle with any one, the road is fpacious, and all may walk at their eafe; it is an orderly alliance, of which morality is the knot, drawing together, by the fame motives and hopes held in common, that chain of duties and fentiments which unite the virtues of men to the ideal model of all perfection.

Virtue,

Virtue, which guards us from the snares of our senses, and checks our blind desires, is besides the basis of the most precious wisdom; but it is not the interest of a day, or the pleasures of a moment, that it protects, it is the whole of life, that it takes under its superintendency; it is, to speak metaphorically, the vindicator of futurity, the representative of duration, and becomes, to the feelings, what foresight is to the mind. We must then, with respect to private manners, consider virtue as a prudent friend, taught by the experience of all ages, who directs our steps, and never lets the flambeau waver, whose salutary light ought to guide them. Our tumultous passions dispute the honour of partaking the government: it is necessary a master should assign to each its proper limits, one who who can keep in peace all these petty domestie tyrants; which reminds us of the image of Ulysses, arriving suddenly in the midst of the hundred kings who had taken possession of his palace.

N   Virtue,

Virtue, some will say, severe in its judgments, and austere in its forms, would it not deprive us of the greatest happiness, the pleasure of being beloved? I reply, that virtue, in its most improved state, has not this character; I represent it to myself as a just sentiment of order, far from banishing all other comforts, it leads to them: thus, benevolence and forbearance, which agree so well with human weakness; the social spirit so consistent with our nature; urbanity in discourse and manner; that amiable expression of a heart, which seeks to unite itself with others; all these qualities, very far from being strangers to virtue, are its attendants and brightest ornament.

Virtue allies itself to all the ideas which can give extent to our mind, and early in life accustoms us to discern relations, and to sacrifice frequently our present affections to distant considerations; it is, of all our sentiments, that which carries us farthest out

of

of ourſelves, and conſequently has the near-
eſt reſemblance with abſtract thinking. It
is then, through the aſſiſtance of virtue,
that a man acquires all his knowledge of
his ſtrength and all his grandeur. Vice, on
the contrary, concentres us in a little ſpace;
it ſeems to be conſcious of its own deformity,
and fears all that ſurrounds it; it endeavours to fix on a ſingle object, on a ſingle
moment, and would wiſh to have power to
draw into a point our whole exiſtence.

I muſt ſtill add, that virtue, by uniting a
motive to all our actions, and by directing
towards an end all our ſentiments, habi-
tuates our mind to order, and juſtneſs of
conception; and prevents our wandering
in too great a ſpace: thus I have often
thought, that it was not only by his vices,
that an immoral man is dangerous in the
adminiſtration of public affairs; we ought
to fear him alſo as unable to comprehend a whole, and for his want of capacity
to rally all his thoughts and direct them
towards any general principle: every kind

N 2   of

of harmony is unknown to him, every rule is become a burthen; he is busy, but only by starts; and it is by accident that a man, always versatile, stumbles on what is right.

It may then truly be said, that morality serves as ballast to our sentiments, its aid enables us to go on without being agitated continually by the caprices of our imagination, without being obliged to turn back at the first appearance of an obstacle.

Virtue then enlarges the mind, gives dignity to the character, and invests it with every thing becoming. Of all the qualities of men, the most rare, the most apt to create respect, is, that elevation of thought, sentiment, and manners; that majestic consistency of character which truth alone can preserve, but which the least exaggeration, the most trivial affectation, would disconcert or banish. This resembles not pride, and still less vanity, as one of its ornaments is, that it never seeks for the homage of others: the man endowed with real dignity,

nity, is placed above even his judges ; he accounts not with them, he lives under the government of his confcience, and, proud of fuch a noble ruler, he does not wifh for any other dependence : but as this grandeur is entirely within himfelf, it ceafes to exift, when he dictates to others what he expects from them ; it can only be reftrained in its. juft limits by virtues which do not pretend to dazzle.

It is to the fame principle, that men owe that noble refpect for virtue, the moft graceful ornament of a great foul; they owe to it alfo that fimplicity in thinking and fpeaking, that happy habit of a confcience not in want of being on its guard. A man truly honeft confiders difguife as a detractor, and defires to appear as he really is ; it is not his intereft to conceal his weakneffes, for in a generous heart they are almoft always united to fomething good; and perhaps franknefs would have become the policy of his mind, if it had not been one of the qualities of his character.

There

There is, in every virtue, a kind of beauty which charms us without reflection : our moral fenfe, when it is improved by education, is pleafed with that focial harmony which the fentiments of juftice preferves. Thefe enjoyments are unknown to men, whofe felfifhnefs renders them infenfible to every kind of concord, and they appear to me to deferve our contempt in one effential point; it is, that they profit by the refpect others have for order, without being willing to fubject themfelves to the fame rules, and without declaring publickly their intention; it feems to me, that, in this view, a defect of morality is indeed a breach of the laws of hofpitality.

In fhort, talents, thofe faculties of the mind which belong more immediately to nature, can never be applied to great things without the aid of morality; there is no other way of uniting the intereft of men, and of attaining their love and refpect. Honefty refembles the ancient idioms, according to which you muft know how to fpeak, when you

you wifh to be underftood by the generality; and a language is never well known,
but by conftant practice. The underftanding is fometimes fufficient to acquire
an afcendency in circumfcribed relations;
you there take men one by one; and you
often engage them by proportioning yourfelf to their depth: but on a vaft theatre,
and principally in public adminiftration,
where we have need of captivating men in
a body, it is neceffary to fearch for a band
which will embrace all; and it is only by a
union of talents and virtue that this chain
can be formed. And when I fee the homage paid by a nation to virtuous characters; when I remark the almoft inftinctive judgment which affifts in difcerning
them; when I fee that they praife and
love only what they can connect to pure
virtue; and noble intention, I return to my
favourite fentiment, and believe I recognize
in thefe emotions the ftamp of a hand
divine.

N 4 After

After having tried to give a feeble sketch of the various recompenses and different satisfactions which seem to appertain to regularity of principles, and propriety of conduct, you will perhaps afk; if you have not a right to conclude from these reflections, that we can attach men to morality by the mere motive of perfonal intereft; I have already mentioned, that I intended to anfwer fuch an objection, and now is the time to do it.

Virtue, in its moft improved ftate; virtue, fuch as we have juft reprefented, is not the work of a moment; it is neceffary that it fhould be called forth and ftrengthened by degrees; but it would be nipped when it firft begins to unfold itfelf, if we deftroyed the fimple opinions which ferve to educate it; if we overturned the only end which can be perceived by all minds; and if we weakened the fentiments which connect it with thofe who refpect the laws of morality, and who promote this cultivation by their commendations and efteem.

Befides,

Besides, it is not virtue only, but virtue united to different motives, which contributes to our happiness. This obfervation is very important, and with great facility you may be made to feel the full force of it. Employment is generally reckoned the fureft fource of agreeable impreffions of which we are fufceptible; but its charm would vanifh, if it did not lead to fome recompenfe, if it did not fhow, in perfpective, an increafe of wealth, an enjoyment for our felf-love, a chance for fame, or fome other advantages of which we are defirous. Vainly, fay fome, that the exercife of our faculties is of itfelf a pleafure; certainly, becaufe that it offers to our view a train of profpects which fucceed each other. But there muft always be a ftrong motive to direct us to the right road, and make us fet off; our bark muft be driven by the wind; in fhort, every kind of labour requires encouragement, although this labour, proportioned to our ftrength, may be more favourable to happinefs then floth and idlenefs; and this truth would ftrike us.

us ſtill more, if we had ability to analyze a ſentiment with ſufficient attention, to diſtinguiſh clearly the happineſs which is annexed to action and employment, from that which neceſſarily relates to the end and to the motive of that action.

The reflections, which I have juſt made, may be applied to virtue; we can eaſily, in ſtudying its different effects, perceive, that it is an excellent guide in the courſe of life; but we diſcover, at the ſame time, that it has need, as well as employment, of a ſpur, a ſimple encouragement on a par with our underſtanding: it is in religion that virtue finds this encouragement, and we ſhall not be able to ſeparate it from the motives and hopes it preſents, without diſconcerting every connexion it has with human happineſs.

It will be eaſy to perceive the great benefit which muſt ariſe from morality; but at the ſame time it muſt be remarked, that to follow its dictates with confidence and firmneſs, knowledge and
ſtrong

ftrong powers of reflection are neceffarily required in the ftudy of fo compounded a truth: we are then in want of a
motive to excite our firft effort, which
fubjects us to felf-denial, and determines us
to ftruggle with courage againft the dominion of the prefent moment.

In fhort, even when, by the art of fophiftry, fome philofophers have, at length,
thrown into confufion the true principles
of order and happinefs; when, by the force
of addrefs, they have led us to doubt about
the kind and degree of power which it is
neceffary to affign to religion, it fhould not,
however, be the legiflators of the nation
who ought to lend an ear to their fubtle
diftinctions.

Metaphyfical fentiments and ideas are
not proper for ftatefman, but in their own
defence; to affift them to guard themfelves
from the afcendency of brilliant errors, and
to confirm the refpect due to ufeful truths:
but when they have to guide minds, when
they

they wifh to excite activity, it is always, if they are wife, the moft fimple idea that they will make ufe of; and they will be very careful not to despife thofe habitual principles, to which time, ftill more then knowledge, has given a fanction. Thefe are fo many leffons, which long experience feems to have gradually difengaged from every thing foreign to natural morality and the fecret fentiments of men.

CHAP.

C H A P. VII.

On Religious Opinions, in their Relation with
Sovereigns.

MANY nations, either by choice, or neceſſity, have depoſited their wills in the hands of an individual; and have thus erected a perpetual monument to the ſpirit of diſcord, and injuſtice, which has ſo frequently reigned amongſt men. It is true, that from time to time they have wiſhed to recollect that they were capable of knowing themſelves their true intereſt; but monarchs miſtruſting their inconſtancy, have taken care to fortify the ſprings of authority, by ſurrounding themſelves with ſtanding armies; and they have only left them the power of being diſguſted with ſlavery: ſoldiers and taxes have ſupported each other; and through the aſſiſtance of this correſponding action, they have become maſters and directors of every thing. How

much

much good and evil depend on them? We then neceſſarily wiſh them to poſſeſs a vigo- rous morality, proportioned to their immenſe duties ; but what force will your morality have, if they perceive at laſt, that it is not ſupported by a divine ſanction ; if they conſider it as a human inſtitution, which they have power to break, and which they are in the habit of modifying? At leaſt they will have the liberty, like other men, to examine if their private intereſt agrees with that of the public, and their conduct will depend on the reſult of this calculation.

I will acknowledge, that at the point of elevation, where kings find themſelves placed, they ought not to be acquainted with thoſe paſſions which proceed from our petty competitions ; but how many other ſentiments have they not to repreſs? And with what celerity it is neceſſary to do it ; ſince they do not experience any contradic- tion, they are not, like us, obliged to reflect and confider ! Beſides, though foveriegns are ſuppoſed to be ſheltered by their ſituation,

from

from the irritations of felf-love, and from
the defires of fortune and advancement,
they are "not, however, difengaged from
every paffion of this kind; it is towards
other princes that they feel them; and envy,
ambition, and revenge, become often very
dangerous, as they affociate with thefe paffions thofe of the nation they govern, by
means of a war. It is then that, freed from
religious ties, and fure of not accounting
with any body, they would find morality a
very ingenious invention, to render the
maintenance of public order more eafy, and
to preferve the fubordination which fecures
their power; but, would not acknowledge
fuch a mafter for themfelves, and would difpenfe with bowing to its dictates.

You will fay, undoubtedly, that a virtuous king would be recompenfed by the
applaufe of his fubjects: but I have already fhown, that the influence of public
opinion would be very weak, if the principles of morality, which ferve to guide this
opinion, were not fupported by religion.
We

We fhould alfo obferve, that elogiums ·and applaufe, homage fo encouraging to·private men, have not an equal power over princes, who cannot, like individuals, confider this fuffrage as an earneft, or forerunner, of exaltation; it is by the continual view ·of the advantages and triumphs of others, that the defire of refpect and diftinction is continually kept alive; and it may, perhaps, proceed a· little from the ftimulation ·of envy, or at leaft from thofe jarring pretentions,·and from thofe ftruggles of felf-love, of which fociety alone is the theatre. Princes without rivals are not ·fubject to the fame impreffions; and the flattery they have fo early imbibed, and the praifes which are lavifhed on them from the fim-ple motive of hope, all ferve to render them lefs fenfible to deferved applaufe;· ·in fhort, this exaggerated praife foon becomes a dull monotony, which extinguifhes,· by its uniformity, · that emulation which ·a juft homage fometimes infpires.· There would ·be then ·great danger in repofing. too much on the power of public opinion, if ·we ·were· to

confider

confider it as a check able to replace with princes the compreffing force of religion. '

I muft now make an effential remark: thofe who furround a monarch, often miflead his judgment by the nature and the application of the elogiums which they lavifh on him. The praife of men, in a monarchy, always has a taint of flavery: thus, in fuch countries, a look, a word from the prince, which feems to efface, for an inftant, the diftance that feparates him from his fubjects, delights them; and their enthufiafm in thofe moments ferves to perfuade the monarch, that it is fufficient for him to fmile, to render his people happy: dangerous illufion, fad effect of fervility: in fhort, in confequence of the character which is impreffed by an habitual yoke, men are pleafed with exalting the power of him to whom they are obliged to fubmit; they love to fee their fervile companions multiplied; and as the greater part of them have feldom any accefs to the prince, vanity perfuades them, that in af-

feting

fecting to partake of the royal grandeur, they contract a kind of familiarity with it; therefore, without reflecting whether it will be more in the power of the fovereign to make them happy, when, by enlarging his dominions, he fhall have more fubjects, and of courfe more duties to fulfil, they celebrate, above all, the conquering warrior, and thus invite princes to prefer the purfuit of military glory to every other; and, as the multitude can quickly comprehend this kind of merit; as the gaining of a battle is a fimple idea, eafily conceived by men of every condition and turn of mind, it happens, by this reafoning, that thefe triumphs are the moft highly extolled; and even that men, on account of them, can excufe every other failure, broken treaties, violated oaths, alliances abandoned—In fhort, fuch is the mad folly of our praife, that the tranquillity of the ftate, the repofe of the people, the mild benefits of peace, appear no more than the laft confequence of the labours and the fuccefs of a monarch; and even hiftory frequently reprefents this fortunate time, as

the

the days of obfcurity in which heroes
of blood and carnage are educated; kings,
difcontented with their deftiny, are warriors
through ambition, and happy by the vic-
tories, to which we annex our firft honours, and the moft noble wreaths of
fame.

It is thus, however, that the prevailing
opinion, and the rumour of renown, can
fometimes deceive princes, though incon-
confiftent with the inftructions of morality and the legiflation of yore, which
point out the true intereft of the people
as the firft object of a fovereign's anxious
folicitude; and inftead of a founding name,
and dazzling qualities, enforce thofe requifite
to form the guardian and protector of the fe-
ilcity of the public; duties of a vaft extent,
and which are difcharged by the fecret labours of paternal vigilance, ftill more than
by the noife of the drum and the inftruments of deftruction.

Let

Let us confider, however, the influence the opinion of the world will have on fovereigns, in directing only our views towards the interior functions of adminiftration. An effential obfervation prefents itfelf at firft to the mind: it is, that the thirft for glory is efpecially felt when a great abufe is to be reformed, and when we can hope to make regularity fucceed to confufion; but when this tafk is fulfilled, and that it is only neceffary to preferve and fupport what is good, the love of renown has not fufficient aliment, and it is then that the virtue of princes becomes the only faithful guardian of the public intereft. A reign, fuch as we have formed an idea of, would carry away from the following ones every fubject of dazzling fplendour; and it would be neceffary that new troubles and fears re-animated the fentiment of admiration, to give it its ancient afcendency and original force.

We fhould be able alfo, and this picture would be very different, to figure

to

to..ourfelves a period,. when, by the fuc-;. ceffive. degradation .of character, the opi- nion of the public would no longer in- dicate the way to fame, nor refound to excite ambition; the recompenfes it offers would not be a motive fufficiently powerful to influence men. Thus, in a country, in a metropolis, where covetoufnefs feemed tri- umphant, where every body would appear to purfue that fortune which is only ac- quired by intrigue, and the vices of thofe who beftow it, refpect for the real intereft of the people, and attention to lighten their burthens, would no longer purchafe renown. In like manner, in a country where defpo- tifm reigns, and the people are accuftomed to proftrate themfelves before power, they would acknowledge no other idol; we fhould not there be able to acquire a contemporary fame by elevation of character, by temper- ing with wifdom the exercife of authority, and allowing the citizens to enjoy that de- gree of freedom, which does not degene- rate into licentioufnefs. It is then mora- lity, and morality alone, which comes at

all

all times, and in all circumftances, to refift the revolutions of habit and opinion, of which hiftory furnifhes examples, and of which men are ever fufceptible.

I ought not to neglect another very important confideration : princes, by the elevation of their rank, and influence on the national manners, find that they are in that fingular fituation, where one is more called to direct the reigning opinion, than to receive inftruction and encouragement from it : thus we are impelled to wifh, that a monarch fhould have principles which flow from his heart, and which depend on his reflections, from which he may be able to derive, at all times, a force properly his own, a natural courage. It is neceffary for a prince to inveftigate and decide on his own conduct ; and a fublime morality fhould nourifh in his heart an ideal model of perfection, with which he can continually compare the opinions of the world and the private judgment of his confcience.

In

In ſhort, and this laſt reflection which I have made will apply, in a general manner, to the preceeding remarks; the opinion of the public, the juſt complaints of the peoٍ. ple, are ſometimes a long while in reaching the prince; they ring in the kingdom before he hears the rumour; they wander round the palace, but the whiſpers do not reach him; vanity, pride, and every vice excludes them; the old courtiers ſneer, and the inſignificant purſuers of credit or faٍ. vour amuſe themſelves by indulging their turn for ridicule. The miniſters, who are followed by the clamour, are often importuned by it; and when it reaches their maſter, find ſome method to weaken its impreſſion, attributing theſe commotions to private paſſions, and giving the name of cabal to a juſt indignation againſt vice. Yes, ſuch is the unhappy fate of princes, that the peace of a ſtate is often tottering, before the opinion of the world reaches them, and diſcovers the truth; a new conſideration, very proper to convince us, that the power of opinion can never equal in

utility

utility thofe grand principles of morality, which, by the aid of religion, are fixed in the hearts of men, to give them laws, without diftinction of birth, rank, or dignity.

But if, from fovereigns, we carry our views to thofe who fhare their confidence, we fhall perceive ftill more the abfolute neceffity of an active and-governing morality. Minifters, without virtue, are more to be feared than fovereigns indifferent to public good; newly come out of the crowd they know better than the monach the felfifh ufe that they can make of all the paffions and vices; and as they are connected with fociety, as they have a continual relation with the different orders of the ftate, their corruptions are propagated, and their dangerous influence fpreads to a great diftance. Attacked, neverthelefs, by the public, they become ftill more mifchievous in their means of warding off danger, for defpairing of difguife before the attentive eyes of a whole people, they turn their addrefs

against

against the prince; they study, they pry into his weakneſſes, and artfully encourage thoſe which may protect or cover the de-fects of their character; they apply them-ſelves, at the ſame time, to adorn immo-rality with every grace which can render it amiable, and they endeavour to make virtue hateful, by delineating it as auſtere, impe-rious, unſociable, and almoſt incompatible with our morals and manners: it is thus that miniſters, not reſtrained by principles, occaſion not only the miſery of a country whilſt their influence laſts, but they poiſon the ſource of public felicity, by weakening in the monarch his ſentiments of duty, di-verting his good diſpoſitions, and diſcou-raging, if I may ſay ſo, his natural virtues.

In ſhort, the picture which I have juſt drawn will produce another important obſer-vation: the prince, after having wandered out of the path of true glory, may return, when he pleaſes, to the love of virtue and great-neſs; all the avenues are open to him, all hearts ready to welcome him, we have an inclination to love him, and deſire to

esteem

efteem him, whom fate has placed at the
head of the nation; and who, invefted with
the majefty which he borrows from a long
train of anceftors, exhibits himfelf furrounded by all the enchantments of a dia-
dem; we adopt with pleafure any interpretation which can excufe his conduct; we
impute to ill counfels the faults which he
has commited; and we are eager to enter
with him into a new contract of efteem and
hope. It is not the fame with minifters;
a like indulgence is not due to them, becaufe they cannot throw the blame on
others, and all their actions proceed from
themfelves; when they have once loft the
opinion of the public, their depravity will
increafe daily; becaufe, to maintain their
poft they are obliged to redouble their intrigues and diffimulation.

I have maturely reflected: the religion
of princes, of minifters, of government in
general, is the firft fource of the happinefs
of the people; we defpife it, becaufe it is
not our invention, and we often give the
preference

preference to thofe artifices of the mind, which feduce us as being our own work; and perhaps they are wanted, after having loft fight of this fure and faithful guide, this companion of true genius, which, like it, prefers eafy and fimple means. Yes, this exalted virtue, refembling fuperior abilities, rejects equally thofe weak refources and inventions, which derive not their origin from an elevated fentiment or grand thought; and, whilft one obliges a ftatefman to refpect honour, juftice, and truth, the other difcovers the union of thefe principles with the juft means which ftrengthen authority; and with the true glory and durable fuccefs of politics; in fhort, whilft one renders him anxious about the happinefs of the people, the other fhows how, from the bofom of this happinefs, they would fee rife infenfibly an agreement of interefts and of wills, of whofe extenfive ufe we are ftill ignorant.

If we wifh to dwell a moment on the private happinefs of princes, we fhall readily

dily perceive, that they have a real want of the encouragement religion affords. Their distinguished authority appears, indeed, to their mind, a singular privilege; they believe this power should extend to every thing, and they indiscretly endeavour to accelerate the moments of enjoyment; but as they cannot change the law of nature, it happens, that in delivering themselves up to every thing which seduces their imagination, they experience as quickly the sad langour of indifference, and the oppression of apathy.

Kings, in the exercise of their intellectual faculties are exposed to the same extremes; providence having placed them on the pinnacle of fortune, they consequently have not been led from one view to another, and know not those gradations which actuate their subjects in the name of vanity, self-love, or fortune.—Alas! we obey so quickly, and their desires are so soon gratified, that their taste and inclinations cannot be renewed with the quickness necessary to enable them to

fill

fill the irkfome void which fo frequently occurs. If the magnificent end which religion offers were to be obfcured, and if, henceforth, we were to confider it as a fallacious illufion, unworthy of our attention, kings would foon attain to that term when the future would appear to their mind a barren uniformity, a fpace without colour or form.

The numerous duties of princes, undoubtedly, afford a continual fource of fatisfaction; but it is neceffary that they fhould be able to connect all their obligations to a grand idea, the only one which can conftantly animate their actions and thoughts, who have need of neither favour nor advancement from their fellow-creatures. And how much would it contribute to their happinefs fometimes, to imagine themfelves between this world, in which they are weary of their own power, and that magnificent future; the fublime contemplation of which would carry them, with a new charm, to the exercife of their authority! What pleafure then would flow

from

from this authority, the fource of fo much good!—What pleafure would they not find in more clófely imitating the divine benefi-cence, the moft comfortable of all ideas, and what a moment for him, when particularly confcious of the prefence of the exalted friend of the whole human race, he fhould be able to reflect, in the morning, on the people he was going to make happy; and in the evening, on thofe he had actually done good to. What a difference between thefe delicious moments, whofe influence the nation feels, and thofe infignificant levees, only known to courtiers, in which the monarch is the fpectacle, and taftes the fad pleafure of feeing fo many men cringing before his own image. What a difference, even be-tween thefe rapturous fenfations, and thofe raifed by flattery, or the dazzling parade which furrounds him, in the midft of which he cannot difcern himfelf, whether he is a great man, or only a king.

In fhort, we ought to acknowledge, that the more extenfive the horizon, which opens

before

before fovereigns, the greater is the number of duties prefented to their reflections, the more they muft feel the want of that fuftaining power fo infinitely fuperior to their own ftrength : they are confcious of the difproportion which exifts between the extent of their authority and the means en-trufted to human nature; and it is only by fupporting themfelves againft that myfte-rious pillar, erected by religion, that they can be firm, and confider without affright, that Providence has called them to regulate and direct the deftiny of a whole empire. It was when profoundly meditating on the exiftence of a God; reflecting on the influence and various relations of fuch a grand thought, that Marcus Aurelius difcovered all the extent of his duties, and felt, at the fame time, the courage and the will to ful-fil them. The happy and conftant agree-ment of his actions and principles made his reign an illuftrious example of wifdom and morality.

We muft confefs, that it is to virtue, fupported by every fentiment which

it

it imprints on the human heart, that we
fhould wifh to confide the facred depo-
fite of public happinefs ; this alone is
always faithful and vigilant, furpaffes the
fpur of praife, and, by the afcendency
of a great example, leads men to the
knowledge of every thing they ought to
admire.

C H A P.

CHAP. VIII.

An Objection drawn from the Wars and from the Commotions which Religion has given Rife to.

I SHALL prefent, at firft, this objection in all its force, or rather I will not feek to weaken it; it would be needlefs to recal to the memory of men all the evils that have happened during a long feries of years, with which we have reafon to reproach the blind and favage zeal of religious fanaticifm. Every one has prefent to his mind thofe multiplied acts of intolerance which have fullied the annals of hiftory; every one knows the fcenes of difcord, of war, and fury, which theological controverfies have caufed amongft men; they have been in-formed of the fatal confequences which thefe enterprizes have brought in their train, and which the rare virtues of a great king have not been able to juftify. In fhort, to maintain, in all ages, a remem-brance of the fatal abufes which have been

P

com-

committed in the name of the God of
Peace, it would be fufficient to defcribe
thofe direful days, when fome different te-
net produced a fentence of profcription, and
the frightful fignal of the moft cruel fren-
zies.

It is thus then, that in all times, by an
abfurd tyranny, or by a ferocious enthufiafm,
triumphs have been contrived for the eager
detractors of religion. Let us examine,
however, if the deductions that they wifh
to draw from thefe errors of the human
mind, are founded on reafon and juftice.

I fhall not ftop to obferve, that religion has oftener been the pretext, than the
true motive, of the unhappy convulfions of
which it appears at prefent the fole origin; or ftop to recal the various political
advantages, which could only arife from
fuch a grand principle of action; thofe auguft teftimonies are commemorated in hiftory: I fhall only borrow the fupport of
reafon,

reafon, and fhall bound my difcuffion to a few fimple reflections.

Do you think, that by relating the different abufes of authority we could prove the advantage of anarchy? Could we decry every fpecies of jurifprudence, by recounting all the ills which have been produced by chicane? Should we be able to throw an odium on the fciences, by recalling all the fatal difcoveries which are owing to our refearches? Would it be proper to ftifle every kind of felf-love and activity, by reciting the different crimes which covetoufnefs, pride, and ambition have given rife to? And ought we, then, to defire to annihilate religion, becaufe fanaticifm has made an inftrument of it to diftrefs the human fpecies? All thefe queftions are fimilar, and all fhould be refolved in the fame manner: thus we may fay with refpect to them, that in all our interefts and paffions, it is by acquired knowledge, and the light of reafon, that right is feparated from wrong; but we

P 2 ought

ought never to confound their proximity with a real identity.

Fanaticifm and religion have not any connection, though very often thefe ideas are found united. It is not the worfhip of the common Father of men ; it is not the morality of the gofpel, whofe precepts lead to goodnefs and forbearance, which infpires the fpirit of perfecution ; we fhould attribute it to a blind madnefs, refembling all thofe wild errors and crimes which difhonour humanity. But fince, at prefent, the exceffes to which men abandon themfelves do not induce us to condemn, as a misfortune, all the fentiments of which the criminal paffions are only the extreme, why do we wifh to refufe religion the gratitude which is its due, becaufe fometimes it has given birth to hatred and unhappy divifions ? It would be neceffary rather to remark, that intolerant zeal is, of all the errors of the human mind, that on which the progrefs of our knowledge appears to have had moft influence. In fact, whilft fanaticifm,

4   gradually

gradually weakened, feems to be now verg-
ing to its decline, the diforders connected
with the common paffions of ambition, love
of wealth, and thirft of pleafure, remain in
all their force. However, what fentiment,
what predominant idea, has a greater claim
to pardon for its miftakes than devotion?
By what an infinite number of benefits the
pure fpirit of religion makes amends for the
abufes which fpring from the falfe interpretation of its precepts. It is to this fpirit,
as we have fhown, that men owe the ftability of public order and the firm principles
of juftice: it procures the indigent the fuccours of charity, and virtue its encouragement; oppreffed innocence its only refuge,
and fenfibility its deareft hopes. Yes, the
pure fpirit of religion furrounds us on every
fide, it makes the charm of folitude, the
band of fociety, the invigorater of intimate
affections; and can we calumniate it and
wifh to deftroy it, on recollecting the tyrannic opinions of fome priefts and fovereigns, whofe principles and conduct we now
deteft?

P 3

I fhall

I fhall further remark, and afk why men denounce a fentence of reprobation againft religion, and give as the motive, the ancient wars of which it has been the origin; whilft they never conteft the importance of commerce, though rivers of blood have been continually fhed for the fmalleft advantage on this account? Can they be fo miftaken in their judgment, as to compare a few pecuniary advantages, which one political ftate never enjoys, but at the expence of another, with thofe, as precious as they are univerfal, of which religion is the origin and fupport?

In fhort, among the various arguments that are employed to attack thefe opinions, the moft frivolous, undoubtedly, is that which derives all its force from the errors and faults of which the prefent times do not furnifh any example. What fhould we fay if, at the moment when a fuperb edifice was firm on its foundation, we fhould be exhorted to level it with the ground, by a relation of all the accidents its erection occafioned?

Throwing

Throwing then a painful retrofpect on the period of hiftory, when religion was made the pretext of wars and cruelty; let us oppofe to the return of thofe fanguinary fcenes, let us oppofe to the fpirit of intoler‑ance all the force of wifdom, and the in‑ftructions of that religion which they pre‑tend to ferve by a blind zeal. But far from freeing us from the refpect which we owe to fuch falutary opinions, which men have abufed, let us take advantage of experience, as a new defence againft the wanderings of our imaginations, and the furprifes of our paffions *.

* I fhould have enlarged this chapter, if I did not intend to make fome general reflections on intolerance in another part of this work.

P 4 CHAP.

CHAP. IX.

Another Objection examined. The Sabbath.

I DO not intend to place among the objections I ought to discuss, nor in the
number of arguments, that it is important
to examine, the various opinions on such
and such parts of religious worship, nor the
difficulties raised against the adoption of
some dogmatic notion, thought essential by
some, and considered with indifference by
others: it is not a treatise of controversial
theology which I wish to compose; and it
is still less the doctrines of one particular
church, which I would oppose to that of
another; all of them connect morality to
the commands of a Supreme Being; they
all of them see in the public worship the
respectful expression of a sentiment of love
and gratitude towards the Author of Nature. Thus, those who might think they
perceived some imperfections in the system,

or

or in the forms of worſhip, adopted in a nation, ſhould not uſe this objection to diſpute the utility of religion, ſince the reflections, which have been juſt made on its importance, may be applied equally to the doctrines of all countries, and the principles of every ſect.

I ſhall dwell then on the only difficulty which intereſts, without diſtinction, the different religions of Europe.

The eſtabliſhment of public worſhip, and the neceſſity of conſecrating at leaſt one day in every week, occaſions, ſay ſome, a ſuſpenſion of labour too frequent; and this ſuſpenſion injures the ſtate, and diminiſhes the reſources of the people.

I may at firſt obſerve, that ſuch objections would appear very weak, if compared with the great advantages which men owe to religion! An increaſe of wealth can never outweigh order, morality, and happineſs. But I muſt go further to prove, that

that a day of reft, devoted amongft us to public worfhip, cannot injure the political ftrength; and that fo far from being contrary to the interefts of the people, it protects and favours them; and as I invariably pre-fer fuch interefts to all others, I fhall begin by demonftrating, in a few words, the juft-nefs of this propofition.

We fhould be miftaken if we thought, that in a given fpace of time, men forced, by the inequality of conditions, to live by their labour, would, by obferving the precepts of religion, better their fituation, if they were not obliged to reft from labour one day in every week.

It is neceffary, in order to perceive this truth, to examine, firft, what is now the meafure of wages; it is not an exact pro-portion between labour and its reward. In fact, if we confulted only the light of rea-fon and equity, no one, I believe, would dare to decide, that the moft fcanty necef-faries is the juft price of fatiguing and painful

ful labour, which commences at the dawn,
and does not finifh till the fetting of the
fun : we fhould not be able to maintain,
that in the midft of his enjoyments, and in
the bofom of luxurious idlenefs, the rich
ought not to grant any other retribution to
thofe who facrifice their time and ftrength
to increafe their revenue and multiply their
enjoyments. It is not then by the principles of common fenfe or reflection, that
the wages of the generality have been fixed;
it is a compact eftablifhed by power, a yoke
to which the weak muft fubmit. The
poffeffor of a vaft domain would fee all his
riches vanifh, if numerous labourers did not
come to cultivate his eftate, and carry into
his ftore-houfe the fruit of their toil; but,
as the number of men without property is
immenfe, their concurrence, and the preffing need that they have to labour for a
fubfiftence, obliges them to receive the law
from him who can, in the bofom of eafe,
wait quietly for their fervices; and it refults from this habitual relation between
the rich and poor, that the wages for hard
labour

labour are conftantly reduced to .the· moft fcanty allowance, that is to fay, to what is only fufficient to fatisfy their daily and in-difpenfable wants.

This fyftem once fettled, if it were pof-fible, that, by a revolution in our nature, men could live and preferve their ftrength without allotting every day fome hours to repofe and fleep, it is beyond doubt, that the work of twenty hours would be re-quired for, the fame wages now granted for twelve.

Or, by an affimilation, agreeing with the hypothefis I have juft mentioned, fup-pofe that a moral revolution permitted ·la-boures to work the feventh day, they would confequently, in a .fhort time, require of them the extraordinary labour at the former rate; and this levelling would · take place through the gradual diminution of the price .of labour. The clafs of fociety, which, in exerting its .power,. has· regulated · the prefent wages, not according to reafon and equity,

equity, but according to the neceffities of the labourers, would quickly difcern its own intereft; and that when a day more was paid for, the people could bear a diminu- tion of the feventh part of their wages, and be in their old ftate. Thus, though before the change had thoroughly taken place, all thofe who live by labour would think that they had acquired a new refource; yet they would foon be brought to their former condition; for it is the fame with focial order as with the law of equilibrium in nature, which combines ranks and places, every thing according to the immutable law of the proportion of force.

Men, devoid of property, after having been fome time deceived, would only get an increafe of work by the abolition of the Sab- bath; and as this truth does not prefent itfelf naturally to the mind, we ought to confider, as an effential fervice of religion, its having fecured the greater number of men from a degree of oppreffion, to which they would

would have run blindly, if they had been
at liberty to make a choice.

The daily labour of one clafs of fociety
furpaffes the reafonable meafure of its
ftrength, and haftens the days of decripi-
tude; it was then abfolutely neceffary that
the cuftomary courfe of thefe labours fhould
be, for a time, fufpended; but as the people, preffed by wants of every kind, are expofed to be feduced by the flighteft appearance of advantage, it was further neceffary to their happinefs, that the interrup-
tion of thier fatigues, fixed by a religious
duty, appeared not to them the voluntary facrifice of fortune, and did not leave in them
any regret. In fhort, they are pleafed when
they think of thofe days of reft, which produce a little alteration in their manner of
living; and they require that alteration, not
to be depreffed by a continual train and re-
petition of the fame occupations. Thus,
were you to affert artfully, that the people
are not as comfortable of a Sunday, as during the week, it would be at leaft true,

that

that one is softened by the expectation of the other; there are people so very wretched, and probably, on that account, so bounded are their defires, that the moft trifling variety is a fubftitute for hope. It feems to me, that the hearts of the common people may be fometimes cheered with the thought of being once a week dreffed like their fuperiors; when they are abfolute mafters of their time, and can fay,—and I alfo—I am free *.

* Thefe various reflections are very neceffary in the place where I live; fince, for a fhort time, labourers have been permitted to work, at Paris, of a Sunday. We fee this publicly done at the new bridge, which is building over the Seine, as if a work of mere convenience was in fuch hafte, that the laws fhould be difpenfed with to accelerate its execution. The labourers, fome will fay, are glad to gain a day every week. Undoubtedly, becaufe they fee only the prefent inftant, they have reafon to think fo; but it is the duty of government to confider, in a more comprehenfive point of view, the intereft of the people, of that part of fociety, which is fo blind, or fo limited in its calculation; and the church fhould examine alfo, if the fudden alteration of a practice fo ancient, may not give rife to an idea, that the fpirit of religion is grown feeble. For the nations where this fpirit is beft preferved, have the greateft refpect for the Sabbath.

I muft

. .I muſt now examime the ſecond propoſi-
tion which I have mentioned.

You have made obvious, ſome will ſay,
that an augmentation of the days of labour
would occaſion a reduction of the wages
allowed for it; we may then reaſonably aſk,
if this reſult would not favour commerce,
and contribute, in ſome reſpect, to increaſe
the political ſtrength? Undoubtedly you
may conſider under this point of view, the
diminution of the reward of induſtry; but
the political ſtrength being always a relative idea, and derived from compariſons with other ſtates, this ſtrength can
never be augmented or diminiſhed by a cir-
cumſtance common to all the countries of
Europe. Were a barbarous ambition to
aboliſh in one ſtate the Sabbath, the abolition would probably procure it a degree of
ſuperiority, if it was the only one that
adopted ſuch a change; but as ſoon as
others followed their example, the advantage would diſappear. However, the ſame
arguments ought to ſerve to convince us,
that

that thofe countries, where the intervals of inaction occur oftener, have necessarily a political difadvantage, with regard to others, where Sunday and a few folemn feafts are the only days of reft prefcribed by government.

We may conclude from thefe obfervations, that fo far from finding fault with religion for appointing a day of reft, devoted every week to public worfhip, we ought to acknowledge with pleafure, that fuch an inftitution is a benevolent act, extended to the moft numerous clafs of the inhabitants of the earth, the moft deferving our confideration and protection; from which we require fo much, and return fo little: towards that unfortunate clafs, whofe youth and maturity the rich profit by, and abandon them when the hour is come, when they have no more ftrength left but to enable them to pray and weep.

Q   CHAP:

CHAP. X.

*An Obfervation on a particular Circum-
ftance of public Worfhip.*

IT is not fufficient, that fovereigns are perfuaded of the influence of religion on the
morality and happinefs of men ; they ought
to make ufe of proper means to maintain this falutary action ; and, of courfe,
every part of public worfhip becomes of
the greateft importance.   Educated in a religion, thought by fome to approach nearer
the firft ideas of chriftianity, yet as it has
adopted feveral principles by no means confonant with the Catholic faith, it would be
unwife in me to difcufs any of the queftions
which divide the two churches ; and I
fhould do it without any good accruing
from it, fo much are we difpofed to refer
to early prejudices, the ideas which are
moft intimately blended with the fentiments
and feeling of a man ; we like to take a

general

general view, and this method agrees with our indolence; but it leads us often aftray. I think, however, that the minds of the people are now fufficiently enlightened, to permit me to advife the fuperiors of both church and ftate, to examine attentively, if it is not full time to make more ufe of the vulgar tongue, and if we are not warned, by the prefent depravity of morals, to alter the manner of performing divine fervice in this refpect.

It is only during an interval of the grand mafs that the prieft addreffes to country people fome words of exhortation in their own language; it was natural to confider this moment as the moft proper to difpofe the mind to refpect and attention; but perhaps, even the pomp of an auguft ceremony, by attracting ftrongly the imagination, withdraws the generality from the importance of the other parts of divine worfhip; and it frequently happens in country places, that many people go out of the church during the fermon, and return at the moment of confecration.

Q 2   I think

I think alſo, that public prayers ſhould always be in the vulgar tongue, and they might eaſily be made intereſting and affecting, as there are not any religious diſcourſes which ſympathize more with human weakneſs; and as our wants and anxieties may be made uſe of to raiſe us towards the Supreme Being, the beſt of all bands might be choſen to win the multitude.

I muſt obſerve beſides, that part of the country people, eſpecially in harveſt time, and other ſeaſons, when the huſbandman is particularly buſy, aſſiſt only at early maſs, and then they ſee but a part of the religious ceremonies *. And, if the practice and liberty of working on a Sunday was more extended, the inhabitants of the country, ſtill more confined to the firſt maſs, would hear neither prayers nor inſtructive diſcourſes in their own language during the whole year.

Certainly there muſt be ſomething altered in theſe religious inſtitutions in order

* This maſs is commonly called a low maſs.

to

to make them more efficacioufly ferve to fupport morality, and comfort the moft numerous clafs of the human race. Country people, whofe labour produces our wealth, ought to be taken care of with paternal anxiety; and fince they are not expofed to thofe diforderly paffions which find nourifhment in a metropolis; fince mild and prudent means ftill fuffice to maintain them in the habit of duty; both the fuperiors in church and ftate have to anfwer, in fome meafure, for the corruption of their manners and difpofitions.

CHAP.

CHAP. XI.

*That the single Idea of a God is a sufficient
Support of Morality.*

AFTER having shown that morality
has need of a supernatural support,
you have reason to expect, that I should
explain the intimate and immediate relation
which unites religion to the love of virtue,
and the observance of order. I will endeavour, then, to discuss this important
question; and in order to arrive at the
truth, I shall follow first the course of those
simple sentiments and natural thoughts,
which guide the mind and the heart of
man, in every climate and country under
heaven.

It is easy to unite all the moral legislation,
and the entire system of our duties, by means
only of the idea of a God.

The

The universe, notwithstanding its magnificence and its immensity, would be a mere nothing, if its Supreme Author had not peopled it with intelligent beings, capable of contemplating so many wonders, and of receiving happiness from them; but the faculties with which we are endowed, consciousness of possessing them, and the liberty to act, all announce to us that we are united to a grand combination, that we have a part to take on the vast stage of the world.

The most simple reason, that which resembles instinct, would have been sufficient to enable us to take care of the body, and to have concentred us in ourselves; more would not have been necessary for those who have so little to do. Thus, when I see that the mind is susceptible of continual improvement, when I see that men enjoy the power of assisting each other, and of communicating their ideas, in a manner so much superior to other animals; when I fix my attention on our social dispositions, and on all the relative qualities which com-

Q 4   pose

poſe our nature, I cannot avoid thinking, that we have a plan of conduct to follow towards others, and that in our pilgrimage on earth we muſt be circumſpect, having obſtacles to conquer, ſacrifices to make, and obligations to fulfil.

Men then appear to be led to religion by the moſt excellent gifts of nature, and by all that they have in them of the ſublime; but we ought to remark, as a ſingular re-ſemblance, that their wants alſo, and their extreme weakneſs, lead them to the ſame object.

Whatever may be my emotions, when I reflect on the preſent imperious laws to which I am obliged to ſubmit, and when I recal to mind the grandeur and magnifi-cence which I have been a witneſs of, I raiſe continually my ſoul towards the Sove-reign Director of events, and am led by inſtinct, as well as by a rational ſentiment, to addreſs my prayers to Him. It appears to the unfortunate, when they view ſo

many

many wonders which their underſtanding cannot graſp, that ſo little is wanting to guard them from the dangers which threaten them, they implore the commiſſeration of Him whoſe formidable power burſts from all ſides. But, while they admire and adore, they muſt imitate His perfections, and not expect mercy when they ſhow none. Purity of heart only can render an intercourſe with the Supreme Being intereſting; and prayers are merely a ſolemn kind of mockery, when they do not produce virtue and forbearance, when they do not render us kindly affected to each other; our very ſtate of dependence, our wants and weakneſſes, ſhould bind us to thoſe beings who equally ſhare the bleſſings ſo liberally beſtowed, and have the ſame evils to endure. Thus diſcontent, the fear of futurity, the anxiety cauſed by misfortunes, all the ſentiments, which engage men to diſturb ſocial order, take another character, or are at leaſt ſenſibly modified; when, from their firſt ſuffering, they can elevate their wiſhes to God, but dare not do it,

it, with a heart fullied by criminal intentions. .. ·.

It is not only prayer which leads us to
religion; another communication with the
Supreme Being, gratitude, produces the fame
effect. A man, perfuaded of the exiftence of
a fovereign power, and who gladly connects
with the divine protection his fuccefs and
happinefs, feels, at the fame time, a defire
to exprefs his gratitude; and not being able
to do any thing for him who beftows all,
he feeks to form an idea of the perfections
of that Supreme Being, in order to comprehend the fyftem of conduct moft conformable to his attributes. At firft, what
reflections poffefs our mind, what emotions
agitate our fouls, when we contemplate the
univerfe? When we refpectfully admire
that magnificent harmony, which is the
incomprehenfible refult of an innumerable
multitude of different powers: ftruck with
this vaft whole, where we difcover an
agreement fo perfect, how is it poffible for
us to avoid confidering order as a diftinct
mark

mark of the wisdom and of the design of Omnipotence? And how is it possible for us not to think, that we render him the most worthy homage, at the time we make use of the free intelligence which he has endowed us with. Then in the composition of a social structure, a work which has been entrusted to us, we shall try to penetrate the ideas of wisdom and order, of which all nature presents such a grand example; then, in establishing the relations which unite men, we shall carefully study the laws of moral order, and we shall find them all founded on the reciprocation of duties, which submit to a regular movement different jarring personal interests. In short, the idea of a God, Creator, Regenerator, and Preserver of the Universe, by invariable laws, and by a train of the same causes and the same effects, seems to call us to the conception of a universal morality, which, in imitation of the unknown springs of the natural world, may be as the necessary tie of this succession of intelligent beings, who always, with the same passions,

come

come to pafs and repafs on the earth, to
feek, or to fly, to affift, or to hurt each
other, according to the ftrength or the
weaknefs of the knot which unites them,
and according to the wifdom or inconfiftency of the principles which direct their.
opinions.

The attentive ftudy of man and of his
nature ought to contribute to confirm in
us the idea which we have juft pointed
out. We cannot, in fact, confider the
prodigious difference which exifts between
the minds and characters of men; we
cannot fix our attention on the length
to which this difference may be carried,
by the perfectibility of which they are
fufceptible; we cannot, in fhort, reflect
on a like conftitution, without being induced to think, that the counterpoife of
thefe extraordinary means of force and
ufurpation muft proceed from reafon, from
that fingular authority which only can eftablifh, between men, relations of juftice
and convenience, proper to maintain an
equilibrium

equilibrium and harmony in the midſt of
ſo many diſparities: it is thus, that reſpect
for morality ſeems evidently to make a part
of the general view and primitive idea of
the Supreme Diſpoſer of the univerſe. And
what pleaſure ſhall we not find in the perſuaſion, that the cultivation of virtue, that
the obſervance of order, offers us the means
of pleaſing our Divine Benefactor! It is by
that alone that we can hope to concur,
however feebly, in the execution of his
grand deſigns; and in the centre of ſo
many bleſſings, ſurrounded by ſo many
ſigns of a particular protection, how highly
ought we to value this means of communication with the Author of our exiſtence? Thus, then, the homage of adoration and gratitude which we render to
the Deity, leads us to a ſentiment of reſpect
for the laws of morality; and this ſentiment, in its turn, ſerves continually to
maintain in us the idea of a Supreme Being.

Independent of the reflections which we
have juſt preſented, morality, conſidered in

all

all its extent, has need of being ftrengthened by this difpofition of the foul, which
makes us interefted in the happinefs of
others ; and it is befides, in one of the moft
glorious perfections of the Deity, that we
find the firft model of this precious fentiment.   Yes, we cannot deny it : either our
exiftence proceeds from no caufe, or we
owe it to the goodnefs of the Supreme Being.   Life, fome will fay, undoubtedly is
a mixture of pains and pleafures : but, if
we are candid we fhall confefs, that thofe
moments, when it ceafes to appear to us a
benefit, do not often occur in life: in youth,
exiftence is thought the greateft blefling,
and the other feafons of life offer pleafures
lefs animated, certainly, but which agree
better with the progrefs of our underftanding, and the increafe of our experience.

It is true, that in order to free ourfelves
from a fentiment of gratitude, we often think
that we would not accept of a renewal of
life, on condition of our running over a fecond time our career, and returning ftep by
ftep

ftep in the fame track. But we fhould confider, that we do not fix a juft value on the
benefits which we have received; for when
we take a retrofpective view of life, we fee
it ftripped of its two principal ornaments,
curiofity and hope; and it is not in this
ftate that it was given to us, and that we
have enjoyed it.

It is, perhaps, not in our power to replace ourfelves, by contemplation, in the
fituation where the imagination made our
chief pleafure, a flight breath has eafily
effaced it from our memory: it is evident
that we enjoy life, becaufe we look forward with affright to the moment when
we fhall be forced to renounce it; but, as
this happinefs is compofed of prefent pleafures, and thofe which we anticipate, we
ceafe to be good judges of the value of life,
when this future profpect is not prefented
to our eyes, but under the form of the paft;
for we know not how to appreciate, with a
languifhing recollection, that which we have
loved in the moment of hope.

Physical

Phyfical evils are not either the end of the condition of our nature, they are its accidents: the happinefs of infancy, which fhows in its primitive purity the works of the Deity, vifibly point out the goodnefs of the Supreme Being; and how can we avoid believing, that we owe our origin to a benevolent defign, fince it is a defire of happinefs, which has been given to ferve as the motive of all our actions? We fhould indeed fpeak well of life, if we had not corrupted its comforts by artificial fentiments, which we have fubftituted inftead of nature; if we had not fubmitted fo many realities to pride and vanity; if, inftead of affifting each other to be happy, we had not employed our thoughts to make others fubmit to us. Undoubtedly there are fome fufferings annexed to our exiftence, as in the natural world there are apparent defects. Let us employ our minds on the moft exalted fubjects, and we fhall no longer be a prey to envy and difcontent.

It is on the confideration of detatched events; it is in fome particular circumftances, that

we

we raife doubts about the goodnefs of God; but we immediately difcern it when we compare particulars which wound us, with the great whole of which they make a part; we difcover then, that the misfortunes which we are fo quickly offended with are a fimple appendage of a general fyftem, where all the characters of a beneficent intelligence are evidently traced. It is neceffary then to view the whole of life to difcover the intention of the author of nature; and in meditating in this manner, we fhall return always to a fentiment of refpect and gratitude. This fimple idea is very extenfive in its application; it feems to me, above all, that it ferves to confole us under the ills of life; the man who is penetrated by it can fay to himfelf, the tranfitory evil to which I am fubject, is perhaps one of the inevitable effects of this univerfal harmony, the moft noble and the moft extenfive of all conceptions. Thus, in the moments when I bemoan my fate, I ought not to think myfelf forfaken, I ought not to accufe Him, whofe infinite wifdom

R   is

is prefent to my view, Him whofe general laws have fo often appeared to me a vifible expreffion of real goodnefs.

It is in vain, fome will fay, it is in vain that you would wifh to make us attend to thefe confiderations ; we only remark, that our earthly happinefs is at leaft infeiior to that which our imagination fo readily forms the picture of; and we do not perceive, in fuch a difpofition, the union of perfections which ought to be afcribed to the Supreme Being.

This objection is prefented under different forms in the writings of all the enemies to religion ; and they have drawn confequences, fometimes againft the goodnefs of God, his power, his wifdom, and juftice. It is· neceffary, clearly to explain this difficulty, to be in a ftate to form to· ourfelves an idea of the perfection of an Infinite Being ; but in all our attempts, we only carry to the extreme every quality which we conceive ; inftead of that, perfection in the works of

the

the Creator, probably confifts in a kind of gradation and harmony, the fecret of which we cannot either embrace, or penetrate; and we ought ftill more to be on our guard, when we form any conception of the eſſence of the Deity, as by confining ourſelves ſolely to reconcile his ſovereign power with his perfect goodneſs, we ſhould never fix the boundary when theſe two properties will be in an equilibrium: for after having exhauſted every ſuppoſition, we might ftill aſk, why the number of rational beings is not more extended? We might aſk, why every grain of ſand is not one of thoſe beings? why there is not a number equal to that infinite diviſibility of which we form the idea? In ſhort, from extreme to extreme, and always in arguing on the ſovereign power, the leaſt inanimate atom, the leaſt void in nature, would appear a boundary to the goodneſs of the Supreme Being. We ſee then to what a point we may wander, when we abandon common ſenſe for the vague excurſions of a metaphyſical ſpirit.

R 2   I think,

I think, if no other proofs could be found, the power of God would be fufficient to demonſtrate his goodneſs; for this power informs us every inſtant, that if the Supreme Ruler of the World had intended the miſery of rational beings, he would have had, to fulfil this intention, means as rapid as numerous. He needed not have created worlds; nor have made them ſo convenient and beautiful; a terrific gulph, and eternal darkneſs might have been fufficient to collect together thoſe unfortunate beings, and make them feel their miſery. Let us not dwell on theſe gloomy ſubjects, let us follow a juſt emotion of gratitude; we ſhall be eager then to render homage to that indelible character of love and goodneſs which we ſee ſtamped on all nature. An unknown power opens our eyes to the light, and permits us to view the wonders of the univerſe: it awakens in us thoſe enchanting ſenſations which firſt point out the charms of life; it enriches us with that intellectual gift which re-aſſembles round us paſt ages, and the time to come; it confers, in an early hour,

an

an empire, by endowing us with thofe two fublime faculties, will and liberty; in fhort, it renders us fenfible to the real pleafure of loving and being beloved; and when, by the effect of a general plan, of which we have but an imperfect conception, it fpreads here and there fome difficulties in the road of life; it feems to wifh to foften them, by fhowing us always the future through the enchanting medium of the imagination. Could it be then without any intereft or goodnefs, that this magnificent fyftem was conceived, and preferved by fo many fuperb demonftrations of wifdom and power? What fhould we be in the fight of the Eternal, if he did not love us? We do not adorn his majeftic univerfe, or lend to the dawn its magnificent colours; neither have we covered the earth with a verdant carpet, or bid the celeftial bodies revolve in the immenfe expanfe; he afked not counfel of us —we fhould be nothing in his eyes, if he was indifferent to our gratitude, and if he took not any pleafure in the happinefs of his creatures.

R 3   In

In fhort, were we to turn our attention from fo many ftriking proofs of the goodnefs of God; were they to be effaced from our memory, we fhould ftill find, in the receffes of our heart, a fufficient evidence of this comfortable truth, we fhould perceive that we are good and affectionate, when not perverted by paffion; and we fhould be led to think, that fuch an inclination in beings who have received every thing, muft neceffarily be the feal of their Divine Author. In order to exalt this fentiment, we muft refer it continually to the idea of a Supreme Being; for there is, we doubt not, a correfpondence of inftinct and reflection between our virtue and the perfections of him who is the origin of all things; and provided we do not refift our natural emotions, we fhall perceive from thofe very perfections all that is fufficient to excite our worfhip and adoration; above all, whatever is neceffary to ferve as an example for our conduct, and to afford principles of morality.

I ought

I ought now to examine fome important objections; for why fhould I fear to prefent them? a love for fyftems and opinions ought not to exift, in treating a fubject on which fo many have expatiated, and which belongs equally to all men. Though we are allowed, when feeking truth eagerly, to wifh to find it united to the fentiments which form our happinefs, and the principles which are the foundation of public order.

We admit, fay fome, that there are many perfections peculiar to the Supreme Being, the ftudy and knowledge of which ought to ferve to fuftain the laws of morality; but one of the effential properties of the divine effence overfets the whole ftructure, it is prefcience: for, as God knows before-hand what we are to do, it follows, that all our actions are irrevocably determined; and thus man is not free. And, if fuch is his condition, he deferves neither praife nor cenfure; he has no means of pleafing or difpleafing the Supreme Being, and the ideas of good and evil, of virtue and vice,

R 4, are

are abfolutely chimerical. I fhall, at firft, make a very fimple reply to this objection, but a very decifive one : it is that, if againft appearances you fhould happen to perfuade me, that there now exifts an abfolute contradiction between the liberty of man and the prefcience of the Deity, it is on the nature and extent of this prefcience that I fhall raife my doubts; for, forced to choofe, I fhould rather miftruft the judgment of my own mind, than that of an internal perfuafion. It is by thefe fame confiderations, that it will always be impoffible to prove to men that they are not free: we could only fucceed with the affiftance of reafoning, and reafoning being already a beginning of art, a kind of exterior combination of reflections, this means, in fome meafure out of us, would not have power to eradicate a fentiment which feems the firft that we are confcious of.

We foon difcover the limits of our faculties, in the efforts which we make to acquire a juft idea of the divine prefcience,:

we

we can very well fuppofe, that God forefees with certainty what we only conjecture about, and in extending without end the bounds which occur to our mind, we fhall proportion in our imagination, the knowledge of the Creator to the immenfity of fpace, and to the infinity of time; but beyond thefe vague ideas we fhall err in all our fpeculations. How is it poffible, that men, who know not even the nature of their own fouls, fhould be able to determine the nature of prefcience? How is it poffible, that they can know whether this prefcience is the effect of a rapid calculation of him, who embraces at one glance the relations and effects of every moral and natural caufe? how can they difcern, whether this prefcience, in an Infinite Being, is diftinct from fimple knowledge? How can they know whether that Being, by a property beyond our conception, does not exift before and after events, whether he is not, in fome manner, the intellectual time, and whether our divifions of years and ages, would

would not difappear before his immoveable exiftence and eternal duration.

It refults, however, from thefe confiderations, that on account of our extreme ignorance we cannot accurately define prefcience; but we are reduced to examine whether this prefcience, confidered in a general manner, is incompatible with the liberty of man.

This opinion, I think, fhould not be adopted. Prefcience does not determine future events, for the mere knowledge of the future makes not the future. It is not prefcience which neceffitates the actions of men, becaufe it does not change the natural order of things; but all future events are fixed, whether forefeen or not; for conftraint and liberty conduct equally to a pofitive term: thus, all that will happen is as immutable as that which is paft, fince the prefent was the future of yefterday, and will be to morrow the paft. It is then abftractedly certain, that an event, either forefeen foreſeen or not, will take place ſome time; but if liberty is not contrary to this inevitable certainty, how would it be more ſo, becauſe their exiſts a Being who is acquainted previouſly with the preciſe nature of events? We may then ſay, with truth, that the knowledge of the future is no more an obſtacle to liberty, than the remembrance of the paſt; and prophecies, like hiſtories, are only recitals, whoſe place is not the ſame in the order of time; but not having any influence on events, do not conſtrain the will, cannot enſlave the ſentiments, or ſubject men to the law of neceſſity.

We will confeſs, however, that if preſcience was founded on the poſſibility of calculating the actions of men, like the movements of an organized machine, liberty could not exiſt; but then it would not be preſcience which oppoſed this liberty, it would be becauſe we are automatons; for with ſuch a conſtitution we ſhould be without liberty, were even the Supreme Being

Being not to have any knowledge of fu‑
turity.

It is in vain, in order to convince us
we are not free, that fome would reprefent
us as neceffarily fubmitting to the impulfe
of various exterior objects; comprehending,
among thofe objects, every thing that is
fubtle in moral ideas, and uniting them
under the general name of motives, and
giving afterwards to thefe motives a phy‑
fical force which we are bound to ohey;
but to be free, is it neceffary that we act
without motives? then man would be in‑
deed evidently a piece of mechanifm. It
is certain, that we are, in all our actions,
determined by reafon, tafte, or a caufe of
preference; but it is our mind which com‑
prehends thefe various confiderations, which
weighs, compares, and modifies; it is our
mind which liftens to the counfels of virtue,
and which replies to the language of our
paffions; it is in order to enlighten itfelf
that it borrows from the memory the fuc‑
cours of experience; it is then our mind
which

which prepares, compofes, and improves every thing which we term motives, and it is after this intellectual labour that we act. There is too much order, unity, and harmony in our thoughts, to allow us to fuppofe them the mere effect of exterior objects; which, under the form of ideas, come without order to imprefs themfelves on our brain; and until we are made ac-quainted with the works of chaos, we fhall believe with reafon that every where there is that unity, that order; that there is a faculty capable of re-affembling every thing that is fcattered, and uniting to one end all that is mixed without defign.

As foon as we are impelled to believe, that there is a mafter of all our perceptions, and that we feel this mafter act, how is it pof-fible not to be certain that it is our mind which acts? It is then, in breaking loofe from its operations, that we are ftripped of our liberty, and that we at length fuppofe that our will is the neceffary confequence of all exterior objects, as if it were the co-

lours,

lours, and not the painter, which produced a picture. However, if we fecure our mind from that dependence to which fome wifh to reduce it, our actions will not obey thefe irrefiftible emotions ; for if they grant that we have liberty of thought, we have free will.

We ought to confider our fenfes as mef-fengers, which bring to our mind new fub-jects of reflection ; but they are in fuch a manner fubordinate to the fublime part of ourfelves, that they act only under direc-tion ; fometimes the ruling principle com-mands them to bring reprefentations of the beauties of nature, to examine affiduoufly the regifters of the human mind, to take the rule and the compafs, and render an exact account of that which it defires to know with precifion ; fometimes they are taught to acquire more power, and when the foul wifhes to communicate with men, when it wifhes to addrefs pofterity, it orders them to perpetuate in indelible characters all that it has maturely combined, all that it has difcovered,

difcovered, and all it hopes· to add to the treafures of our knowledge.· Is it not the mafter rather than the flave of our fenfes, or the blind play of their caprice?

There is befides another obfervation, which feems to contraft with the abfolute empire, that fome are willing to grant to exterior objeéts over the powers of our foul; for it is in the filence of meditation that the aétion of our mind is not interrupted :, we experience that we have the power of re-calling paft ideas, and that we can conneét thofe ideas with the profpeét of the future, and to various imaginary circumftances of which we compofe this piéture ; our reflec-tion is then the refult, but not the work of thofe exterior objeéts we are acquainted· with. Thefe two words, work and refult, which in fome acceptations have a great re-femblance, have here very different mean-ings; and it is only in confounding them, that the objeétion againft the exiftence of. our liberty is favoured., We cannot form, any judgment, without previoufly difcuffing every

every argument proper to throw a light on the fubject; and the refult of fuch enquiries determines our will; but thefe enquiries are themfelves the work of our mind.

In. fhort, all the degrees which lead to the end of our intellectual refearches, are fimple antecedents, and not abfolute motives : there is, in the operations of our mind, as in every thing which is not immoveable, a train of caufes and effects; but this train does not characterize neceffity more than liberty.

In reftoring thus to our foul its original dignity, do you not perceive, that we approach nearer to nature, than in adopting thofe fyftems and explications which affimilate our intellectual faculties to the regular vibrations of a pendulum? or would you like better ftill to compare them to thofe little balls which go out of their niches to ftrike our brain, which by various ramifications, produce that fhock which impels our will? I fee, in all this,

4   only

only childifh figures, put in the place of thofe names which indicate at leaft, by their abftraction, the indefinite extent of the ideas which they reprefent, and the refpect they merit. It is eafy to call a motive a little moving ball; it is eafy to call uncertainty or repentance the combat of two of thefe balls, till the arrival of a third forms a determination; and the concurrence of many to. the fame point excites, in us, an impetuous. paffion: but who fees not that, after having endeavoured to debafe the functions of the mind by thefe wretched comparifons, the difficulty remains undiminifhed?

In fhort, if the meditations and the refearches of our minds, on the exiftence and the nature of our liberty, prefents us only impenetrable clouds and obfcurity, is it not fingular, that in the midft of this darknefs we fhould reject all the information of our inftinctive fentiments, which only can clearly explain every thing that we in vain fearch for. by other means? What

S   would

would you say of a man born blind, who would not be directed by the voice? We are assuredly better instructed in the constitution of our nature by our feelings, than by metaphysical arguments! they compose an internal part of the essence of our soul; and we ought to consider them, in some measure, as a sally of the incomprehensible formation, whose mysteries we cannot penetrate. Such a doctrine, which came to us from a divine hand, is more deserving of confidence than the interpretations of men. There are secrets which philosophers try in vain to explain, all their efforts are useless to represent by comparison, that which is alone and without resemblance.

One would think, that nature, guessing the false reasoning which would mislead us, has purposely bestowed an inward conviction of the existence of our free will, in composing our natural life of two movements very distinct: one depends on a necessity, whose laws we are not acquainted with, and do not govern; whilst the other

is

is entirely fubmitted to the government of
our reafon. Such a comparifon would be
fufficient to convince us, if we fought
merely for the truth.

When Spinofa defired to throw contempt
on our inftinctive perceptions, he faid, it is
the fame as if a weather-cock; at the very
moment it was the plaything of the winds,
believed itfelf to be the caufe, and confequently that it had free will. What figni-
fies fuch an argument, unlefs it is to prove,
that it is poffible to fuppofe a fiction fo perfect, that it would apparently be equivalent
to a reality? But I would afk, by what
foolifh defign of an intelligent being, or even
by what fortuitous affemblage of blind nature, is it that man fhould have every moment a will precifely conformable to his
actions, if there is not a real correfpondence
between every part?

We could oppofe to the hypothefis of
Spinofa another argument; which would
lead to a conclufion abfolutely contrary;
that is, if the moft apparent liberty may be

only

only a fiction, by a particular concurrence
of our will with an action ordained; it is
also inconteftible, that were we to fuppofe
the exiftence, or fimple poffibility of a free-
will, we could not have a different idea of
:it,: than that which we have already; and
the liberty of God· himfelf would not appear
to our thoughts under any other form. It
is very effential to remark, that when we
reflect about our faculties, we with eafe
imagine a fuperior degree of intelligence, of
knowledge, of memory, of forefight, and of
every other property of our underftanding;
liberty is the only part of ourfelves to which
our imagination cannot add any thing.

I fhall not purfue other fubtle arguments,
which have been produced, to corroborate
my opinion; it is not to fome men, but to
all, that I defire to fpeak, becaufe I wifh to
be univerfally ufeful: I fhall then always
dwell on the principal reflections, whenever
they appear to me fufficient to influence the
opinion of found minds, and to fix them on
thofe important truths which are the fureft
foun-

foundation of public happiness. Self-love might induce many to follow a question as far as it would go, and vainly glory in spinning it out; but self-love, applied to profound meditations, is itself a great subtilty.

Let us examine other arguments used to combat principles which we have established. It is in vain, some will say, to endeavour to prove the existence of a God, as a real support of the laws of morality; all this system will fall to pieces, if we are not informed, at the same time, in what manner this God rewards and punishes.

I shall observe, at first, that such an objection cannot make a very deep impression, but when it is connected in our minds with some doubt of the existence of a Supreme Being: a question that I shall not yet treat; for supposing an internal conviction of this last truth, supposing, in all its force, the idea of a God present to our thoughts; I ask, whether in order to please Him, we

S 3   should

fhould not have need of knowing precifely
the period when we could perceive diftinct
figns of his approbation and beneficence?
I afk, again, whether, to avoid incurring
His difpleafure, it would be equally neceffary for us to know how, and in what
manner, He would punifh us? Undoubtedly
not: for in taking a comprehenfive view of
the rewards and punifhments which may
proceed from a Supreme Being, ftruck
with His grandeur, and aftonifhed by His
power, the vague idea of infinity would
obtrude; and this idea, fo awful, would
fuffice to govern our fentiments, and fix
our principles of conduct. We fhould be
careful not to propofe conditions to Him
who has drawn us out of nothing, and we
fhould wait with refpect for the moment,
when, in His profound wifdom, He may
think proper to make us better acquainted
with His attributes. Men may fay to each
other, fecure my wages, I want them on fuch
a day, I demand them on fuch an hour; they
barter things of equal value, and during a
fhort fpace of time; but in the intercourfe of
man

man with the Deity, what a difference!—
The creature and the Creator—the child of
dust and the fource of life—a fleeting moment and eternity—an inperceptible atom
and the Infinite Being!—our underſtanding
is ſtruck by the contraſt! How then ſhould
we adapt to ſuch difproportions the rules
and notions which we have introduced into
our trivial tranfactions? You require that in
order to feel the defire of pleaſing the Supreme Being, He ſhould every moment
beſtow gifts on thoſe, who, by their ſentiments and actions, appear worthy of his
goodneſs; and, to infpire the fear of
offending Him, you wiſh that, without
delay, He would let His vengeance cruſh
the wicked. Certainly you would be ſcrupulous obfervers of His will on ſuch conditions, for lefs ſtable hopes and fears detain you fervilely near a monarch; and I
may venture to ſay, that you would be
equally attentive to the Ruler of the World,
if, in order to reward or puniſh you, he
was to alter the laws of nature.

But

But do we not, you may add, see that God does not interfere in any manner to direct things here below : you do not perceive Him ; but do you more clearly discover the power which gives life and motion ? It is not because He does not exist, but because He is above the flight of your mind. We do not know what to say to a man who rejects the opinion of the existence of a God ; for without that guide all our ideas are wandering, and have not any other connexion but that of the wildest imagination ; but if you grant that the world had an origin, if you suppose a God, creator and preserver, what arguments would you use to induce us to believe that this God has no relation to us ; that He does not take any notice of us, and that He is thus separated from the offspring of His intelligence and love ?. You add, vice is every where triumphant, an honest man often languishes in despondency and obscurity ; and you cannot reconcile this injustice with the idea of a Divine Providence ! One may at first deny the assertion which

which forms the bafis of this reproach, or difpute at leaft the eonfequences that are drawn from it: thefe ideas of triumph and abafement, of fplendour and obfcurity, are fometimes very foreign to the internal fenti-ments, which only conftitute happinefs and mifery; and for my part, I am perfuaded, that if we take for a rule of comparifon, not fome particular fituation, or fome, fcat-tered events, but the whole of life, and the generality of men; we fhall then find, that the moft conftant fatisfactions attend thofe minds which are filled with a mild piety, firm and rational, fuch as the pure idea of the Deity ought to infpire; and I am equally perfuaded, that virtue, united to this piety, which knows how to foften every facrifice, is the fafeft guide in the path of life. Perhaps, ignorant as we are of our nature and deftination, it is not our intereft that uninterrupted rewards fhould ex-cite us to virtue; for if this virtue were our title and hope with God for the prefent, and the time to come, we ought not to defire that it fhould degenerate into an evident calcu-lation,

lation, into a fentiment bordering on felfifhnefs. It would then be very difficult to
give a proper definition of liberty, if, by
the effect of rapid juftice, a conftant proportion of good and evil, accompanied
every determination of our mind; we fhould
then, morally as well as phyfically, be
impelled by an imperious inftinct, and the
merit of our actions would be abfolutely
deftroyed.

I mean by all this to afk, what would be
our merit or demerit, if our life is only for
an inftant, and if nothing is to follow? The
perfuafion of the exiftence of a God, without a certainty of the immortality of our
foul, cannot impofe any obligation; but the
real connexion between thefe two ideas is
too frequently overlooked.

Undoubtedly, left to our underftanding,
this word certainty is not made for us, or at
leaft it is not applicable to our relation with
the Deity, and to the judgment we form
of his defigns and will. We are too far
                                        removed

removed from the High and lofty One, who inhabiteth eternity, to pretend to measure His thoughts by our bounded views. They are covered with a veil, and we always obfcurely difcern that which is hid in the depths of His wifdom: but the more this God, whom we adore, efcapes by His immenfity from our conceptions, the lefs have we a right to limit His perfections, in order to refufe Him the power of tranf-porting our exiftence beyond the narrow circle fubmitted to our view; and I know not how it would be poffible to perfuade us, that this action of the Deity would furpafs in grandeur the creation of the world, or the formation of animated beings: the habit of obferving a great wonder may weaken our aftonifhment, but fhould not eradicate our admiration.

We cannot reach, but by reflection, to thofe events of which the future is ftill the depofitory; but if every thing which furrounds us attefts the grandeur of the Supreme Being; if the mind, in its medita-

4   tions

tions, without terror, approaches the confines of infinity, why miftruft that he can per-
form in favour of men, a magnificent union
of Omnipotence and perfect goodnefs? Why
reject, as an abfurd confidence, the idea of
another exiftence? We fee, without aftonifhment, the feeble chryfalis force its way
from the tomb it wove for itfelf, and appear
under a new form. We cannot be antici-
pated witneffes of the perpetuity of our intelligence; but its vaft extent would appear
to us, were we not familiarized with it, a
greater phœnomenon than duration.

In fhort, why do I refift an idea of a
continuation of exiftence, fince I am forced
to give credit to my birth? There is a
greater diftance from nothing to life, than
from life to its fequel, or renewal under a
new form: I am clearly acquainted with
the commencement of exiftence, I know
death only by conjecture. We now enjoy
the light and bleffings brought to us by a
beneficent heavenly Teacher; could it be,
that he alone would be a ftranger to his
own

own glory and virtues ? I cannot fay, why this contraſt makes an impreſſion on me; but it is among the number of ſuperficial ideas which occur to my mind, when I reflect on this ſubject.

A comforting thought ſtill ſtrikes me, the natural order of the univerſe appears to me a finiſhed ſyſtem : we perceive a perfect regularity between the revolution of the heavenly bodies, an invariable ſucceſſion in vegetable life, an almoſt incredible preciſion in that immenſe quantity of volatile particles ſubmitted to the laws of affinity; and think every thing in its right place, and that all fulfil exactly their deſtination in the grand and complete ſyſtem of nature.

But if we turn afterwards our attention on the multitude of beings inferior to men, we ſhall diſcover alſo, that their action is as complete and conformable in every reſpect to the faculties they are endowed with, ſince they are governed by an imperious in-ſtinct. Full of theſe ideas, ſtruck with
aſtoniſh-

aftonifhment at the appearance of an harmony fo general, have we not juft grounds
to prefume, that man, tranfported into infinite fpace by his intelligence; that man,
fufceptible of improvement, and continually
combatting obftacles; that man, in fhort;
this moft noble work of nature, only commences in this fublunary world his race?
And, fince all which compofes the material order of the univerfe appears to us in
an harmony fo admirable, ought we not
then to conclude; that the moral order in
which we perceive fome things vague and
not determinate; that the moral order
is connected with another life more fublime and more aftonifhing than the other
parts of creation, and will one day be ulti-
mately developed? This fingular difproportion between the harmony of the phyfical
and apparent confufion of the moral
world, feems to announce a time of equilibrium and completion; a time when we
fhall all know its relation with the wifdom
of the Creator, as we already perceive the
wifdom of His defigns, in the perfect agreement

ment of the innumerable bleffings on future with the prefent wants of man, and
every other animated creature.

The grandeur of the human mind is indeed a vaft fubject of reflection; this marvellous conftitution feems to remind us perr-
petually of a defign proportioned to fuch a
noble conception; it feems almoft unnecef-
fary that God fhould have endowed the foul
with fuch noble faculties for fuch a fhort
life as ours, to fulfil its limited plans and
trivial purfuits: thus every thing authorizes
us to carry our views further; were I to fee
fuch men as Columbus, Vefputius, Vafco
de Gama, in a fhip, I fhould not fuppofe
that they were mere coafters.

Some try to deftroy our hopes, by endeavouring to prove, that the foul is material,
and that it ought to be affimilated to every
thing which perifhes before us; but the
forms only change, the vivifying force does
not perifh; perhaps the foul refembles it,
but with this difference, that as it is compofed

pofed of memory, reflection, and forefight,
it exifts only by a feries of confequences,
which forms the diftinct attributes and particular character of its effence : it follows
then, that it cannot be generalized like the
blind force which animates in a univerfal-
manner vegetation ; but that every foul is
in fome meafure a world to itfelf, and that
it ought to preferve feparately an identity
of intereft, and confcioufnefs of preceding
thoughts. Thus, in this fyftem, the cor-
poreal body, which diftinguifhes us to the
eyes of others, is only the tranfitory habitation of that foul which is not to die ; of that
foul fufceptible of continual improvement,
and which, by degrees we can have no
idea of, will probably approach infenfibly
to that magnificent period, when it will be
thought worthy of knowing more intimately the Author of Nature.

How can we conceive the action of the
foul on our fenfes, without a point of contact ? and how conceive that contact,
without the idea of matter ? For, it is only

by

by experience we are acquainted with the necessity of it to occasion a motion; and without that previous knowledge, the rapidity with which one body sometimes strikes another, could only have been represented by the length of time necessary for its approach to it: however, if we had not any metaphysical knowledge of the cause of motion, and if experience only guided our judgment in this respect, why resist an idea that there is within us a faculty which acts of itself? the intimate feeling which we have of it, is certainly an argument for its existence. We cannot, besides, maintain, that a like property may be opposite to the nature of things; since if we adopt the system of the creation of the world, this property may proceed, like all others, from the Divine Power; and if we admit, on the contrary, the irreligious opinion of the eternity of the universe, there must have been from eternity a general movement without impulsion, without exterior contact, or any cause out of itself;

T

and

and the action of our fouls might be fubject to the fame laws.

The idea of the neceffity of a contact, to effect a movement, would never have oc-curred, if we had bounded our obfervations to the influence of our ideas on our deter-minations, and the influence of thofe deter-minations on our phyfical being. In fhort, the laws of attraction and repulfion are fub-ject to great exceptions; which excep-tions may ferve to fupport the fyftem of the fpirituality of the foul. We may be al-lowed to fay, that there exifts a vacuum in the univerfe, fince, without this vacuum, there could not have been any motion? It is known that this motion depends on the laws of attraction but how can attraction act through a vacuum, unlefs it is by a fpiritual force, which acts without contact, and notwithftanding the abfolute interrup-tion of matter? It is then this force, or its equivalent, that I may adopt to define the caufe of the impreffions of which our fouls are fufceptible.

Let

Let others explain, in their turn, by what material communication, the fight of a few immoveable characters, traced on in-fenfible marble, difturbs my foul. It is very eafy to comprehend by what mecha-nifm the eye diftinguifhes thefe characters; but there ends the phyfical action, for we cannot attribute to that action, the general power of producing fenfations in the mind, fince, perhaps, many other men may con-fider the fame characters, without receiving any impreffion.

It is very poffible, that our intellectual preceptions have not any connection with motion, fuch as we conceive it. Our in-terior nature, which we diftinguifh by the name of immaterial, is probably fubject to laws very different from thofe which govern nature in general; but as we are obliged to ap-ply to the myfteries of our fouls, thofe expref-fions which ferve to delineate or to interpret the phœnomena fubmitted to our infpec-tion; thefe expreffions, and their continual ufe, have infenfibly habituated us to certain

opinions,

opinions, about the caufes and developement of our intellectual faculties. It is thus that, after having ufed the words motion, reft, agitation, and action, to difcriminate different affections of our fouls, of which we know very little, we have afterwards affimilated them, foolifhly, to our moral nature, to all the ideas which were reprefented by thefe denominations; and even death itfelf, of which we have not any clear knowledge, but by the diffolution of our phyfical being; death, an image borrowed from things which are under the infpection of our fenfes, has not, perhaps, either relation or analogy with the nature and effence of our fpirit; all thefe are incomprehenfible fecrets, not mixt with any thing we are acquainted with.

We act, in this refpect, like men born deaf, who apply to founds thofe terms which they were accumftomed to ufe, to exprefs the fenfations the other fenfes produced.

I fhall

I fhall only add another obfervation to the ideas on which I have juft dwelt: perhaps we fhould never have thought of applying the words which exprefs action and motion, to all the operations of our fouls, if we had not at firft divided our fpiritual being into a great number of dependencies, fuch as attention, reflection, thought, judgment, imagination, memory, and forefight; and if afterwards, in order to render intelligible the variable relations of thefe abftract parts of our mind (thefe parts of a unit which we have taken to pieces, though it compofed that fingle being ourfelf) we had not been obliged to have recourfe to fome plain expreffions, like thofe of action, motion, attraction, and repulfion; but this familiar ufe of thefe expreffions, in order to explain the accidents of our intellectual fyftem, very much refembles the ufe which we make of X in Algebra, to expefs unknown terms.

In fhort, were we to fubmit the action of our fouls to the laws of a particular

move-

movement, forming one of the dependencies of the great one, we fhould ftill have to explain the caufe of the confcioufnefs that we have of this action, which Atheifts refufe to nature itfelf, at the very moment they make it the God of the Univerfe. Were reafoning able to fubject all the operations of our mind to the impreffions of external objects, we could not rank under the fame laws, that confcioufnefs which we have of our exiftence, and of the different faculties of the foul. This confcioufnefs is not an effect, or the production of any known force, fince it has been always in us independant of any external object, confequently we cannot inveftigate it. The conception of the exiftence of our fouls, is as incomprehenfible to us as that of eternity; what a profound thought, which even our imagination cannot embrace!

Let us admit, however, for a moment, that all the operations of our fouls are determined by fome impulfion, whatever it may be, we fhall ftill be ftruck with the abfolute

lute difference which exifts, according to our knowledge between the regular movements of matter, and the almoft infinite and unaccountable emotions of our hearts and minds; fo variable and fo differently modified, that the attention is loft in the examination of them. And after having vainly endeavoured to conceive the union eftablifhed between our thoughts and exterior objects, we have ftill to form an idea of the actions of thefe thoughts on themfelves, their progreffion and connection; our mind led aftray, loft in fuch a meditation, leaves us only a confcioufnefs of our weaknefs, and we feel, that there is an intellectual altitude which the human faculties can never reach.

We diftinguifh, in a fingle character which our judgment can decypher, an abfolute difference between foul and matter: we cannot avoid reprefenting the latter as infinitely devifible, whilft, on the contrary, all the efforts of our imagination could never divide that indivifible unit which

compofes

compoſes the ſoul, and which is the ſovereign over our will, thoughts, and all our
faculties *.

But if we examine again, under another
appearance, the properties of matter, we
know not how to aſſimilate to them the
emotions of our ſoul; for we diſtinctly feel
thoſe emotions, let their number be ever ſo
numerous, when even they act together and
terminate in the ſame center, which is that
Indiviſible Being before alluded to; whereas
matter, by an eſſential property, cannot, in
the ſame inſtant be preſſed or ſtruck in ſe-

* Some ſay, in order to weaken this argument, that
we may attribute to the indiviſible unit all the qualities
of matter, that a round body is really diviſible, but that
roundneſs and impenetrability are not. Such an objection is evidently not juſt. Roundneſs and impenetrability are only qualities, and theſe qualities, when
merely abſtract, are neceſſarily invariable : thus, it is
as impoſſible to divide it, as it is to multiply and increaſe it; but my ſoul, my thoughts, the conſciouſneſs
that I have of my own exiſtence, forms a particular
and perſonal being; and if it were of the ſame nature as matter, ought to be equally diviſible.

veral

veral manners, unlefs it is in parts which
have a tendency to different centres.

There is not then any refemblance between the impreffions that our fouls receive,
and the various effects which may be attributed to the action of all the material fubftances of which we can form·any conception: they are always connected with
the idea of fpace and extent; but that centre, where all our perceptions meet, that
Judge, who dictates laws in the internal
empire, whofe revolutions we only know,
that laft Director of our will, this Indivifible Being, at the fame time our friend and
mafter, is not to be found in any compounded idea; and this unity fo fimple,
ought neceffarily to convince us, that nothing which is fubmitted to the dominion of
our fenfes, can ferve as a type of the idea
which we are to form of the foul.

We difcover the traces of this truth,
when we fix our attention on the comparifons with which our fpiritual unit,

3   our

our identical felf, is continually occupied: we imagine it feated on a throne, ·liftening, and examining the various reafons which ought to determine its action; we fee it, like Nero,· yielding fometimes to Narciffus, and fometimes to Burrhus; but at the fame time we diftinctly perceive all the counfel-lors, all the flatterers, all the enemies which furround it; we never remark but a fingle, mafter in the midft of the tumult and the intrigues of this court.

. Whilft our foul then is thrown into mo-tion by contemplation, and by the imper-ceptible modification of a fugitive idea, as well as by every thing which is oppofed to material action, why fhould we not fuppofe that it is purely intelligent and fpiritual? It muft be confeffed, that fometimes our cor-poreal infirmities influence our minds; but this relation is not a proof of identity, fince our body may be an inftrument intrufted to our foul, one of the organs which it is to make a tranfitory ufe of. The continuity of exiftence, confidered abftractedly, certainly

is

Is in the univerfe a fimple and natural ftate; and the temporary exiftence is perhaps the only one which is heterogeneous and accidental; the foul feems too noble to be affimilated to the latter ftate, it may exift in a different manner when joined to a material fubftance, but that connection does not make it lofe its original effence.

It is to be acknowledged, that it is through the medium of our fenfes we know all the force of our exiftence; and that they are thofe parts of our mixt being which ftrike us moft during a little while; and it is perhaps by a law of the fame kind that we fee men, ingroffed by a great paffion, entirely ftrangers to every other moral affection; but, why fhould it be contrary to the nature of things, that the foul, once ftripped of its terreftrial cloathing, fhould be acquainted with the nature of its exiftence, and at the fame time perceive thofe truths which now are obfcured by clouds. An innate fire languifhes a long time unknown in a rough ftone, that ftone is

ftruck

ftruck, and we fee iffue out a fplendid light; this is perhaps a faint picture of the ftate in which our foul is when death breaks its fetters.

' In fhort, in a matter fo obfcure every fuppofition is admiffable, which affures us that the foul is not on earth in a ftate of enchantment, or in a kind of interruption of its ordinary exiftence. All that we fee of the univerfe is an affemblage of incomprehenfible phœnomena; and when we wifh to difcover the conclufion, through the aid of the ideas moft on a level with our intelligence, we wander perhaps from truth; fince, according to appearances, it is in the depths of infinity that it repofes. •

I doubt, whether we can allow the authority of thofe metaphyfical arguments which are made ufe of to defend the fpirituality of the foul to be decifive; but they are fufficient to repulfe the different attacks of materialifts. The moft evident opinion to me is, that we are too weak to comprehend

hend the fecret we fearch for. We have, according to our petty knowledge, divided the univerfe into two parts, fpirit and matter; but this divifion ferves only to diftinguifh the little we know from that which we have no knowledge of; there is perhaps an infinite gradation between the different properties which compofe motion and life, inftinct and intelligence; we can only exprefs the ideas conceived by our underftandings, and the general words which we make ufe of, ferve only to detect the vain ambition of our mind; but with refpect to the univerfe, in confidering its immenfity, we fhall find, that there is fufficient fpace for all the fhades and modifications we have no idea of. We confefs, that it is the connection between our phyfical powers and intellectual faculties, and the action that they feem to have on each other, which nourifhes our doubts and anxieties; but without this relation, without the appearance of our fall, all would be diftinct in the fate of man, all would be manifeft. It is then, becaufe that there is a fhade in the

midft

midſt of the picture, which continually catches our attention, that we have need to collect the light of the mind and the feelings, in order to ſee in perſpective our deſtiny; and it is from this motive that we find it neceſſary, above all, to be penetrated with the idea of a God, and to ſearch for, in his power and goodneſs, the laſt explication which we want.

There is, in the judgments of men, a contraſt which I have often been ſtruck with. Thoſe people, who, at the ſight of the immenſity of the univerſe, at the view of the wonders in the midſt of which they are placed, fear not to attribute to our intellectual faculties the power of interpreting and underſtanding every thing, and even the capacity of attaining almoſt to the hidden ſecrets of our nature; theſe ſame people are neverthelefs moſt eager to ſtrip the ſoul of its true dignity, and the moſt obſtinate in refuſing it ſpirituality and duration, and every thing elſe which can exalt it.

But

But happily, thefe refufals or conceffions fix not our fate: the nature of the foul will always be as unknown as the effence of the Supreme Being; and it is one of the proofs of its grandeur, to be wrapped up in the fame myfteries which hide from us the univerfal fpirit. But there are fimple ideas and fentiments, which feem to bring along with them more comfort and hope than metaphyfical arguments.

We cannot profoundly meditate on the marvellous attributes of thought; we cannot attentively contemplate the vaft empire which has been fubmitted to it, or reflect on the faculty with which it is endowed, of fixing the paft, approaching the future, and bringing into a fmall compafs the expanded views of nature, and of containing, if I may ufe the phrafe, in one point the infinity of fpace, and the immenfity of time; we cannot confider fuch a wonder, without continually uniting a fentiment of admiration to the idea of an end worthy of fuch a grand conception, worthy of Him whofe wifdom we adore.

adore. Shall we, however, be able to difcover this end, in the paffing breath, in the
fleeting moments which compofe life? Shall
we be able to difcover it in a fucceffion of
phantoms, which feem deftined only to
trace the progrefs of time? Shall we, above
all, perceive it in this general fyftem of deftruction? and ought we to annihilate in the
fame manner the infenfible plant, which perifhes without having known life; and the
intelligent man, who every day explores the
charms of exiftence? Let us not thus de-
grade our fate and nature; and let us judge
and hope better of that which is unknown.
Life, which is a means of improvement,
fhould not lead to an eternal death; the
mind, that prolific fource of knowledge,
fhould not be loft in the dark fhades of for-
getfulnefs; fenfibility and all its mild and
pure emotions, which fo tenderly unite us
to others, and enliven our days, ought not
to be diffipated as if it were the vapour of a
dream; confcience, that fevere judge was
not intended to deceive us; and piety and
virtue are not vainly to elevate our views
towards

towards that model of affection, the object
of our love and adoration. The Supreme
Being, to whom all times belong, feems already to have fealed our union with futurity
by endowing us with forefight, and placing
in the receffes of our heart the paffionate
defire of a longer duration, and the confufed
fentiment which it · gives of obtaining it.
There are fome relations ftill obfcure, fome
connections between our moral nature and
futurity; and perhaps our wifhes, our hopes,
are a fixth fenfe, a faint fenfe, if I may be
allowed to exprefs myfelf fo, of which we
fhall one day experience the fatisfaction.
Sometimes alfo I imagine, that love, the
moft noble ornament of our nature, love,
fublime enchantment, is a myfterious pledge
of the truth of thefe hopes; for in difen-
gaging us from ourfelves, tranfporting us
beyond the limits of our being, it feems the
firft ftep towards an immortal nature; and
in prefenting to us the idea, in offering to
us the example of an exiftence out of ourfelves, it feems to interpret by our feelings
that which our minds cannot comprehend.

U   In

In ſhort, and this reflection is the moſt
awful of all, when I ſee the mind of man
graſp at the knowledge of a God; when I ſee
him, at leaſt, draw near to ſuch a grand idea;
ſuch a ſublime degree of elevation prepares
me, in ſome manner, for the high deſtiny
of the ſoul; I ſearch for a proportion between this immenſe thought and all the intereſts of the world, and I diſcover none;
I ſearch for a proportion between theſe
boundleſs meditations and the narrow pic-:
ture of life, and I perceive none: there
is then, I doubt not, ſome magnificent
ſecret beyond all that we can diſcern;
ſome aſtoniſhing wonder behind this cur-
tain ſtill unfurled; on all ſides we diſcover the commencement of it. How imagine, how reſolve the thought, that all
which affects and animates us, all which
guides and captivates us, is a ſeries of
inchantments, an aſſemblage of illuſions?
The univerſe and its majeſtic pomp would
then have been only deſtined to ſerve as the
theatre of a vain repreſentation; and ſuch
a grand idea, ſo magnificent a conception
would

would have had for an object a mere dazzling chimera. What would then have
fignified that mixture of real beauties and
falfe appearances ? What had fignified that
concourfe of phantoms, which, without
defign or end, would be lefs admirable than
a ray of light, deftined to enlighten our
abode ? In fhort, what had fignified in men
that union of fublime thoughts and deceitful hopes ? Guard us from giving credit to
fuch a fuppofition ! Is it to Him then, whofe
power has not any limits, that we dare to
attribute the artifices of weaknefs ?- Should
we have feen every where order, defign, and
exactnefs, as far as our underftanding can
reach, and as foon as we are arrived at the utmoft boundary of our faculties, fhould we
ftop the views of the Supreme Intelligence,
and imagine that all is finifhed, becaufe futurity is unknown ? Alas ! we endure but
a moment, and we prefume to know the
paft and the future ! But grant us only the
idea of a God ; do not deprive us of our
confidence in Him ; it is in relying on that
grand truth, that we fhall be able to guard

our

our hopes againſt all the metaphyſical arguments which .we are not immediately
prepared to anſwer.

Would you objeć̵t, that hope is not ſufficient to determine men to the obſervance of
morality, and to ſubjeć̵t them to the ſacrifices which the praćtice of virtue ſeems to
impoſe ? What then attraćts them, in all
the buſtle of life, unleſs it is hope ; what
is it that renders them greedy of honour
and of fortune, unleſs it is expećtation ?
And when they obtain the objeć̵t of their
wiſhes, they have frequently only the imaginary advantages hope created. Why then
would you aſk for a demonſtrated certainty,
in order to devote yourſelf to all the re-
ſearches which the human mind can conceive to be the moſt grand, the moſt worthy of an ardent purſuit ? On the contrary,
the moſt trifling degree of expećtation ſhould
become a motive of encouragement. And
what is it, of all our intereſts, which could
be put in competition with the moſt fugitive idea, with the ſlighteſt hope of pleaſing

the Mafter of the World, and maintaining the intercourfe which feems to be indicated by our natural fentiments, and by the firft perceptions of our minds ?

I would wifh to go ftill further, and I would demand, not of all men, but of fome at leaft, if, were even this life to be their only heritage, they would think themfelves freed from the defire of pleafing the Sovereign Author of Nature. The moment that is given us to know and admire Him, would it not ftill be a bleffing ? We celebrate the memory of thofe princes who have done good to men ; are we not to do the fame with Him to whom we are indebted for our exiftence ; to Him who has contrived, if I may be allowed to fay fo, the various enjoyments we are fo unwilling to detach ourfelves from ? Shall we dare, weak and ignorant as we are, to meafure the wifdom, and calculate the power of our Benefactor, and rafhly reproach him for not having done more for us ? This would be the language

U 3   of

of ingratitude. But, as I have ſhown, our ſentiments have not been put to this teſt; and it is on more liberal terms that we have been admitted to treat with the Supreme Being: He has ſurrounded us with every thing that can encourage our expectations; He allows us, by contemplation, to attain almoſt a knowledge of his perfections; He lets us read them in that collection of glory and magnificence which the univerſe diſplays; He permits us to perceive his power and goodneſs, infinity and happineſs; and by that ſucceſſion of ideas he has guided our wiſhes and our hopes. How grand is the contemplation of the Eternal, they who have ſenſibility can tell! But this idea ſhould be very early implanted in the human heart, it is neceſſary that it ſhould be connected with our firſt feelings, that it ſhould riſe by degrees, in order to gain ſtrength before men are thrown into the midſt of that world which boaſts of being freed from childiſh prejudices; leſt, hurried along by its levity, they follow every

day

day a new mafter, and render themfelves the flaves of pleafure and vanity.

And that which is to maintain, amongft men, the principles firft inculcated, is public worfhip, an idea as beautiful as fimple, and the moft proper to vivify all that is vague and abftract in reafoning and inftruction! public worfhip, in affembling men, and in turning them without public fhame to their weakneffes, and in equalifing every individual before the Mafter of the world, will be, in this point of view a grand leffon of morality; but this worfhip, befides, habitually reminds fome of their duty, and is for others a conftant fource of confolation; in fhort, almoft all men, aftonifhed and overwhelmed by the ideas of grandeur and infinity, which the appearance of the univerfe, and the exercife of their own thoughts, prefent to them, afpire to find repofe in the fentiment of adoration which unites them in a more intimate manner to God, than the developement of their reafon ever will.

We

We fhould guard ourfelves carefully from
defpifing the emotions of piety, which
cannot be feparated from its advantages;
and philofophers themfelves know not how
far they would go, when they try to reduce
the interefts of men to the narrow circle
of demonftrated truths; that which we
perceive confufedly, is more precious than
all we have a certain knowledge of; that
which we anticipate, is of more value than
the bleffings fcattered round us. Thus, we
fhould be miferably impoverifhed, if they
could retrench from the various comforts which we fhall never poffefs, but
through the aid of the imagination. However, if we take this imagination as a guide
and encouragement, when we are engaged
in the purfuits of fortune and ambition,
and if the wife themfelves find that to be good
which ferves to nourifh our paffions, why
would you reje¢t it, when, fimply more
grand and more fublime in its objeét, it becomes the fupport of our weakneffes, the
fafeguard of our principles, and the fource
of our moft interefting confolations?

It

It is the part of legiflators to ftudy thefe truths, and to direct towards them the fpirit of laws, and the uncertain courfe of opinions. How honourable is it for them to be called to form the auguft alliance which is to unite happinefs with morality, and morality with the exiftence of a God!

CHAP.

C H A P. XII.

That there is a God.

THAT there is a God ! How is it poffible to avoid being penetrated with
an awful refpect in uttering thefe words ?
How reflect on them without the deepeft
humility, and even an emotion of furprife,
that man, this weak creature, this atom difperfed in the immenfity of fpace, under-
takes to add fome weight to a truth, of
which all nature is the fplendid witnefs ?
However, if this truth is our fupreme good,
if we are nothing without it, how can we
banifh it from our minds ? Does it not conftrain us to dwell continually on the fubject ? Compared with it, all other thoughts
are infignificant and uninterefting ; it gives
birth to, and fuftains all the fentiments on
which the happinefs of an intelligent creature depends. I confefs I tremblingly difcuffed the different objections which are

employed

employèd to deftroy our confidence in the exiftence of a Supreme Being; I dreaded the melancholy which thofe arguments produced; I was afraid to feel the impreffion of it myfelf, and thus to hazard the opinion moft dear to my heart, and moft effential to my happinefs; it appeared to me, that a few general ideas, fupported by lively feelings, would have been fufficient for my tranquillity; and without an intereft more extended, without the defire of oppofing, according to my powers, a fpirit of indifference and falfe philofophy, which is every day gaining ground, I fhould never have ftepped beyond my circle. But, I am far from regretting the part I have taken: I have ran over, without much trouble, thofe books where the moft pernicious doctrines are ingenioufly diffemminated; and have thought that a perfon, endowed with common'fenfe, on whom metaphyfical fubtleties were obtruded, would refemble thofe favages who are brought fometimes amongft us, and who, from the depraved refinement of our morals and manners,

manners, have often recalled us, by some natural reflections, to those simple principles which we have abandoned, to those ancient truths whose vestiges are loft.

The whole structure of religion would be overturned, if, by the strength or artifices of reasoning, men could destroy our confidence in the existence of a Supreme Being: morality, being detached from the opinions which sustain it, would remain a wavering, unsupported notion, only defended by a policy, whose power time would insensibly weaken. A fatal languor invading every mind, where would be that universal interest, that sentiment felt by all men, and proper to form a general alliance between them? Then those, who, with pure intentions, can only be guided and sustained by an intimate persuasion, would retire sad, and leave to others the care of supporting moral order by fictions and falsehoods; they would pity that dismayed race, called to appear and pass away like flowers, which bloom but for a day; they would despise
thofe

thofe animated phantoms which only come to make a buz with their vanity and trivial paffions, and fall in a little while into eternal oblivion. All that appears beautiful in the univerfe, and excites our enthufiafm, would foon lofe its fplendour and enchantment, if we perceived nothing in this brilliant fcene but the play of fome atoms, and the uniform walk of blind neceffity; for it is always becaufe a thing may be otherwife, that it acquires a claim to our admiration: in fhort, that foul, that fpirit, which vivifies man, that faculty of thought which furprifes and confounds thofe who reflect, would only appear a vain movement, if nothing was before, or was to follow, if fome unknown breath, or general intelligence, did not animate nature. But we have dwelt too long on thofe gloomy thoughts; reaffume your light and life, admirable works of God; come and confound the pride of fome, and comfort others; come and take poffeffion of our fouls, and direct our affections towards Him whom we ought to love,

towards

towards Him who is the eternal model of perfect wifdom, and unlimitted goodnefs !

I fhall not endeavour to prove that there is a God, by reciting all the wonders the works of nature difplay to our eyes ; feveral celebrated writers have already done it, and have miffed their aim. Infinity can only be reprefented by aftonifhment and refpect, which overwhelms all our thoughts : and when we labour to explain the fucceffive and varied picture of the wonders of nature, this change of objects is more calculated to relax our admiration than to increafe it ; for any change cafes our mind, by affording thofe relaxations which our weaknefs has need of; and if we were to inveftigate only one phœnomenon, we fhould foon difcover, the utmoft extent of our faculties. We find the limits of our underftanding in the examination of the organization of the fmalleft infect, as well as in obferving the faculties of the foul ; and the myfteries of the fimpleft vegetation is as far above the reach

of

of our intelligence, as the principal agent of the univerſe.

It is then as a hymn of praiſe to the Supreme Being, and not as neceſſary in-ſtruction that I freely follow the courſe of my thoughts. I ſhall begin by throwing a rapid glance on the principal characters of wiſdom and grandeur, which we are all equally ſtruck with, when we contemplate the wonder of the univerſe.

What a fight is that of the world! What a magnificent picture for thoſe who can be rouſed out of the ſtate of indif-ference, in which habit has thrown them. We know not where to begin, or ſtop, when we expatiate on ſo many wonders; and the moſt noble of all is, the faculty which has been beſtowed on us of admiring and conceiving them. What an aſtoniſhing and ſublime relation is that of the innume-rable beauties of nature, with the intelli-gence which permits us to enjoy, and to be made

made happy by them! What relation
so surprising, as that of the order and
harmony of the universe, with the moral
intelligence which enables us to anticipate
the enjoyments of wisdom and unclouded
knowledge! Nature is immense, and all
that it contains, all that it spreads with so
much splendour, seems within the reach of
our sensibility, or the powers of our mind;
and these faculties, invisible and incomprehensible, unite to form, that wonder of
wonders, which we call felicity. Let not
these plain words turn our attention from
the magical ideas which they represent. It
is because the grand phœnomena of our existence cannot either be defined or expressed
many ways, that they are so much more
wonderful; and those words, used by
common consent, soul, mind, sensation,
life, happiness, and many others besides,
which we pronounce so slightly, confound
not less our understanding, when we wish
to discuss the essence of the properties of
which they are the sign. It is for this
reason,

reafon, among feveral others, that the admiration of particulars, in the works of nature, is always infufficient for thofe who have fenfibility, as fuch admiration is neceffarily placed between two ideas fufceptible of being known; ideas which we connect through the aid of our own knowledge; but the charm of our relation with the wonders which furround us, arifes from experiencing every inftant the impreffion of an infinite grandeur; and feeling the neceffity of flying to that mild refuge of ignorance and weaknefs, the fublime idea of a God. We are continually carried towards this idea by the vain efforts which we make, in order to penetrate the fecrets of our own nature; and when I fix my attention on thofe aftonifhing myfteries, which feem to terminate, in fome manner, the power of our thoughts, I reprefent them with emotion, as the only barrier which feparates us from the infinite fpirit, the fource of all knowledge.

Men

Men endowed with the greateſt genius, perceive quickly the bounds of their faculties when they wiſh: to.go very far in the ſtudy of abſtract metaphyſical truths; but the ſimpleſt and leaſt exerciſed mind, can diſtinguiſh the proofs of that order, which announces with ſo much ſplendour the end and deſign of ſovereign wiſdom. It ſeems, that all the knowledge proper to intereſt men has been placed within their reach. The learned aſtronomer, obſerving the courſe of our globe round the ſun, perceives the cauſe of that regular ſucceſſion of repoſe and vegetation, which ſecures the earth its fecundity, and adorns every ſeaſon with renewed beauties; but the ſimple cultivator, who ſees the treaſurers of the earth renovated every year, and anſwer, with ſingular preciſion, to the wants of animated beings, is not leſs a witneſs of a phœnomenon which is ſufficient to excite his admiration and gratitude! Newton analyzed light, and calculated the ſwiftneſs with which it runs over the immenſity of ſpace; but the ignorant herdſman, who ſees, when he wakes, his hut enlightened by the fame rays which animate all nature, is equally benefitted by them. The indefatigable anatomift attains a juft idea of our inimitable ftructure, and the ingenious texture of our different organs; but the man moft devoid of inftruction, who reflects an inftant on the pleafures, and the variety of the fenfations, which we find ourfelves fufceptible of, partakes the bleffing equally.

The tranfcendent knowledge of fome people, is a degree of fuperiority which difappears when contrafted with the incomprehenfible grandeur of nature; when we contemplate infinity, thofe talents which exalt one man above another are no more feen; and probably it is beyond the limits of our intelligence that the greateft wonders of nature begin. The knowledge of all ages has not explained what is the imperious authority of our will over our actions, nor how our thoughts could reach the moft remote ages, how our fouls could inveftigate

X 2   that

that innumerable multitude of prefent ob-,
jects, of recollections and anticipations;
neither has it informed us how all thofe
excellencies of the mind, fometimes remain unknown to itfelf, nor how they
are fometimes at its command, iffuing
out of their long obfcurity, and fucceeding
each other with method, or are profufely
poured forth. At the fight of thefe aftonifhing phœnomena, we think man pre-
fumptuous, when, puffed up with pride,
he miftakes the meafure of his ftrength and
wifhes to penetrate into the fecrets, whofe
confines are fhut by an invifible hand. He
fhould be content to know, that his exiftence is united to fo many wonders; 'he
fhould be fatisfied with being the principal
object of the liberality of nature, and he
fhould adore with reverential refpect that
powerful Sovereign, who beftows fo many
bleffings on him, and who has made him
to fympathize with all the powers of heaven and earth.

The

The globe on which we live runs over every year a fpace of two hundred millions of leagues; and in this immenfe courfe, its diftance from the fun, determined by immutable laws, is exactly proportioned to the degree of the temperature neceffary to our feeble nature, and to the fucceffive return of that precious vegetation, without which no animated being could fubfift.

That celeftial body, which fertilizes the feeds of life fhut up in the bofom of the earth, is, at the fame time, the fource of that light which opens to our view the glorious fight of the univerfe. The rays of the fun run over in eight minutes about thirty millions of leagues: fuch an impetuous motion would be fufficient to pulverize the largeft maffefs of matter; but, by an admirable combination, fuch is the incomprehenfible tenuity of thefe rays, that they ftrike the moft tender of our organs, not only without wounding it; but with a meafure fo delicate and precife, that they excite in us thofe extatic fenfations, which are the

X 3   origin

origin and the indifpenfable condition of our greateft enjoyments.

Man, in immenfity, is only an imperceptible point; and yet, by his fenfes and intelligence, he feems in communication with the whole univerfe; but how pleafant and peaceable is this communication! It is almoft that of a 'prince with his fubjects: all is animated round man, all relates to his defires and wants; the action of the elements, every thing on earth, like the rays of light, feems to be proportioned to his faculties and ftrength; and whilft the celeftial bodies move with a rapidity which terrifies our imagination, and whilft they hurry along in their courfe our dwelling, we are tranquil in the bofom of an afylum, and under the protecting fhelter allotted us; we enjoy there in peace a multitude of bleffings, which, by. another wonderful affinity, ally themfelves to our tafte, and all the fentiments we are endowed with.

In

, In fhort, and it is another favour, man is permitted to be, in fome things, the contriver of his own happinefs, by his will and ingenuity; he has embellifhed his habitation, and united feveral ornaments to the fimple beauties of nature; he has improved, by his care, the falutary plants; and even in thofe which feemed the moft dangerous he has difcovered fome wholefome property, and carefully feparated it from the envenomed parts which furrounded it; he can foften metals, and make them ferve to augment his ftrength; he obliges the marble to obey him, and affume what form he defires; he gives laws to the elements, or circumfcribes their empire; he ftops the invafion of the fea; he reftrains the rivers in their natural bed, and fometimes obliges them to take a different courfe, in order to fpread their benign influence; he erects a fhelter againft the fury of the winds, and by an ingenious contrivance, makes ufe of that impetuous force, which he could not at firft dream of de-

fending

fending himself from; even the fire, whofe terrible action feems to prefage deftruction, he fubjugates, and renders it, if I may fo exprefs myfelf, the confident of his induftry, and the companion of his labours.

What a fource of reflections is this dominion of the mind over the moft dreadful effects of the movement of blind matter. It feems as if the Supreme Being, in fubmitting thus to the intelligence of men the moft powerful elements, chofe to give us an anticipation of the empire which His fovereign wifdom has over the univerfe.

However, it is in the influence of our fpiritual faculties on themfelves, that we obferve, above all, their admirable nature; we fee, with aftonifhment, the perfections which they acquire by their own action. Intelligence, confidered in a general manner, undoubtedly is a great phœnomenon; but it is a ftill greater wonder, to fee the thoughts

thoughts of a man reach, by the moft ingenious means, the knowledge of others,
and form an alliance between the past and
prefent productions of the mind. It is by,
fuch an alliance that the fciences have been
improved, and that the mind of man has
been acquainted with all its ftrength. The
mighty of the earth cannot break this affociation, nor fubject to their tyrannic divifions the noble heritage of knowledge; this
gift, fo precious, preferves the ftamp of a
divine hand;—and no one has yet been able
to fay it is mine.

The moft noble ufe that has ever been
made of the admirable union of fo many
talents, and fo much knowledge, was to demonftrate how every thing in nature relates
to the idea of a firft caufe; which forcibly
announces a defign full of wifdom, and a
beneficent intention; but now, unhappily,
thefe proofs of the exiftence of a God are
not fufficient; imperious philofophers have
laboured to fubvert every thing founded on
the connection and wonderful harmony of
the

the fyftem of nature; it is not fufficient to oppofe to thefe new opinions the mere au-thority of final caufes; they do not conteft that there is a perfect conformity between our defires and wants, between our fenfes and the bounties of nature; they do not conteft, from the cedar to the hyffop, from the infect to man, that there is a beauty of proportion in the whole, which is to be found equally in the relation that objects have with each other, as well as in their different parts; but this admirable har-mony, in which the pious man, the man of feeling, perceives with delight the ftamp of an eternal intelligence; others lefs fortunate, undoubtedly, obftinately prefent it to us as a fortuitous collifion, as a play of atoms agi-tated by a blind movement, or as nature it-felf, exifting thus from all eternity. What trouble they take to invent and defend thefe fyftems deftructive of our happinefs and hopes! I prefer my feelings to all this philo-fophy; but, to avoid an encounter would be to favour their prefumption, and give addi-tional ftrength to their opinions.

Thus

Thus I fhall treat the moft important queftion that man can confider. I fhall endeavour firft to fhow, that the different conjectures on the origin of the world all centre in the fingle opinion of the eternal and neceffary exiftence of every thing which is; and I fhall afterwards compare the bafis of that fyftem with the reafon of that happy and fimple belief which unites the idea of a Supreme Being with all we fee and know; in fhort, to the univerfe, the moft unlimitted of our conceptions,

CHAP.

C H A P. XIII.

The same Subject continued.

WHEN we see the authors of the different systems, concerning the formation of the world, reject the idea of a God, under the pretext, that this idea is foreign to the nature of our perceptions, should we not have a right to expect some better substitute for it? But, far from answering our expectations, they abandon themselves to all the wanderings of the most fantastic imagination. In fact, whether we refer the origin of the universe to the effect of hazard, the fortuitous concourse of atoms, or whether we establish another hypothesis derived from the same principle, it is necessary at least to suppose the eternal existence of an innumerable multitude of little particles of matter, placed without order in the immensity of space; and to suppose, afterwards, that these atoms, disseminated

nated

nated to infinity, attracted each other, and
correfponded by the inherent properties of
their nature; and that there refulted, from
their adhefion, not only organized, but intelligent faculties; it is neceffary, in fhort,
to fuppofe, that all thofe incomprehenfible
atoms have been fettled with admirable order through the effect of a blind motion,
and by the refult of fome of the poffible
chances in the infinity of accidental combinations. Indeed, after fo many fuppofitions
without example or foundation, that of an
Intelligent Being, foul and director of the
univerfe, had been more analogous and more
confonant with our knowledge.

Let us return to the hypothefis we have
juft mentioned. We fhall then recognize
the trifling habit of the mind; it is accuftomed to proceed from fimple to compound
ideas, every time it meditates, invents, or
executes: thus, by an inverfe method, the
compofers of fyftems have thought, that,
in order to connect the univerfe to its origin, it was fufficient to detach, by the exercife

ercife of thinking, all its parts, and to break
and fubdivide them afterwards to infinity;
but whatever may be the tenuity of thefe
atoms, their exiftence, having organized and
intellectual properties, which we fhould be
obliged to grant them, would be a wonder
almoft equal to thofe phœnomena which
furround us.

When we fee a plant grow, embellifhed
with different colours, we only think of the
period when its vegetation may be perceived
by our fenfes; but the feed of this plant,
or if you like better, the organized atoms,
the firft principle of this feed, would have
offered alfo a grand fubject of admiration,
if we had been endowed with the faculties
neceffary to penetrate into the occult fecrets of nature. But perhaps, in transform-
ing into an imperceptible powder all the
parts of matter, which have been collected
to compofe the world, we have only before
our eyes a fugitive vapour, to which even
our imagination cannot reach; and thofe
who unfortunately love and defend this ad-

4   miration,

miration, 'find befides, in the fyftem of divi-
fible atoms, means to defer, according to'
their fancy, the moment of their aftonifhment.

All thefe fantaftic combinations ferve
only to lead us aftray in our refearches;
and I do not think it a matter of indifference to make a general obfervation.
The ftudy of the firft elements, of all
the fciences which we acquire, fuch as
geometry, languages, civil legiflation, and
feveral others, appear to us the fimpleft
parts of our inftruction. It is not the
fame, when we feek to know the laws
of the phyfical world; for the works of nature never appear more fimple than in their
compounded ftate; they are then, to our
mind, that which harmony is to the ear;
it is the agreement of all parts which forms
a union perfectly proportioned to our intelligence. Thus, man, for example, that
wonderful alliance of fo many different faculties, does not aftonifh our underftanding, but appears to us in one point of view,
a fimple

a fimple idea ; but we are troubled, and, as it were, difmayed, when we try to ana- lyze him, or mount to the elements of his liberty, will, thought, and all the other properties of his nature.

We only advance towards infinity, and confequently towards the moft profound darknefs; when we deftroy the world in or- der to divide it into atoms, out of the midft of which we make it iffue afrefh, after hav- ing rallied all we have difperfed.

Let us admit, for a moment, that there exifts organized and intelligent atoms, and that they are fuch, either by their nature, or by their adhefion to other atoms. We are now, of all thefe fcattered atoms, to compofe the univerfe, that mafter-piece of harmony, and perfect affemblage of every beauty and variety; that inexhauftible fource of every fentiment of admiration ; and in rejecting the idea of a God, creator and pre- ferver, we muft have recourfe to the power of chance, that is to fay; to the effects of

an

an unknown continual motion, which, without any rule, produces, in a limited time, all the combinations imaginable; but, in order to effect an infinite variety of combinations, it is not only neceſſary to admit a continual motion, but befides, to fuppofe this continual motion changes its direction in all the parts of fpace fubject to its influence. The exiſtençe of fuch a change, and a fimilar diverfity in the laws of motion, is a new fuppofition which may be ranked with the other wild ones.

However, after thefe chimerical fyſtems have been granted, we are not freed from the difficulties which the notion of the formation of the world by a fortuitous concourfe of atoms produces.

It is difficult to comprehend how particles of matter, agitated in every manner, and fufceptible, as has been fuppofed, of an infinity of different adhefions, fhould not have formed fuch a mixture, fuch a contexture, as would have rendered, the har-

Y   monious

monious compofition of the univerfe in all. its parts, impoffible.

When we reprefent to ourfelves, abftract-edly, the unlimmitted number of chances that may be attributed to a blind move-ment, the imagination, unable to conceive, is left to guefs how an infinite number of atoms, endowed with a property of uniting themfelves, under an infinite diverfity of movements, could compofe the heavenly bo-dies; but, as long before that period, when fuch an accidental throw would become pro-bable; thefe fame atoms might have formed an innumerable multitude of partial combi-nations; if one of thefe combinations had been incompatible with the harmony and compofition of a world, that world could not have been formed.

The fame confiderations may be applied to animated beings: chance might have produced men fufceptible of life, and the tranfmiffion of it, long before chance gave them all the faculties which they enjoy;

and

and if they had been formed with only four fenfes, they could not have acquired a fifth; for the fame reafon that we do not fee a new one fpring up. Befides, the chance which might have produced living beings, muft have always preceded the chance which afforded thofe beings every thing neceffary for their fubfiftence and prefervation.

It may indeed be fuppofed, that atoms affembled in a manner incompatible with the difpofition of the univerfe, have been feparated by the continuation of the motion introduced into the immenfity of fpace; but this continual motion, fufficient to fever that which it has joined, would it not have deftroyed that harmony which has been the refult of one of the fortuitous chances to which the formation of the world has been attributed?

Will fome object, that all the parts of matter, once united in the maffes and proportions which conftitute the heavenly bo-

dies,

dies, have been maintained by the impreffion of a predominant force at the fame
time invariable? But how is it poffible to
reconcile the exiftence and dominion of fuch
a force with that continual motion, which
was requifite for the compofition of the
univerfe?

It may be alfo demonftrated, that the formation of worlds, by the chances of a blind
motion, and their regular continuity of exiftence, are two propofitions which difagree.
Let us explain this idea. The play of atoms,
neceffary in order to produce the unformed
mafies of the heavenly bodies, being infinitely lefs complicated than that which is
neceffary to produce them, inhabited as they
are with intelligent beings, muft have happened long before the other. Thus, in
the fyftem of the compofition of the univerfe, by the fortuitous concourfe of atoms,
it is neceffary to fuppofe, that thefe atoms,
after having been united to form the heavenly bodies, have been fevered, and united
again,

again, as many times as was neceffary; to produce a planet inhabited by intelligent beings.
Since beings thus endowed add nothing to the
ftability of the world, fince they do not contribute to the grand coalition of all its parts;
why the fame blind motion which has united,
diffolved, and affembled fo often every part
of the earth, before it was compofed, fuch
as it is; why does it not produce fome alteration now? It fhould again reduce to
powder our world, or at leaft, let us perceive the commencement of fome new
form.

It is not only to a world inhabited by
intelligent beings, that the arguments, juft
mentioned, may be applicable; for we
perceive around us an innumerable multitude of beauties and features of harmony, which were not neceffary to the
prefervation of our world, and which,
according to every rule of probability,
would never have exifted, unlefs we
fuppofed, that the earth has been formed,
diffolved, and reproduced, an infinity of

times,

times, before having been composed such
as we see it; but then I would ask, why
there are no vestiges of those alterations,
and why that motion has stopped?

It would be possible, however, by the
assistance of a new supposition, to resolve
the difficulty I have just mentioned; some
may say, that the union, and the successive
dispersion of the universal atoms, are executed in a space of time, so slow and insensible, that our observations, and all those
which we have from tradition, cannot inform us whether there will not be a se-
paration of all the parts of the universe,
by the same causes which have occasioned
their adhesion.

It is obvious, that transporting us into
infinity and admitting such a series of ar-
bitary suppositions, they are not indeed exposed to any rational attacks; but, making
equally free with infinity, in order to oppose nonsense to nonsense, why may I not
be allowed to suppose, that in the infinite
combi-

combinations arifing from perpetual motion, men have been created, deftroyed, and again called into being, with the fame faculties, remembrances, thoughts, relations, and circumftances; and why each of us feparated from our former exiftence, only by a fleep, whofe duration is imperceptible, fhould not be in our own eyes immortal beings? Infinity permits the fuppofition of this abfurd hypothefis, as it authorifes every flight of the imagination in which time is reckoned for nothing. We fee, however, how we rifk running into error, when with our limited faculties we wifh to fubject the incomprehenfible idea of infinity, and boldly adjuft it to the combinations of finite beings.

Let us produce, however, another objection. It may be faid, that our planet is the refult of chance; but is not this chance improbable, if we fuppofe that there exifted in the infinity of fpace, an infinite number of other affembled atoms, equally produced by the firft throw of the dice,

which

which reprefent all the poffible forms, and imaginable proportions? And I would alfo afk, by what laws, all thefe irregular bo-dies, neceffarily fubject, by reafon of their number and maffes, to an infinity of. move-ments, have not difconcerted the planetary fyftem formed, at the fame time as they were, by chance?

I ought to obferve, above all, that the order which we are acquainted with, is a proof of univerfal order; for, in immenfity, where one part is nothing compared with the whole, no part, without exception, could be preferved, unlefs it was in equili-brium with every other.

Thus, whether *an infinite fucceffion of chances* be fuppofed, to which the entire mafs of atoms has been uniformly fubject, or whether the firft general throw is thought fufficient, but divided *into an infinity of different fections*, our reafon op-pofes invincible difficulties to the refult which

which some want to draw from these various systems.

In short, we must observe, that in order to understand the accidental formation of a world, such as we are at liberty to suppose, the eternal existence of every kind of organized and intelligent atoms, must have preceded the formation of that world. I must again observe, that when they are obliged to such wonderful first principles, and to admit, in the beginning, a nature so astonishing, we can scarcely conceive how they can make it act suddenly a foolish part, in order to finish the work of the universe: a more exalted supposition, would have prevented their drawing a conclusion so absurd.

It seems to me, that notwithstanding the immensity which has given rise to so many ridiculous notions about the formation of the world, they have such a resemblance to each other, that we can scarcely discern any difference;

difference; and considering the little circle
which the imagination runs over, when it
applies its force to deep conceptions, we
think we discover something supernatural in
its singular weakness: the authors of these
systems seem to have a slavish turn of thinking, and the marks of their chains are very
visible; it is always atoms, and atoms that
they make play together, either at different
times, or all at once; in infinite space; but
when some want to form ideas of liberty
and will, as they do not know in what manner to analyze these properties, they suppose
them pre-exifting in the elementary parts,
which they made use of to create their universe; and they prudently take care not to
grant any action to liberty and will; in order
to prevent any resistence to those notions on
which they build their universe.

They would not render either more simple or credible, the blind production of
worlds, by supposing not only innumerable
multitude of organized atoms, but, even an
infinite

infinite diverfity of molds to hold the atoms,
and of which force chemical analogy gives us
an idea. Such a fyftem, which might ferve
to explain a few fecondary caufes of our
known nature, is not applicable to the firft
formation of beings; for with fuch an affemblage of molds and atoms, all the great difficulties would ftill fubfift. In fact, how
fhould the different molds have claffed themfelves properly, in order to form the moft
fimple whole, but which befide required a
fixed meafure and gradation of ranks? The
mold deftined for the organized atoms, of
which the cryftalline is to be compofed,
how is it poffible it fhould have placed
itfelf in the centre of that mold which is to
form the pupil of the eye, and this laft on
that one which is to form the whole, and fo
on, by an exact gradation, whofe divifions
and fubdivifions are innumerable?

Were they to fuppofe an infinite fucceffion of molds, of which the largeft attracted the fmalleft, in the fame manner as
the

the molds attracted the atoms; this fuppofition, lefs ridiculous than any other,
is not fufficient to model, even in imagination, the moft unimportant phœnomena of
nature; it is neceffary, befides, that by the
direction of a wife and powerful force, the
molds, and the atoms which belong to
them, fet themfelves in motion, without
confufion; it is neceffary that thofe deftined
to compofe the exterior fibres fhould not
obftruct the paffage of thofe molds calculated to form the interior organs; in fhort,
that every one of thofe in its courfe and expanfion, fhould artfully obferve thofe delicate fhades which blend or feparate all the
parts of the fimpleft of nature's works.

We are already acquainted with a force
which acts in all directions, which difpofes
every thing in due order, tends towards an
end, ftops, begins again, and finifhes, every
moment, a complicated work; and this is
the intelligent will, and certainly we have
reafon to be aftonifhed, that the only faculty
we

we have an intimate confcioufnefs of, is the one. philofopher's turn from, when they inveftigate the admirable order of the univerfe.

I allow, that they may, at the fame time they reject the idea of a God, admit, as a principle, the eternal exiftence of a mechanical force, which, by an incomprehenfible neceffity, directed, towards a wife end, every thing that was at firft confufedly fcattered in the immenfity of fpace; but this new fuppofition would form an hypothefis fimilar to the fyftem of the eternal exiftence of the univerfe; in fact, the eternal exiftence of all the elements, of all fubftances, forces, and properties which were neceffary to produce a certain order of things, would be a phenomenon as incomprehenfible as the exiftence of that order itfelf.

We muft add, that thefe two phœnomena would be feparated in our thoughts only

only by an indivifible inftant, an inftant that we can neither defcribe nor imagine in the extent·of the time reprefented by eternity; for any chofen period would be ftill too late by an infinity of ages. The neceffary effect of an eternal caufe has not, like that caufe, any period to which we can fix its commencement.

We thus perceive, under another point of view, how vain and ridiculous are the fantaftic operations, they imagine, before the exiftence of the world, and which are attributed fometimes to the difordered movements of chance, and fometimes to the regular laws of blind neceffity.

There is then but one hypothefis to be oppofed to the idea of a God : it is the fyf- tem of the eternal exiftence of the univerfe. Such an atheiftical fyftem will always be more eafily defended than any other, becaufe that being founded on a fuppofition without bounds, it does not require to be embraced

by

by reasoning, like all the hypothetical ideas, by which men make nature act according to an order of their own invention. We will, in the next chapter, consider this system, and discuss it by every means in our power.

CHAP.

C H A P. XIV.

The same Subject continued.

THOSE who maintain that the world subsists of itself, and that there is not a God, say, in favour of their opinion, that if the eternal exiftence of the univerfe over-whelms our underftanding, the eternal exiftence of a God is a ftill more inconceivable idea; and that fuch a fuppofition is only another difficulty, fince, according to a common mode of judging, a work the moft wonderful appears a phœnomenon lefs aftonifhing than the knowledge of which it is the refult.

Let us firft fix our attention on this argument. It is ufelefs to afk, what is meant by another difficulty in infinity; thofe ideas which are reprefented by familiar expreffions, neceffarily derived from comparifon, are only admiffable in the narrow circle of our knowledge; out of it, thofe ideas have not any application, and we cannot fix any

degrees

degrees in the immenfity which exceeds the bounds of our views, and in thofe unfathomable depths which are out of the reach of our intellectual powers.

Undoubtedly, our mind is equally loft, both in trying to form a diftinct idea of a God, and in endeavouring to defcribe the eternal exiftence of the world, without any caufe out of itfelf: however, when we try to glance our thoughts towards the firft traces of time; when we try to rife almoft to the beginning of beginnings, we feel diftinctly that, far from confidering the eternal exiftence of an intelligent caufe as increafing the difficulty, we only find repofe in that opinion; and inftead of forcing our mind to adopt fuch an opinion, and thinking we wander in an imaginary fpace, we find it, on the contrary, more congenial with our nature; whilft order unites itfelf to the idea of a defign, and a multiplicity of combinations to the idea of an intelligence. Thus we rife from little to great things, and reafoning by analogy, we fhall more eafily

Z   conceive

conceive the exiſtence of a Being endowed
with various unlimitted properties, which
we in part partake ; we ſhall, I ſay, more
eaſily conceive ſuch an exiſtence, than that
of a univerſe, where all would be intelligent, except the firſt mover. The workman, undoubtedly, is ſuperior to the work :
but according to our manner of feeling and
judging, an intelligent combination, formed
without intelligence, will always be the
moſt extraordinary, as well as the moſt in-
comprehenſible phenomenon.

It is not indifferent to obſerve, that according to the ſyſtem I combat, the more
the world would appear to us the admirable
reſult of wiſdom, the leſs power ſhould we
have to draw any deduction favourable to
the exiſtence of a God, ſince the author of
a perfect work is not ſo eaſily traced as the
feeble re-iterated labours of mediocrity.
Thus, all thoſe who particularized the
beauties of nature, would ſtupidly injure
the cauſe of religion, and weaken our belief in the exiſtence of a Supreme Being.

It

It feems to me, 'that it is eafy to perceive what an ill-founded argument that muft be which leads us to a conclufion fo abfurd.

The attentive view of the univerfe fhould make us miftruft the judgment, which we form, of that which is the moft fimple in the order of things; for all the general opeー rations of nature arife from a movement more noble and complicated than we can eafily form an idea of. We fhould furely find, contrary to a perfect fimplicity of means, that a circuit of two hundred millions of leagues, which our globe makes every year, is neceffary, in order to produce the fucceffive changes of feafons, and to affure the re-production of the neceffary fruits; we fhould find, that the diftance of thirty-four millions of leagues, between the fun and the earth, was neceffary to proportion the rays of light to the delicacy of our organs. However, if even in the narrow circle we traverfe, we do not difcover any conftant application of that fimple order, of which

we

we form an idea, how could such a principle serve to guide our opinions, at the moment when we elevate our meditations to
the first link of the vast chain of beings;
when we undertake to examine, whether,
throughout the immensity of the universe,
there exists, or not, an intelligent cause?
What would become, in that immensity, of
the insignificant phrase, *it is one difficulty
more?* The buzzing fly would be less ridiculous, if capable of perceiving the order
and magnificence of a palace, it asserted,
that the architect never existed.

Every thing indicates, that, according to
our different degrees of sense and knowledge, what is simple, and what is easy,
have a very different application; we may
continually observe, that these expressions
are not interpreted in the same manner, by
a man of moderate abilities and a man of
genius; however, the distance which sepa-
rates the various degrees of intelligence with
which we are acquainted, is probably very trifling in the universal scale of beings. All our
reflections

reflections would lead us then to prefume,
that beyond the limits of the human mind,
the fimple is compounded, the eafy our
wonderful, and the evident our inconceivable.

After having examined the principal arguments of the partifans of athieftical fyftems, which we now attack; let us change
the fcene, and in the midft of the labyrinth, in which we are placed, try to find
a clue for our meditations.

We are witneffes of the exiftence of the
world, and intimately acquainted with our
own; thus, either God or matter muft
have been eternal; and by a natural confequence, an eternal exiftence, which is an
idea the moft incomprehenfible, is, however, the moft inconteftible truth. Obliged
now, in order, to fix our opinion, to chufe
between two eternal exiftences, the one intelligent and free, the other blind, and void of
all confcioufnefs, why not prefer the firft? An
eternal exiftence is an idea fo aftonifhing, fo

Z 3 much

much above our comprehenfion, that we decorate it with every thing fublime and beautiful, and nothing deferves more thofe decorations than thought.

Would it not be ftrange, that in our fyf-matic divifions, it was only to thought, and confequently to all that was moft ad-mirable in our nature, that we refufe eter-nity, whilft we grant it to matter and its blind combinations ? What a fubverfion of all proportion! that we fhould believe in the eternal exiftence of matter, becaufe it is prefent to our eyes, and yet not admit the eternal exiftence of an intelligence; whilft that which we are endowed with becomes the fource of our judgment, and even the guide of our fenfes!

And by what other fingularity we fhould grant the faculty and the confcioufnefs of intelligence, only to that fmall part of the world which is reprefented by animated beings ? Thus, the whole of nature would be below a part; and if no fpirit animated the

the univerſe, man would appear to have reached his ultimate perfection; though we ſee in him but a faint ſketch, a weak ſhadow of ſomething more complete and admirable; we perceive that he is, to ſpeak thus, at the commencement of thinking; and all his cares, all his efforts, to extend the empire of that faculty, only inform him, that he tends continually towards an end, from which he is always diſtant; in ſhort, in his greateſt exertions he feels his weakneſs; he ſtudies, but he cannot know himſelf; he makes a few petty diſcoveries, ſees ſome trifling wheels, whilſt the main ſpring eſcapes his ſearch: he is fallen into the world, like a grain of ſand thrown by the winds; he has neither a conſciouſneſs of his origin, nor a foreſight of his end; we perceive in him all the timidity and miſtruſt of a dependent being; he is conſtrained, by inſtinct, to raiſe to heaven his wiſhes and contemplations; and, when he is not led aſtray by an intoxicating reaſon, he fears, ſeeks to adore a god, and rejects with diſ-

dain

dain the rank which audacious philofphers affign him in the order of nature:

I muft alfo add, that the fentiment of admiration, which I cannot ftifle, when I turn my attention on the fpiritual qualities we are endowed with, would be infenfibly weakened, if I was reduced to confider man himfelf as a fimple growth of blind matter; for the moft aftonifhing production would only infpire me with a tranfitory emotion, unlefs I can refer it to an intelligent caufe: I muft difcover a defign, a combination, before I admire; as I have need to perceive feeling and affection, before I love.

But as foon as I fee in the human mind the ftamp of Omnipotence; and it appears to me one of the refults of a grand thought; it reafumes its dignity, and all the faculties of my foul are proftrate before fuch a wonderful conception.

It is then united with the idea of a God, that the fpiritual faculties of man attract my homage and captivate my imagination; in reflecting on thefe fublime faculties, ftudying their admirable effence, I am confirmed in the opinion that there exifts a fovereign intelligence, foul of nature, and that nature itfelf is fubject to its laws: yes, we find in the mind of man the firft evidence, a faint fhadow of the perfection which we muft attribute to the Creator of the Univerfe. What a wonder indeed is our thinking faculty, capable of fo many things yet ignorant of its own nature! I am equally aftonifhed, by the extent and limits of thinking; an immenfe fpace is open to its refearches, and at the fame time it cannot comprehend the fecrets which appear moft proximate with it; as the grand motive of action, the principle of intellectual force, ever remains concealed. Man is then informed, every inftant, of his grandeur and dependance; and thefe thoughts muft naturally lead to the idea of Omnipotence. There are, in thofe limits of our knowledge and ignorance, in that confufed and conditional light, all the evidence of defign;

defign; and it feems to me, fometimes, that I hear this command given to the human foul by the God of the univerfe: go to admire a portion of my univerfe, to fearch for happinefs and to learn to love me; but do not try to raife the veil, with which I have covered the fecret of thy ex-iftence; I have compofed thy nature of fome of the attributes which conftitute my own effence, thou wouldft be too near me, if I fhould permit thee to penetrate the myf-teries of it; wait for the moment deftined by my wifdom; till then, thou canft only reach me by reverence and gratitude.

Not only the wonderful faculty of think-ing connects us with the univerfal intelli-gence; but all thofe inconceivable proper-ties, known by the name of liberty, judg-ment, will, memory, and forefight; it is, in fhort, the auguft and fublime affemblage of all our intellectual faculties. Are we, in fact, after the contemplation of fuch a grand phœnomenon, far from conceiving a God? No, undoubtedly, we have within

us

us a feeble image of that infinite power : we seek to difcover; man is himfelf a univerfe, governed by a fovereign; and we are much nearer the Supreme Intelligence, by our nature; than by any notion of the primitive properties of matter; properties, from which fome wifh to make the fyftem of the world and its admirable harmony flow.

It feems to me, that our thinking faculty is too flightly treated in the greater number of philofophic fyftems; and fome have been fo afraid of honouring it, that they will not admit it to be a fimple and particular principle, when the fubject of the queftion is the immortality of the foul; nor will they confider it as a univerfal principle, when they difcufs the opinion of the exiftence of a God.

It is equally fingular, that they wifh to compofe of matter a foul endowed with the moft fublime qualities; and they pretend, at the fame time, that the world, in which we

see

fee intelligent beings, had not for a contriver and principal any being of the fame nature: this fuppofition, however, would be as rea-fonable as the other is weak; but it feems to me, that 'they like better to attribute order to confufion, than to order itfelf.

We feek to penetrate the fecret of the exiftence of the univerfe; and when we re-flect on the caufes of that vaft and magni-ficent difpofition, we can only attribute it to what feems the moft marvellous and ana-logous to fuch a compofition, thought, in-tention, and will. Why then fhould we retrench from the formation of the world all thofe fublime properties? Are we to act fparingly in an hypothefis in which all the wonders of nature are concentred? It is by the fpiritual faculties with which man is endowed, that he remains mafter of the earth, that he has fubdued the ferocious animals, conquered the elements, and found a fhelter from their impetuofity: it is by thefe faculties that man has conftructed fociety

ciety, given laws to his own paffions, and that he has improved all his means of happinefs; in fhort, nothing has ever been done, but by the aid of his mind; and in his fpeculations on the formation of the world, and on the admirable relations of all the parts of the univerfe, that which he wifhes not to admit, and will dare to reject is the intelligent powers and action of thinking. It feems like men difputing about the means which has been made ufe of to erect a pyramid, who name all the inftruments, except thofe that they found at the foot of the edifice.

Habit only turns our attention from the union of wonders which compofe the foul; and it is thus, unfortunately, that admiration, lively light of the mind and feelings, does not afford us any more inftruction. We fhould be very differently affected, if, for the firft time, we contemplated the meaneft part of this admirable whole! But even then, in a little time, the ftrong conviction of the exiftence of a God would be worn away,

4

away; and become what it is at present. But, let me be permitted, in order to render this truth more ſtriking, to have recourſe, for a moment, to fiction. Let us imagine men, as immovable as plants, but endowed with ſome one of our ſenſes, enjoying the faculty of reflection, and enabled to communicate their thoughts. I hear theſe animated trees diſcourſe about the origin of the world, and the firſt cauſe of all things; they advance, like us, different hypotheſis on the fortuitous movement of atoms, the laws of fate and blind neceſſity; and among the different arguments, employed by ſome, to conteſt the exiſtence of a God, creator of the univerſe; that which makes the greateſt impreſſion is, that it is impoſſible to conceive how an idea ſhould become a reality; or how the deſign of diſpoſing the parts ſhould influence the execution, ſince the will being a ſimple wiſh, a thought without force has not any means to metamorphoſe itſelf into action: but in vain would theſe immovable ſpectators of the univerſe wiſh to change their ſituation, to

raiſe

raife a fhelter againft the impetuofity of the winds, or the fcorching heat of the sun; yet then it would be evidently abfurd to imagine the exiftence of a faculty effentially contrary to the immutable nature of things. Let however, in the midft of this converfation, a fupernatural power appear, and fay to them, what would you think then, if this wonder, whofe exiftence you regard as impoffible, fhould be executed before your eyes; and if the faculty of acting, according to your own will, was to be fuddenly given you? Seized with aftonifhment, they would proftrate themfelves with fear and refpect; and from that inftant, without the flighteft doubt, would believe they had difcovered the fecret of the fyftem of the world; and they would adore the infinite power of intelligence, and it is to a like caufe we fhould attribute the difpofition of the univerfe. However, the fame phenomenon which would appear above belief, and out of the limits of poffibility, to thofe who have never

never been a witnefs of it, that wonder exifts in our world; we fee it, we experience
it every inftant; though the force of habit
weakens the impreffion and eradicates our
admiration.

,The hypothefis I have juft mentioned,
might even be applied to the fudden acqui-
fition of all the means proper to communicate ideas; and to the prompt difcoveries
of the other properties of our mind; but
feveral of thefe properties conftitute, in fuch
an effential manner, the effence of the foul,
that we cannot, even in imagination, feparate
them, any more than we can detach action
from will, and will from thought. There
are fome fpiritual faculties, and thofe the
moft wonderful, which we cannot define,
and which we fhould not have even fuppofed to exift had we not poffeffed them;
and if it had been poffible to have known
them before we were endowed with them,
the inventors of fyftems would have pointed
out this aftonifhing means, as the only one
applicable

applicable to the compofition of the admirable harmony of the univerfe.

We fhall be led to the fame reflections, when ceafing to expatiate on the
greateft wonders of our nature, we bound
ourfelves to confider the human mind at
the moment when its action may be perceived. To render this obfervation clearer,
let us follow a man of genius in the
courfe of his labours, and we fhall fee him
at once embrace a multitude of ideas, compare them, notwithftanding their diftance,
and form from fuch a mixture a diftinct refult proper to direct his public or private
conduct; let us confider him extending and
multiplying thefe firft combinations, and
connecting them, by an invifible web, to
fome fcattered points which his imagination
has fixed in the vaft regions of futurity;
with the affiftance of thefe magic fuccours
we fee him approaching the time which
does not yet exift; but we fee him, in his
career, aided by accumulated knowledge,
more fubtle than the rays of the fun

and

and yet separated, with an admirable order ;
more fleet and dispersed than the light va-
pours of the morning, and still subject to
the will of that inconceivable power,
which, under the name of memory, heaps
up the acquisitions of the mind, in order to
assist it afterwards in its new acquirements :
but let us examine still further this man of
genius, when he deposits, by means of writing, his different reflections ; and let us ask,
how he knows quickly, that an idea is new,
and that a style has an original turn ? Let
us again enquire, how, in order to form
such a judgment, he makes with celerity a
recapitulation of the thoughts and images
employed by others, to illustrate the subjects
they have treated, whilst years and ages
were rolling away ; in short, let every one,
according to his strength, try to penetrate
into these mysterious beauties of the human
understanding ; and let him enquire afterwards about the impression which he receives from a like meditation. There is,
perhaps, as great a difference, if I may be
allowed to say so, between the most perfect
vegetable

vegetable and the human mind, as between it and the Deity: to extend this idea, we have only to fuppofe, that in the immenfity which furrounds us, there exifts a gradation equal to that we have perceived in the little fpace we are permitted to infpect.

The author of a celebrated work accufes men of prefumption, becaufe, when they endeavour to trace the firft principle of things, by comparing their own faculties with it, they feem to think that they approach it. But, what other part fhould we be able to take, when we are called to reafon and to judge? It is not fufficient that the idea of the Supreme Being may be metaphyfical; it is neceffary further, fome will argue, that we even try to render it abftract, by removing it out of our imagination, and that we feek for, in our judgment and opinions, a fupport which may be in a manner abfent from ourfelves, and abfolutely foreign to our nature. All this cannot be underftood: we confefs that we have not fuffi-

cient

cient ftrength to know the effence and perfection of God, but giving way to abftraction, we extinguifh our natural light, and
deprive ourfelves of the few means we have
to obtain this knowledge ; we can only be
acquainted with unknown things by the
help of thofe we know : we fhall be led
aftray, if we are obliged to take another road ;
and modern philofophers often feek to attack intimate fentiments by arbitrary ideas,
of which an imagination the moft capricious
is the only foundation.

It will then always be furprizing, that
in our contemplations and habits of thinking, the wifdom of the defign, the harmony
of the whole, and the perfection of parts,
are manifeft traces of intelligence ; and yet
that we fhould renounce, fuddenly, this
manner of feeling and judging, in order
to attribute the formation of the univerfe to
the effect of chance, or the eternal laws of
blind neceffity ; and is it poffible, that we
can deduce the fame confequences from an
admirable order, as from wild confufion ?

Facts

Facts so different, principles so contrary, should not lead to the same conclusion; the magnificent system of the universe ought to have some weight, when we conjecture about its origin; and it would be difficult to persuade us, that in investigating the most exalted truths, we ought to consider all the knowledge we acquire by the view of nature as merely indifferent. Men are carried very far, when they reject the arguments drawn from final causes; it is not only a single thought they would destroy; it is the source of all our knowledge they would dry up.

Men insensibly cease to perceive a connexion between the existence of a God, and the different miracles with which we are surrounded; but all would be changed, if God exhibited the numerous acts of his power successively, instead of displaying them all at once; our imagination, animated by such a movement, would rise to the idea of a Supreme Being; it is then, because an accumulation of wonders ag-

A a 3

grandizes

grandizes the univerfe; it is becaufe a harmony, not to be equalled, feems to convert
an infinity of parts into an admirable whole;
and that profound wifdom maintains it in an
immutable equilibrium; it is, in fhort, becaufe infenfible gradations and delicate fhades
render ftill more perfect the wonders of nature, that men are lefs ftruck with aftonifhment, or loft in adoration.

We want, fay you, new phenomena to
determine our perfuafion: do you forget,
that all which is offered to our view already furpaffes our underftanding? If the
leaft miracle was to be effected before you,
you would be ready to bend your proud
reafon; but becaufe the moft grand and
wonderful, which the imagination itfelf can
form an idea of, has preceded your exiftence, you receive no impreffion from it,
all appears fimple to you, all neceffary.
But, the reality of the wonders of the univerfe has nothing to do with the inftant
you are allowed to contemplate them:
your pilgrin.age on-earth, is it not a period

riod imperceptible in the midft of eternity ?
admiration, furprize, and all the affections
of which man is fufceptible, do not change
the nature of the phœnomena which furround him; and his intelligence reflects but
a very fmall part of the wonders of the
univerfe.

We have no need of a revolution
in the order of nature, to difcover the
power of its author; the fibres of a blade
of grafs confound our intelligence, and
when we have grown old in ftudy and obfervation, we continually difcover new objects, which we have not inveftigated, and
perceive new relations; we are ever in the
midft of unknown things and incomprehenfible fecrets.

However, fuppofing, for a moment, the
exiftence of extraordinary miracles which
we fhould be impreffed with; it is eafy to
conceive, that thefe miracles would not have
on men the influence we prefume; for if
they were frequent, and if they happened

only

only at regular periods, their firſt impreſſion, would ſlowly be weakened, and, at
laſt, men would range them in the claſs of
the ſucceſſive movements of eternal matter.
But if, on the contrary, there was a long
interval between theſe miracles, the generations who ſucceeded the actual witneſſes
of them would accuſe their anceſtors of
credulity, or conteſt the truth of thoſe tra-
ditions, which tranſmitted the account of
a revolution contrary to the common courſe
of nature.

Some may ſtill ſay, that, in order to render manifeſt the exiſtence of the Supreme
Being, it would be neceſſary that men were
punctually anſwered, when they addreſs their
prayers; but the influence of our wiſhes
upon events, if this influence was habitual
and general, would it be ſufficient to change
the opinion of thoſe who ſee, with indifference, that innumerable multitude of actions
which are ſo miraculouſly ſubject to our will?
Would they not ſtill find ſome reaſon for
conſidering ſuch an increaſe of power, as
the

the neceffary refult of the eternal fyftem of the univerfe? Thus, whatever might be the meafure of intelligence, added to that we now enjoy, in fhort, though a number of new wonders were accumulated, men could ftill oppofe to that union of miracles the fame objections, and the fame doubts they do not now fear to raife againft the wonders we are daily witneffes of. It is difficult, it is impoffible, to make a conftant or profound impreffion on men who are only fufceptible of aftonifhment in the fhort tranfition from the known to the unknown; they have but a moment to feel this emotion, and it is from the flownefs of their comprehenfion, or the continual fucceffion of the phœnomena fubmitted to their infpection, that the duration of their admiration depends. And, perhaps, our faculties and powers would excite more furprize, if, in in order to fubject our movements to our will, it were neceffary to give our orders, and to pronounce them with a loud voice, as a captain does to his foldiers; however, fuch

·a con-

a conftitution would be a degree lefs wonderful than that we poffefs,

I will anticipate another objection; we
advance gradually, fome will fay, in difco-
vering the fecrets of nature; the power of attraction, that grand phyfical faculty, has only
been known about a century, and obfervations on the effects of electricity are ftill
more recent; every age, every year, adds
to the treafure of our knowledge, and the
time will arrive, perhaps, when, without
having recourfe to any myfterious opinions,
we fhall have explained all the phenomena
which ftill aftonifh us,

It is not at firft conceivable, how our
paft difcoveries, and all thofe which may in
future enrich the human mind, would ever
free us from the neceffity of placing a firft
caufe at the termination of our reflections;
for, the more we perceive of new links in
the vaft difpofition of the univerfe, the more
we extend the magnificence of the work,
and the power of the Creator. A feries of
                                  fuccefsful

fuccefsful exertions may reveal, perhaps, the fecret of fome phyfical properties, fuperior in force to thofe we have experienced: but, even then, all the movements of nature would be fubordinate to a few general laws; and when we fhould diftinguifh thefe laws, the refult of our refearches would demonftrate fimply the exiftence of a greater unity in the fyftem of the world; and this character of perfection would be impreffed, if it was poffible, ftill more on us; for, in a work, fuch as the univerfe, it is the fimple and re- gular relations which announce, above all, the wifdom and power of the Difpofer; becaufe our admiration could never be ex- cited by an affemblage of incoherent ideas, whofe chain would every inftant be broken. But, I know not by what habit or blindnefs it is, that when men have difcovered a principle uniform in its action, and have given to that principle a denomination, they believe that their aftonifhment ought to ceafe: in fact, attraction and electricity are not fo much now fubjects of furprize, as a means to free us from the admiration due to the magnifi-

cent

cent refult of thofe fingular properties; in
fhort, we are habituated to confider, with
indifference, every general effect, of which
we acquire a conception, as if even this
conception was not one of the moft noble
of the phenomena of nature. 'Some will fay;
that men, by degrees, becoming familiarized
with their own minds, defpife all they can
eafily underftand; their competitions are
then the only origin of their vanity; for
when they examine themfelves individually;
or when they judge of men in general, they
have fuch a mean opinion of themfelves, that
they do not highly value their difcoveries.

We ought to place, amongft the number of ideas the moft extenfive and general,
that of Buffon on the formation of the
earth; but this idea, fuppofing it as juft as
it is beautiful, only explains to us one of the
gradations of this fuperb work. I fee the
earth formed by an emanation of the fun;
I fee it animated and become fertile, when
it has received, by flow degree, its temperature; and I fee, befide, iffue out of its lap
all

all the beauties of nature; and that which furprizes me ftill more, all the beings endowed with inftinct or intelligence; but if the elements of thefe incomprehenfible productions had been prepared or fimply difpofed in the fiery body which animates our fyftem, I transfer to it my aftonifhment, and equally have to feek for the author of fo many wonders.

I muft now fix my attention, for a few moments, on the moft metaphyfical part of this work. We can, perhaps, form an idea of a world exifting without a beginning, and by the laws of blind neceffity, provided that world was immovable and invariable in all its parts; but how apply the idea of eternity to a continual fucceffion; as fuch a nature is neceffarily compofed of a beginning and end, we cannot otherwife define the idea of fucceffion; thus, we are conftrained to elevate ourfelves to a firft Being exifting by himfelf, when we have before our eyes a conftant revolution of caufes and effects, of deftruction and life.

It

It is impoffible to have any idea of motion without that of a beginning.

The difficulty would not be removed, by faying, that the whole of the univerfe is immutable, and the parts only fubject to change; for a whole of this kind, without any relation whatever, either real or imaginary, a like whole has only an ideal circumfcription, which, in fact, is not fufceptible of an alteration; but fuch a circumfcription only prefents us an affemblage of pofitive things contained in its circle; and it is not in ftudying thofe, nor in examining the different parts of the unknown whole, which we call the univerfe, that we are allowed to draw confequences, or to form a judgment. Thus, feeing only a fucceffion, we rationally feel the neceffity of a firft caufe.

But, fome will fay, you are entangled in the fame difficulty, when you fuppofe the eternity of a God; for a feries of defigns in an intelligent being fhould lead to the

idea

idea of a commencement, as well as the fuc-
ceffions of the phyfical world.

This propofition, undoubtedly, is not
eafily cleared up, like all thofe. whofe folu-
tion appears to be united to the knowledge
of infinity. We cannot, however, hinder
ourfelves from perceiving, that the phyfical
generations lead us, in a manner fimple and
manifeft, to the neceffity of a firft principle;
and we ought to fearch for this principle
out of ourfelves, fince our nature does not
furnifh any idea of it; whereas, the fucceffive combinations of the mind may relate to
an origin, of which we have not any conception, and which feems united, in fome
manner, to thefe fame combinations. In
fact, we can eafily form a diftinct idea of a
faculty of thought, antecedent to the action
of thinking, and which might even be feparated by fuch intervals as the imagination
could conceive. It is the fame with liberty,
that intellectual power of which we have
the confcioufnefs, at the fame time that it
remains abfolutely idle;

I fhall

I fhall add, that, even in the narrow circle of our thoughts, it is true, the operations of the mind appear to us often depen-
dant on each other; yet, fometimes their
chain is fo broken, that our ideas feem really
to iffue out of nothing; inftead of which,
in every other production, we know, there
is always a vifible tie between that which
is, and that which was. We muft not
forget, that at the very time our ideas appear to us connected, that fucceffion is to
be attributed to our weaknefs and ignorance,
rather than to the mind, confidered in a
general manner. Circumfcribed in all our
means, we are obliged to go continually
from the known to the unknown, from
probability to certainty, from experience of
the paft, to conjectures about the future;
but this gradation, this courfe, ought to be
abfolutely foreign to an intelligence without
bounds, which knows and which fees all at
the fame time; and perhaps we are in the
way of this truth, when we perceive,
amongft us, the claim of true genius, and
the turbulent whirlpool of folly.

In

In fhort, it is not men perfuaded of the exiftence of a God; that we need require to tranfport themfelves beyond, if I may fay fo, the domain of thought, in order to fearch for proofs of their opinion; atheifts alone want fuch an effort, fince they alone refift the influence of the fimpleft fentiments and moft natural arguments; fince they alone bid us miftruft that diftinct connexion which we perceive between the Supreme Intelligence and the perfection of order; that train of caufes and effects, between the idea of a God and all the propenfities of the foul; it is thefe confiderations, intelligible to all, which give new force to our opinions.

Directed by thefe reflections, and wifhing to inveftigate in a ufeful manner the fubject I have undertaken, I fhall not engage in the arguments which turn on the creation of the world. It is fufficient for me to have perceived, that the idea of the creation of the univerfe is not more inconceivable than the idea of its eternity; I am not in-

deed

deed obliged, with those who adopt the last system, to suppose something growing out of nothing; but substituting the idea of an eternal existence, instead of that of nothing, is a thought which equally terrifies my imagination; for my mind knows not where to place that eternity and in order to comprehend it still surrounds it with a vacuum. In the system of a created universe, I see something coming out of nothing, by the will of a Being whom I can form an idea of; but in the system of the eternity of matter, my faculties are absorbed in endeavouring to embrace it; in short, both of these modes of existence appear to me in the midst of a vague infinity, which no human power can conceive; and if sometimes the eternal existence of the universe seems less incomprehensible than its creation, it is only because such an idea eludes examination and precludes reasoning.

The idea of a Creator is undoubtedly equally above our comprehension, but we

are

are led to it by all our feelings and thoughts; and if we are stopped in the efforts, which we make to reach the cause we seek; it is by obstacles which we can even attribute to the will of that power we are searching to discover; instead of that, contemplating the uniform and insipid rotation of an eternal existence, we are almost driven to despair; that is to say; we feel the impossibility of conceiving the nature of things; and the certainty, nevertheless, that there exists not any veil designedly placed between that nature and our understandings.

I must still make some further observations; we see a resemblance of creation in the continual reproduction of all the bounties of the earth; and our moral system offers a still more striking one, in the formation of ideas which did not exist antecedently. Our feelings appear another proof of the same truth; for they have not any evident connexion with the cause that we assign them: thus, without habit we might

see

fee as great a difference between certain exterior emotions and the various affections of our fouls, as we can conceive between the exiftence of the world and the idea of a Creator.

We perceive alfo, that the univerfe has all the characters of a production; characters which confift in the union of a multitude of parts, whofe relations are fixed by a fingle thought. In fhort, even the fucceffion of time announces intelligence; for we know not how to place that fucceffion in the midft of an eternal exiftence. We cannot conceive any different periods in an extent in which there is not a beginning; for before we arrive at any of thefe periods, there muft have been always an infinite fpace; befides, there being no beginning, confidered abftractedly, annihilates the idea of intervals, fince they could not have two fixed points: thus, the introduction of the paft, the prefent, and the future, into the midft

2   of

of eternity, feems due to an intelligent. power, who has modelled this immenfe uniformity; and governs the. nature of ·things,

I ought not to dwell long on thefe re- flections; to give a bafis' to religious opi- nions, it is not neceffary to conceive of creation in its metaphyfical effence; it is fufficient, to believe the exiftence of a Supreme Being, creator and preferver of nature, the model of wifdom and goodnefs, the protector of rational beings, whofe providence governs the world. We lofe all our ftrength when extending too far our meditations, we afpire to know and explain the fecrets of infinity; we then only exhibit to the adverfaries of reli- gion the faint ftretch of our opinions, and the laft ftruggles of a reafon weak- ened by its own efforts; it is much bet- ter to ufe thofe arguments which fenfe and feeling are able. to defend. We fhould candidly confefs, that our nobleft faculties have immutable limits; one degree

more

more would perhaps diffuse a sudden light on the queſtions, whoſe examination diſconcerts us. There is not perhaps any mind accuſtomed to meditation, which has not had ſeveral times pre-ſentiments of this truth; for the firſt glimmering of a new perception ſeems to out-run thinking, and ſuch is its proximity that we imagine one ſtep more would enable us to catch it; but our hope is diſſipated, we cannot graſp the fleeting ſhadow, and fall back again into the ſad conviction of our impotence. Alas! in that infinite ſpace which our intellectual powers try to run over, there are only immenſe deſerts, where the mind cannot find repoſe, or the thoughts meet any aſylum; theſe are the regions whoſe entrance ſeems to have been deſolated, in order that the moſt unbounded imagination might not obtain any knowledge of them; but will you dare to ſay, that there ſtops all intelligence, there finiſhes the myſteries of nature? would you expect to poſſeſs the ſecrets of time in attributing an eternal exiſtence to all we know? Certainly, we are too inſignificant fignificant to promulge fuch decrees, we enjoy too fmall a portion of eternity to determine what belongs to it.

The moft probable thought is, that our reafon is infufficient to reach the explanations we wifh to unfold; the chain of beings above us every inftant reminds us of this truth; and it appears fingular, that perceiving fo diftinctly the bounds of our fenfes, we fhould not be induced to think, that our intelligence, apparently fo extended, may neverthelefs run over a very circumfcribed fpace. Our imagination goes much farther than our knowledge, but its domain is perhaps only a point in what is yet unexplored; and it is neceffary to penetrate thofe unknown regions, to difcover the truths which illuftrate the myfteries that furround us; but there is a Being who knows them, Omnifcience is at the fummit of thofe gradations of intelligence which we trace. We know nothing, we do not difcover any refult but through the affiftance of experience and obfervation; and we

only

only know the world by the little front
feene which meets our view : is it rational
to fuppofe, that only this kind of knowledge exifts in the univerfe ? Men, in the
flow progrefs of their judgment, refemble
children ; but even this condition recals the
idea of a father and a tutor. Every thing
however fhows us, that the phenomena of
nature relate to a grand whole ; we fee that
its difperfed productions are united to fome
general caufe ; it is the fame with human
knowledge ; more admirable than the rays
of light fpread through immenfity, it is
an emanation from the moft perfect light.
In fhort, if fpace, if time itfelf, thofe two
exiftences without bounds, are fubject to
divifion, why fhould we not be induced to
think, that the degrees of knowledge we
experience and conceive, are alfo only a part
of a univerfal intelligence ?

Of all the objections againft the idea of
a God, the weakeft, in my opinion, is that
drawn from the mixture of troubles and
pleafures to which human life is expofed.

A God,

A God, fome will fay, ought to unite every perfection, and we cannot believe in his exiftence, when we perceive limits in his power or goodnefs.

This is a flimfy argument; for, if men do not admit as a proof of the exiftence of a God, all that we difcover of wifdom, harmony, and intelligence in the univerfe, what right have they to ufe an apparent contraft between fovereign power and goodnefs, in order to attribute the formation of the world to chance. Would it be juft, that the defects of a work fhould be brought as a proof againft the exiftence of a workman, whilft the beauty of the fame work was not allowed to fupport a contrary opinion ? We fhould reafon in a different manner; diforder and imperfection merely point out to us a negation of certain qualities; we muft, in general terms, throw an odium on the whole, in order to banifh the idea of an intelligent hand; whereas, to ftrengthen the other opinion, it is fufficient that particular parts announce art and genius. Thus,

when

when we enter a palace, if we find there diftinct marks of talents, we attribute its erection to an architect, even though in a part of the edifice we fhould not diftinguifh any traces of invention.

I have already had occafion to fhow how we are led to thefe incomprehenfible extremes, when we endeavour exactly to proportion the wifdom and power of an Infinite Being, and I fhall not again dwell on this argument: or repeat that from any imaginable hypothefis, we might draw this deduction, that Omnipotence could have produced more happinefs.

There are ideas which appear contrary to reafon, only becaufe we cannot perceive them in one point of view; and we difcover this truth, not only in confidering things which are foreign to our nature, but when we turn our attention on the events which come daily under our infpection. Why do we then fuppofe, that we can comprehend the moft grand and noble thoughts? Is it con-

fiftent

fiftent with the idea of an Infinite Power that
we refufe to credit the exiftence of infinite
goodnefs? Is it confiftent with the idea of Infinite Wifdom that we will not admit the exiftence of Omnipotence? Nay more, is it confiftent with the idea of infinite chances that
we imagine the abfurd fyftems concerning
the formation of the world? We ufe infinity
for every thing, except to place above us an
intelligence, whofe properties and effence
our reafon cannot determine.

We are loft in a boundlefs uncertainty,
when we try to go beyond the limits of human powers. Thus, after having collected
all the forces of our fouls, to enable us to
penetrate the exiftence of a God, we ought
not to exhauft ourfelves in fubtleties, vainly
endeavouring to conceive in a juft acceptation, and under evident relations, various
attributes of an Infinite Being, who has
chofen to make himfelf known to us in a
certain meafure, and under certain forms;
and it is too much to require of the wor-
fhippers of God, to defend themfelves
againft

against those who contest his existence, and dispute about the nature of his perfections. I am far from supposing any obstacle to the execution of his will; but I should be full of the same religious sentiments, if I knew that there existed order and laws in the nature of things, which the Divine Power has a faculty of modifying, and that it cannot entirely destroy. I should not less adore the Supreme Being, if, at the same time, his various attributes were in constant union, it was nevertheless, by degrees, that he produced happiness; I should silently respect the secrets which would escape my penetration, and wait with respectful submission, till the clouds were dissipated which still surrounded me. What then! always in ignorance and obscurity? Yes, always: such is the condition of men, when they wish to go beyond the limits traced by the immutable laws of nature; but the grand truths which we can easily perceive are sufficient to regulate our conduct, and afford us comfort. That there is a God, every thing indicates and loudly announces;

but

but I cannot difcover either the myfteries of his effence, or the intimate connection of his various perfections: I plainly fee in a crowd. the monarch encircled by his guards; I know his laws, I enjoy the order he has prefcribed; but I affift not at his councils, and am a ftranger to his deliberations. . I even perceive, that an impenetrable veil fe-. parates me from the defigns of the Supreme Being, and I do not undertake to trace. them; I commit myfelf with confidence to. the protection of that Being whom I be-. lieve good and great, as I would rely on the. guidance of a friend during a dark night; and whilft I have my foot in the abyfs, I will depend on Him to fnatch me from. the danger and calm my terrors.

If we might be allowed the comparifon, we fhould fay, that God is like the fun, which we cannot ftedfaftly gaze at; but throwing our eyes down, we perceive its rays and the beauties it fpreads around. However, men who, either through a miftruft of their under-ftanding, or the nature of it, have only by their reverence an intercourfe with God, feel

moft

moft forcibly the impreffion of his grandeur; as it is at the extremity of the lever that we ftrongly experience its power.

We confider the general affent of nations and ages, in the opinion of the exiftence of a God, as a remarkable prefumption in favour of that opinion; but fuch a proof would lofe part of its force, if we, in time, regarded as a kind of moral phenomenon, the relation which all men may have with an idea fo fublime, notwithftanding the vifible difparity which exifts between their different degrees of underftanding and knowledge; and this obfervation fhould lead to a thought, that in the midft of the clouds, which obfcure the idea of a God, fenfibility becomes our beft guide: it feems the moft innate part of ourfelves, and in this refpect to communicate, in the moft intimate manner, with the Author of our Nature.

The fight advances before our other fenfes, the imagination goes beyond it; but as it is obliged to trace its own path, fenfibility,

fibility, which bounds over all, goes still further.

The reasoner, in his efforts to attain to profound metaphysical truths, forms a chain whose links rather follow each other, than are joined : the mind of man not being suf-ficiently subtle, and extended, cannot always unite exactly that infinite multitude of ideas which crowd at the determination of our meditations ; sensibility is then the best cal-culated to conceive the sublime truth, which not being composed of parts, is not suscep-tible of section, and can only be compre-hended in its unity. Thus, whilst the mind often wanders in vain speculations, and loses itself in metaphysical labyrinths, the idea of a Supreme Being is impressed, without effort, in a simple heart, which is still, under the influence of nature : thus, the man of feeling, as well as the intelligent man, announces a Supreme Being, whom we cannot discover without loving ; and this union of all the faculties of the soul towards the same idea, this emotion, which

resembles

refembles a kind of inftinct, ought to be connected with a firft caufe; as there is for every thing a firft model.

It is, perhaps, alfo the confufed fentiment of that firft model, which leads us to religion, when we fee a virtuous man. Men, with their fatal fyftems, would alter and annihilate every thing, but the comfortable hopes and thoughts which arife from a profound and rational admiration, will ftill refift that deftruction. They vainly wifh to make us confider fuch a fentiment as the fimple play of blind matter, whilft all within us feems to invite us to fearch for a more noble origin. And how can we avoid feeing, in thefe great qualities of men, noblenefs of foul, elevation of genius, expanfion of heart, love of order, and interefting goodnefs; how avoid feeing, in this rich picture, the reflection of a celeftial light, and concluding from it, that there is fomewhere a firft intelligence. Do rays exift without a centre of light? I know not, but hurried away by thefe reflections, I fometimes think, innate goodnefs,

goodnefs, which we admire as the firft rank in the fcale of intelligent 'beings, in a more immediate manner, leads to the knowledge of the Author of nature; and when this innate morality is found united in fome perfons with a prefentiment of the Divine Nature, there is, in this agreement, a charm which impreffes us; a kind of unknown cha- racter which attracts our refpect: as every tender and fublime thought is roufed by the idea which we form of the fouls of Socrates and Fenelon.

At the fame time, actuated by fimilar fentiments we experience a painful emotion, when we are informed, that there exift men, enemies to all thefe ideas; men, who had rather debafe themfelves and huma- nity, by attributing their origin to chance, than refolve to confider the fpiritual facul- ties which they enjoy as a faint fketch of the fovereign intelligence. Thus, inftead of employing their minds to lend fome force to thefe comfortable truths, or, at leaft pro-

babilities

babilities fo dear, they, on the contrary, difpute their realty, and feek to embarrafs by fophiftry, the doctrines which tend to fortify the firft difpofitions of our nature: we fee the materialifts, rather then elevate themfelves, drag us with them from happinefs and hope; they only grant eternity to the duft, out of which, they fay, we fprung. What honour, however, can they derive from thofe more enlightened views which they boaft of, if they are only the refult of a growth fimilar to that of plants; and if our fpiritual faculties, fo far from being loft, in fome meafure, in the infinite intelligence, fo far from being united to a grand deftiny, are only affociated to this frail ftructure, which is every day, every hour, expofed to various dangers. What credit fhould we derive from thefe faculties, if they only enabled us to defcribe, with precifion, the almoft imperceptible circle of time, in which we live and die: if they only ferved to raife us above our equals during that fhort moment of life, which is baftening to lofe itfelf in endlefs ages, as a light

vapour

vapour in the immenfity of air? How can you fpeak with delight of fame and promotion, when you voluntarily renounce the grandeur arifing from the moft noble origin? You are proud of the celebrity of your country, the renown of your families, and the only glory you defire not partake, is that which enobles the whole human race!

In fhort, I would afk, by what ftrange error of the imagination it is, that in meditating on the exiftence of a God, men do not go further than to doubt it; fince to fupport, to guide our judgment, we have only an underftanding whofe weaknefs we continually experience; fince it is capable of gradual improvement, as knowledge is perpetually accumulating? There exifts not any proportion between the meafure of our knowledge and the unbounded extent which is difplayed before us; there is not any between the union of all our powers and the profound myfteries of nature: how then fhall we dare to fay, that men are

C c 2   arrived

arrived at the pinnacle of knowledge, and that in the endlefs ages to come, there will never break forth a more penetrating faculty than our weak reafon ?

However, were men even to lofe the hope of advancing one ftep in metaphyfical refearches; and perfifted to declare infufficient and imperfect the various proofs of the exiftence of a God; it is not to be contefted, that all other fyftems are furrounded with ftill greater obfcurity, and they would only have a doubt as the refult of their reafoning. But have they ever reflected on the influence a simple doubt has, when that doubt is applied to an idea, whofe relations are without bounds ? Let us try to reprefent an equal probability in a circumftance which only concerns the interefts of this tranfitory life, and we fhall foon fee what force the fame degree of probability would have in the immenfurable relations of the finite to the infinite. Thus, not only an uncertainty, but the flighteft prefumption of the exiftence of a God, would, in the
eftimation

estimation of found reason, be a sufficient foundation for religion and morality. Yes, we might thus humbly pray, though depressed by doubt:—O Thou God who art un_known! sovereign goodness whose image is stamped on our hearts—if Thou existest, if Thou art Lord of this magnificent universe, deign to accept our love and humble homage.——

Undoubtedly, these thoughts are sufficient to inspire with respect and fear beings ignorant of their origin, who have so little to sacrifice and so much to desire, who, on account of their extreme weakness, cannot relinquish some hopes, and must attach themselves to a fixed and predominate idea, which may serve as an anchor in the midst of the inconsistencies and agitations of their minds.

It is, perhaps, because the time when every thing will be explained, is still far distant, that many exaggerate their doubts, and often confound them with a decided

incredu-

incredulity. I form to my imagination, a solemn period, when the inhabitants of the earth will be instructed in the mysteries of their nature and the secrets of futurity; and that some signal phenomenon will mark the awful day proper to fix our attention; and I am intimately persuaded, that, in such a moment, the men most indifferent about religion will appear dismayed, and even recognize that what they took for conviction, was but a wavering opinion, only supported by self-love and a desire of distinction.

At the same time that I form this judgment of the pretended incredulity of several persons, I will venture a reflection of a different kind: it is, that superficial faith in the existence of God, and the opinions, which depend on it, is not equivalent, in effect to doubt retained in proper bounds; and perhaps, if these bounds were determined, the belief of one class of society would be less wavering.

I anti-

I anticipate another objection; thofe doubts, fome may fay, thofe doubts which fo many men cannot fmother, are they not an argument againft the exiftence of a God? for a Powerful Being, fuch as we fuppofe Him, could have infpired a general confidence in that noble truth; He needed not to have recourfe to fupernatural means; His will was fufficient. I confefs, that we can eafily add, in imagination, feveral degrees to our knowledge and happinefs; but that condition of our nature, of which the caufe is unknown, can never be contrary to the the idea of the exiftence of a God: all is limited in our phyfical properties and in our moral faculties; but within thefe confines we fee the work of a Supreme Intelligence, and we difcover every inftant the traces of a divine hand, fufficiently obvious to direct our opinions. Unftable reafoning, concerning what we fhould be, can never weaken the diftinct confequences which arife from what we are.

C c 4   When

When the Laplander, in his cave, hears by chance the diftant echo of thunder, he fays, that *God ftill lives on the high mountain*; and, is it in the very bofom of munificent bleffings, with the light of philofophy, that men would wifh to reject the idea of the exiftence of a Supreme Being? What an abufe of reafon! Infinity ought to overwhelm the moft vigorous and enlightened underftanding, make the wife man timid in his judgment, and inform him what he is; can man do better than give way to the admiration the view of fo many incomprehenfible wonders muft neceffarily infpire, and with fervour feize that chain of miracles which feem to promife to lead to the knowledge of the Creator of them? Can he be more nobly employed, than in tracing an opinion, not only the moft probable, but the moft grand and interefting? Alas! if we fhould ever lofe it—the idea is not to be endured; clouds and thick darknefs would overwhelm the feelings which feem to dart before our reafon, to explore the unknown country

country we pant after, and a melancholy and eternal silence would appear to surround all nature: we should call for a comforter, implore protection—but where is it to be found? We should search for hope, but it is for ever fled—Alas! this is not all, a terrific thought strikes me, I hesitate a moment to communicate it; yet, it seems to me, that we lend new force to religious opinions, when we demonstrate, by various ways, that the principles which destroy those opinions lead to a result contrary to our nature. I will then conclude this chapter by a reflection of serious importance.

If there is not a God, if this world and the whole universe was only the production of chance or nature itself, subsisting from all eternity; and if this nature, void of consciousness, had not any guide or superior; in short, if all its movements were the necessary effect of a property ever concealed in its essence, a terrible thought would alarm our imagination : we should not only renounce the hopes which enliven life, we should not only see continually, advancing towards us the image of death and annihilation, these dreadful anticipations would not be all—an uncertain cause of fear would trouble the mind. In·fact, the revolutions of a blind nature being more obscure than the designs of an Intelligent Being, it would be impossible to discover on what base, in the universe, reposed the destiny of men; impossible to foresee whether, by some one of the laws of that imperious nature, intelligent beings are devoted to perish irrevocably, or revive under some other form; if they are to stumble on new pleasures, or suffer eternally : life and death, happiness and misery, may belong indifferently to a nature whose movements are not directed by any intelligence, are not connected by any moral idea, but solely dependent on a blind property, which is represented by that word, terrible and inexplicable *necessity*. A like nature would resemble the rocks to which Prometheus was bound, that were equally insensible to the agonizing groans of

the

the wretch, and to the joy of the vultures who preyed on his vitals.

Thus, in a like fyftem, nothing would be able to fix our opinion with refpect to futurity, and guard the fenfible part of ourfelves from yielding to fome unknown force: in fhort, can we reply without trembling? nothing,—and of courfe eternal torments might accidentally become our portion.

The momentary experience of life might, perhaps, infpire us with a kind of tranquillity; but what is that in immenfity, but calculations founded on the obfervance of a fhort interval? What is that hope which only a fleeting moment gives weight to? It is as if the fluttering infect, which lives but a day, fhould confider it as a reprefentation of the eternal condition of the univerfe. The mixture of pains and pleafures, to which men are fubject on earth, is not a certain proof of what may happen in other times and places; for unity, equality, and analogy, all thofe fources of probability, and

principle

principles to judge from, are connected with general ideas of order and harmony, but those ideas are not applicable to a nature subject to necessity.

We have some difficulty to assure our-selves of the designs of a Supreme Being: however, by a kind of analogy we shall be able to form an idea of the divine will; and our minds, our feelings, and virtues, all aid us in the search; but were we sprung from an insensible nature, we should not have any con-nection with the different parts of its im-mense extent, and the attentive study of our moral constitution would not throw a light on the various revolutions of which the material world is susceptible. We should only discover, that there would be much less reason to oppose, in imagination, limits to the varied movements of a nature without a guide, than to circumscribe, in some manner, the actions of an Omnipo-tent Being, whose other attributes are also infinite; for the ideas of order, justice, and goodness, which arise from a knowledge of

His

His perfections, feem to trace a circle in the midft of infinity, which the mind of man may perceive. Yes, thefe ideas fubject a great fpace to our contemplations; but what advantage is there in trying to be acquainted with the myfteries of an infenfible nature, or to penetrate the fecret of the motion impreffed by blind neceffity?

Let me repeat it then, as a termination to thefe reflections; all would be obfcure, all mere chance in the fate of man, if we did not attribute the difpofition and prefervation of the world to the omnipotent will of an Intelligent Being, whofe perfections our feelings and thoughts faintly reprefent.

In fhort, when even in the fyftem of the eternity of nature, men were affured that death deftroys individuality, and were they even able to drive away the idea of the continuation or renewal of it, by any fentiment or remembrance; would it be evident, that we fhould be abfolutely indifferent about the torments rational be-

ings

ings · may endure in that space which is reprefented by the idea of infinity and eternity? The metaphyfical idea, which determines us to place our confcioufnefs on that imperceptible and mysterious point, which unites our prefent thoughts to the paft, and our actual fentiments to our hopes and fears; this thought is not fufficient to make us regardlefs of our fate, or render us indifferent to the unknown effects which may refult from the revolutions of a nature, which we are not acquainted with: the anxieties and troubles of the beings who are to live in the ages yet unborn, do not intereft us as belonging to any particular perfon; however, we have, for thofe abftract misfortunes, in this inftance, a fympathy which efcapes reafoning.

I agree, that in the fyftem of undirected nature, happinefs or mifery, tranfitory or without end, have the fame degree of probability: but what a terrifying refemblance! Can we undifmayed confider fuch a chance?

How

How happens it then, that some pretend, that atheism frees us from every kind of terror about futurity ? I cannot perceive, that such a conclusion flows from this fatal system. A God, such as my heart delineates, encourages and moderates all my feelings; I say to myself, He is good and indulgent, He knows our weakness, He loves to produce happiness; and I see the advances of death without terror, and often with hope. But every fear would become reasonable, if I lived under the dominion of an insensible nature, whose laws and revolutions are unknown : I seek for some means to escape from its power; — but even death cannot afford me a retreat, or space an asylum. I reflect, if it is possible, to find compassion and goodness; but here is no prime intelligence, no first cause, a blind nature surrounds us, and governs imperiously. I in vain demand, what is to be done with me? it is deaf to my voice. Devoid of will, thought, and feeling, it is governed by an irresistible force, whose motion is a

mystery

myftery never to be unfolded. What a view for the human mind, to anticipate the deftruction of all our primitive ideas of order, juftice, and goodnefs! Shall I further fay, when even, in every fyftem, the entrance of the future was unknown, I fhould be lefs unhappy and forlorn, if it was to a father, a benefactor, that I committed the depofit of life which I held from him; this laft communication with the Mafter of the World would mitigate my pains; my eyes, when clofing, would perceive His power; that I fhould not lofe all, I might ftill hope that God remained with thofe I loved, and find fome comfort in the thought, that my deftiny was united to His will, that my exiftence and the employments • I devoted myfelf to, formed one of the indelible points of His eternal remembrance; and that the incomprehenfible darknefs I was going to plunge into, is equally a part of His empire. But when a feeling and elevated foul, which fometimes enjoys a fentiment of its own grandeur, fhould certainly know, that dragged by a blind motion, it was going to be

diffipated

diffipated, to be fcattered in that dreary wafte, where all that is moft vile on earth is indifferently precipitated; fuch a thought would blight the nobleft actions, and be a continual fource of fadnefs and defpondency. Save us from thefe dreadful reflections, fublime and cherifhed belief of a God! afford us the courage and comfort we need, and guard our minds, as from fatal phantoms, from all thofe vain fuppofitions, thofe errors of reafoning and metaphyfical fubtleties, which interpofe between man and his Creator! And we, full of confidence in the firft leffon of nature, will take for a guide that interior fentiment which is not thought, but fomething more, which neither reafons nor conjectures; but perhaps forms the clofeft connexion and moft certain communication with thofe grand truths which the underftanding alone can never reach.

D d CHAP.

C H A P. XV.

On the Respect that is due from true Philosophy to Religion.

THE view of the universe, the reflections of our minds, and the inclinations of our hearts, all concur to strengthen
the thought, that there exists a God; and
without power to comprehend this Infinite
Being, to form a just idea of His essence
and perfections, the confused sentiment of
his grandeur, and the continual experience
of their own weakness, are so many imperious motives, which, in all ages and countries, have impelled men to worship a God.
Those natural ideas have acquired new force
by the light of revelation; but it is not in
a metaphysical work that the authenticity
of the Christian religion ought to be dif-
cussed; nor could we add much to the doctrines contained in books composed at different periods on this important subject.

All

All difcuffions which are allied to truths, whofe authenticity depends on facts, are neceffarily confined within certain bounds; and we are obliged to purfue a beaten track, and run over the fame circle, when we enter on fuch a well-known fubject. I fhall then confine myfelf to fome general reflections, and make choice of thofe which are beft adapted to the particular genius of the prefent age, and the modifications which our fentiments receive from predominate opinions; for our judgments, like our impreffions, vary with the change which happens infenfibly in habits and manners: one age is that of intolerance and bigotry; another of relaxation and indifference, or a contempt of all ancient cuftoms: every century, every generation is diftinguifhed by a general character, a character which we take fometimes for new ideas; whilft it is nothing but the natural effect of exaggeration in our preceding opinions. Men are fubject to moral laws, fimilar in feveral refpects to mechanical rules; and with all

their

their knowledge and pride, they remind us of thofe children, who, placed at the extremity of a long balance, rife and fall fucceffively. They can only be fixed by moderate fentiments, which are fuftained by their own force; any other has a borrowed action, and this action is never in perfect equilibrium with truth.

It is in the nature of revelation to appear lefs evident to the mind, in proportion as the proofs of its authenticity are diftant; and if, among the dogmas united to a religious doctrine, fome one contains a myftic fenfe; if, among the forms of worfhip adopted, fome one is not confonant with the fimple and majeftic idea which we ought to have of the Mafter of the World; it would not be extraordinary that this religious inftitution, confidered in its different parts, fhould give birth to controverfies; and we fhould not be exafperated againft thofe, who, after having faithfully examined, ftill have fome doubts. It is in proportion to the extent of our underftanding that God has

has thought fit to manifeft. Himfelf to us;
thus, the exertion of thofe faculties of the
mind cannot be difpleafing to Him. But
reafon left to itfelf, and even when improved by philofophy, fhould, by no
means, lead men to any kind of contempt for religious worfhip in general, or
any of the particular opinions·of which
Chriftianity is the fupport. Any doctrine
which leads to the adoration of the God of
the univerfe is worthy of the refpect of His
creatures: thus, perfons moft difpofed to
conteft the authenticity of the facred books,
ought ftill to love precepts which feem to
come to the aid of the human mind, in order to affift men in the laft efforts which
they make to know more of God; as the
friendly bark, offered to the forlorn wretch
ftruggling on the furface of the immenfe
wafte of waters, on which his feeble hands
have vainly endeavoured to fupport him.

We cannot but have difcovered, that the
fentiments of gratitude and refpect which

infpire

OF THE IMPORTANCE OF

inspire men, the most capable of reflection, with the idea of a God, are intimately connected with the Christian doctrines, such as we find them in the New Testament; and in those moments, when, with the desire of happiness, and the timidity which belongs to our nature, we seek to unite our littleness to supreme grandeur, and our extreme weakness to Omnipotence, the divine perfections which the gospel delineates encourage our hopes and dissipate our fears; religion shows us all that we have need of in our miserable condition, a sovereign goodness, an inexhaustible compassion: thus then, the last link of the Christian faith, like the termination of the deepest meditations, reaches the same conclusion; and religion agrees with philosophy, in the moment when it is most elevated.

However, the Christian and the Deist unite, in some manner, in the ultimate tendency of their thoughts; they meet when they throw their attention on civil society, and when they seek to determine the duties

of

of men; for a wife-man muft ever pay homage to the morality of the gofpel, and the
philofopher could not have imagined a more
reafonable fyftem, or one more conformable
to our fituation *. If it is then true, that
opinions, in appearance oppofite, approach
at their extremities; and if it is true, that
the adoration of a God, and refpect for
morality, form by uniting, the circle of
evangelical doctrines, it very little concerns
the reafonable philofopher, that the Chriftian faith is placed between thofe two grand
ideas; if he thinks he can himfelf explore
the fpace which feparates man from his
Creator, for what reafon would he condemn
with bitternefs the fentiments of thofe who
are-attached to the comfortable fyftem of
interceffion and redemption, of which
Chriftanity has laid the foundation?

In fhort, were they even not to agree in
every opinion with the interpreters of the
Chriftian doctrine, this would not be a fuf-

* I fhall prefent fome reflections on this truth, in
another Chapter.

ficient

ficient reafon for breaking the religious alliance which ought to fubfift amongft men;
an alliance reprefented and rendered authentic, in every nation, by the public worfhip which has been made choice of by the
government. What idea then fhould we
have of the genius or the abilities of a philofopher, who, at the fight of the ceremonies
of the public worfhip which difguft him,
could not rife above them, fo as to confider
them, in fome meafure, as the atmofphere
of religious opinions, which turning his attention from the importance of thofe opinions, could not preferve, at leaft, fome
refpect for all the dependencies of the moft
fublime and falutary thought? It is eafy,
however, to perceive, that, for the generality of men, the duties of morality, religion, and all the exterior homage rendered to the Deity, compofe a whole fo
clofely connected, that the bafis is in danger when the outworks are attacked. The
imagination of the vulgar cannot be guided
in the fame manner as that of the folitary
thinker; and it would be committing a
great

great error, to try to influence the opinions of the generality by the fame confiderations which are fufficient for the man who profoundly reflects : there is a fyftem proportionate to the different faculties of intelligent beings, as there is one applicable to the varied forces of their phyfical nature.

I know nothing more dangerous, than the inconfiderate cenfures of thofe religious ceremonies received and refpected in the country we live in : fome do not think that they are acting wrong when they fpeak flightingly of the various fymbols of public worfhip; yet, if they attentively obferved the kind of minds, and the firft habits of the greater part of thofe to whom they addrefs fuch difcourfes, they would know how eafy it is to wound them in the fentiment which is the fource of all their tranquility, and the fafe-guard of their moral conduct. The deliverer of Switzerland ftruck off with one of his arrows an apple placed on the head of his only-fon; but every one cannot expect to be fo fortunate.

Some

Some would contradict thefe affertions,; by faying, that celebrated men have occa_fioned rapid changes in the church of Rome. without weakening religion. The origin, the circumftances, and the refult of a re-volution fo marked in hiftory, has not any connexion with the prefent queftion; the reformers of the fixteenth century, preaching a new doctrine, openly profeffed religious zeal and a fervent piety: thus, at the fame time that they difapproved of a part of the eftablifhed worfhip, they more rigidly recommended all the fundamental opinions of Chriftianity, and fought to introduce a feverity of manners which even extended to the profcription of feveral indulgences that had not been before condemned : and, in fact, if the new doctrines had not been united to the greateft refpect for the effential principles of the Chriftian religion, they never would have had fo many followers.

They cannot then eftablifh any kind of comparifon between the cenfures poured

forth

forth by the reformers, and the ridicule or contempt of thofe who now infult our moft refpectable opinions; thofe men, who at prefent abound, are fometimes excited by a libertinifm of mind and conduct, by felf-love or the enthufiafm of falfe philofophy, and fome of them are feduced by an air of fuperiority, attached to the principles which they themfelves inftitute. There is a great difference between the grave and ferious courfe of the reformers, and the various evolutions of the active opponents of religion: the latter do not take care to ftop at clearing up a point of doctrine, or a difputed interpretation of fome dogma; it is religion itfelf that they wifh to attack, and if they begin with the outworks, it is in order to undermine it; they take fkilfully their poft, and know when to have recourfe to a tone of pleafantry; which is very dangerous, as it gives an air of confidence to thofe who employ it, and they obtain a kind of afcendancy in avoiding every idea of an equal combat: one is difpofed to think, that it is by difdain that they glance flightly over the fubject;

subject; we cowardly submit to the appearance of their superiority; and that which is in them weaknefs or impotence gives confequence.

Men, in order to exprefs their gratitude to the fovereign Mafter of the World, muft borrow from their imaginations every thing grand and majeftic : thus, when they detach from thofe reverential figns the ideas that they reprefented and preferve, they only difplay a vain gravity, a chimerical pomp; and it is eafy to make a fimilar contraft a fubject of ridicule; but in acting thus, far from making us applaud their talents, they infult, without any fenfe, the habit moft men have acquired of venerating, on the whole, every fyftem of worfhip paid the Supreme Being.

Neverthelefs, the bold and frivolous difcourfes which are permitted againft religion in general, have made fuch a progrefs, that at prefent the perfons who moft refpect thefe opinions, without oftentation or feverity, find themfelves obliged to conceal or moderate their fentiments, left they fhould be expofed to a kind of contemptuous pity, or run the rifk of being fufpected of hypocrify. We are at liberty to fpeak on every fubject, except the moft grand and interefting which can occupy men. What ftrange authority gave rife to this imperious legiflation, which is termed fafhionable? What a miferable confpiracy, that of weaknefs againft Omnipotence! Men are proud of knowing at what hour the king wakes, goes to the chace, or returns; they are very eager to be informed of the vile intrigues which fucceffively debafe or exalt his courtiers; they pafs, in fhort, their whole lives in panting after objects of vanity and badges of flavery; they are continually brought into converfation; and they profcribe, under the dreadful name of vulgarity, the moft remote expreffion, which would recal the idea of the harmonious univerfe, and the Being who has beftowed on us all the gifts of the mind; what is moft excellent in our nature we overlook, to dwell only on the

inflations

inflations of vanity. Ungrateful that we are! Our intelligence, our will, all our fenfes, are the feal of an unknown power; and, is it the name of our Mafter and Benefactor that we dare not pronounce? it is from your modern philofophers that this falfe fhame arifes; you, who fpread derifion over the moft respectable fentiments, and employing in the difpute the frivolous fhafts of ridicule, have given confidence to the moft infignificant of men; you have, for your followers, a numerous race, which is taken promifcuoufly from every rank and age.

We now reckon, amongft thofe who oppofe a contemptuous fmile to religious opinions, a multitude of young people, often incapable of fupporting the moft trivial arguments, and who, perhaps, could not connect two or three abftract propofitions. Thefe pretended philofophers artfully, and almoft perfidioufly, take advantage of the firft flight of felf-love, to perfuade beginners, that they are able to judge at a glance, of the ferious queftions

queftions which have eluded the penetration of the moft exercifed thinkers: in fhort, fuch is in general the decifive tone of the irreligious men of our age, that in hearing them fo boldly murmur about the diforders of the univerfe, and the miftakes of Providence; we are only furprized to fee how much they differ in ftature from thofe rebellious giants mentioned in the heathen mythology.

I believe, however, that if contempt for religious opinions did not produce a ftriking contraft, thofe who profefs to feel this contempt would quickly adopt other fentiments; they only fuperficially attend to the pernicious tendancy of their maxims, whilft they believe themfelves ftill in the oppofition; but if they ever obtained a majority, not having then the fpur of felf-love, they would foon difcover the abfurdity of their principles, and haftily throw them afide.

There

There are, undoubtedly, a great number of eſtimable perſons, who highly value the truths and precepts of religion, yet are a prey to doubt and uncertainty, and who become the firſt victims of the inconſiſtencies of their minds; but men of ſuch a character do not aim at dominion, on the contrary, they rather wiſh to be confirmed by the example of thoſe whoſe confidence is more aſſured; they would conſider with intereſt the ſentiments that unfortunately have made too flight an impreſſion on them; and they would endeavour to ſtrengthen their weak hopes, till they reached the courageous perſuaſion. which inſpires the Chriſtian :———yes, even the enthuſiaſm of piety excites their envy, as it is more delightful to yield to the emotions of a lively imagination, than to ſtruggle with apathy againſt the opinions calculated to diffuſe happineſs. Thus, if amongſt the number of perſons that I have juſt delineated, there were ſome to whom nature had granted ſuperior talents, wit or eloquence, they would carefully avoid exerting them

them to difturb the repofe of thofe peaceable fouls; who calmly rely on religion, and
receive all their confolation from that fource.
A wife man never permits himfelf to fpread
fadnefs and difcouragement, in order to
gratify the ridiculous vanity of exalting
himfelf a little above common opinions, or
to fhow his abilities by making fome ingenious diftinctions concerning particular
parts of the eftablifhed religion; in the fame
manner, as it would be the height of folly
to ftop an army during its march, to difcriminate fyftematically the perfect juftnefs
of the different tones of the warlike inftruments of mufic. The bold and frivolous
opinions of feveral philofophers, have appeared to me to be weak, where they moft
wifh to rife; I mean, in the extent and
loftinefs of their views.

I need not fpeak to thofe who deny even
the exiftence of a God. Alas! if they are
fo unhappy as to fhut their eyes, and not
to admit this refplendant light; if they
have a foul fo infenfible, as not to be af-

E e   fected

fected with the comfortable truths which flow from such a noble thought; if they are become deaf to the interefting voice of nature; if they truft more to their weak reafoning, than the warnings of confcience and fenfibility; at leaft, let them not fpread their difafterous doctrine, which, like the head of Medufa, would transform every thing into ftone. Let them remove from us that frightful monfter, or let his hoarfe hiffing be only heard in the dreary folitude, of which their heart prefents the idea; let them fpare the human race, and have pity on the diftrefs into which they would be plunged, if the mild light, which ferves to guide them, were ever to be obfcured: in fbort, if they really believe that morality can agree with atheifm, let them give the firft proof of it, by remaining filent; but if they cannot abftain from publifhing their opinions, let a remnant of generofity induce them to inform us of their dangerous tendency, by placing in the frontifpiece of their works this terrible infcription of Dante's: *Lafciat' ogni fperanza voi ch' entrate.*

CHAP.

CHAP. XVI.

The same Subject continued. Reflections on Intolerance.

THE surface of the earth represents to us about the two hundred and fortieth part of the surperfice of the different opaque bodies which revolve round the sun.

The fixed stars are so many suns, which, according to all appearance, serve equally to enlighten and fertilize planets similar to those we are acquainted with.

A famous astronomer * has lately discovered fifty thousand new stars in a zone fifteen degrees in length and two in breadth, a space which corresponds with the thirteen hundred and sixty-fourth part of the celestial sphere.

* Dr. Herschel.

E e 2

Thus

Thus, fuppofing that we perceive an equal number of ftars in every other parellel fection of the firmament, the quantity we fhould be acquainted with would rife to near fixty-nine millions.

And if each of thefe ftars were the centre of a planetary fyftem, refembling the one we inhabit, we fhould have an idea of the exiftence of a number of habitable globes, whofe extent would be fixteen or feventeen millions of times more confiderable than the furface of the earth *.

* It may be faid, that the fifty thoufand new ftars perceived by Dr. Herfchel, being the refult of obfer-vation directed to the milky-way, we are not to expect to difcover as great a number in other parts of the heavens of a like extent; but independent of thefe ftars which Dr. H. clearly diftinguifhed, he imagined that there were twice as many more of which he had only an inftantaneous glance. See the Philofophical Tranfactions of the Royal Society, 1774. Dr. H. has probably, fince that time, made new difcoveries; but they have not reached me: I find, in the Tranfac-tions of the Royal Society, of which he is a member, that he confiders the new telefcope as being ftill *in its in-fancy*; thefe are his own words.

However,

However, the ingenious invention which aſſiſts us to explore the vaulted firmament is ſuſceptible of new improvement; and even at the period when it may arrive at the greateſt perfection, the ſpace which our aſtronomic knowledge may have taken poſſeſſion of, will only be a point in the vaſt extent which our imagination can conceive.

This imagination itſelf, like all our intellectual faculties, is perhaps only a ſimple degree of infinite powers; and the images that it preſents are but an imperfect ſketch of univerſal exiſtence.

What then becomes of our earth, in the midſt of that immenſity which the human mind vainly tries to graſp? What is it even now, compared with that number of terreſtrial bodies we can calculate or ſuppoſe?

Is it then the inhabitants of this grain of ſand, is it only a few of them, that have diſcovered the true mode of worſhipping the Creator of ſo many wonders? Their dwel

ling

ling is a point in infinite fpace; the life which they enjoy is but one of the moments which compofe eternity; they pafs away like a flafh of lightning in that courfe of ages, in which generations after generations are loft. How then dare any of them announce to the prefent age, and to thofe to come, that men cannot efcape the vengeance of Heaven if they alter one tittle of the Ritual? What an idea they give of the relation eftablifhed between the God of the univerfe and the atoms difperfed throughout nature? Let them then raife one of the extremities of that veil which covers fo many myfteries, let them confider a moment the wonders on every fide, the ftarry firmament, and the inconceivably dreary immenfity which their imagination cannot embrace; and let them judge, if it is by the exterior form of their adoration, the vain pomp of their ceremonies, that this Omnipotent God can diftinguifh their homage. Is it then, by the pride of our opinions, that we think to reach the Supreme Being? It is more comfortable, more reafonable to be-

lieve,

lieve, that all the inhabitants of the earth have accefs to His throne, and that we are permitted to raife ourfelves to it by a profound fentiment of love and gratitude, as the moft fure and intimate relation between man and his Creator.

Undoubtedly it is neceffary•that public worfhip fhould be conftantly regulated, and that diftinct fymbols fhould be refpected, whofe effential character ought not to vary, that the fentiments of the generality, fo promptly affected by exterior objects, may not be expofed to any alteration; it is neceffary that weak minds eafily find their way, and that they are not embarraffed with doubt and uncertainty; in fhort, it is to be defired, that the citizens, united by the fame laws and political interefts, fhould be fo by the fame worfhip, in order that the facred band of religion may take them all in; and that principles of education fhould be maintained and fortified by example. But as morality is the firft law of princes, and that always clear and diftinct in its motives and inftruc-

E e 4   tions,

tions, it ought to precede the uncertain combinations of the politician. A government is never permitted to aim at any end by unjuſt means, let it be ever ſo deſirable; and I believe that this rule is equally adapted to the opinions of men and their rights. It would be poſſible to conceive a ſyſtem of diſtribution, with reſpect to the fortunes of men, more convenient than any other for the increaſe of public wealth and the power of the ſtate; but though this knowledge ſhould influence the general conduct of government, it receives no right from its diſcernment, to arrange according to its will, the ſituation of every citizen. The ſame principle has greater force applied to opinions: it is reaſonable to ſeek to direct their courſe by ſlow and mild means; but the ſyſtem of unity, which is certainly moſt conducive to the happineſs of a ſtate, would ceaſe to be good, if, in order to eſtabliſh that ſyſtem, violence, or merely conſtraint, was had recourſe to: liberty of thought is the firſt of rights, and the moſt reſpectable dominion is that of conſcience.

They

Some now talk of the union of civil tolerance and religious intolerance; the one protects Proteftants in Catholic countries, and Catholics in Proteftant countries; and the other would forbid every kind of worfhip which is not conformable to the inftitutions of the predominant religion: but upon this plan, if the number of Diffenters was to become confiderable, an important part of the nation would be without worfhip; and the government fhould not appear indifferent to this, fince it is of great importance to mankind to maintain carefully every fupport of morality.

There is nothing more to be faid on intolerance when we confider it in its excefs. We all now know what we ought to think of the feverities and perfecutions which hiftory has tranfmitted an account of, and we know the opinion we fhould form of many acts of intolerance and inhumanity which fome have for a long time gloried in; and we cannot ftifle our indignation at the fight of the faggots that are ftill lighted

round

round thofe unhappy wretches fcattered over the face of the earth, of whom Jefus Chrift himfelf faid, with fo much goodnefs, in the midft of his agonies; *Father forgive them, for they know not what they do.* It is time to abolifh for ever thofe dreadful cuftoms, ignominious remembrance of our ancient phrenfies! O God, are thefe Thy creatures that they dare to torment in Thy name! Is it the work of Thy hand that they facrifice to Thy glory?—Petty tyrants! ferocious inquifitors! do you expect to obtain the favour of Heaven, with a heart hardened, after mutilating the members and tearing the bofoms of thofe whom you can only draw to you by a fentiment of pity? whofe emotions you are not acquainted with? The God of goodnefs rejects fuch offerings—He cannot away with them. Who then will pardon errors, if not men who are continually deceived! Alas! if exactnefs of judgment, or the perfection of reafon, were the only title to divine benevolence, there is not any one who

might

might not caſt down his eyes devoid of all hope.

Thoſe who proudly flatter themſelves, that they alone know the worſhip agreeable to the Supreme Being, loſe all their claim to our confidence, when, guided by a ſpirit of intolerance, they depart ſo viſibly from the character which ought to inſpire the idea of a God, protector of human weakneſs. But the abſurd attempt to inſpire faith by acts of rigour and ſeverity, has been ſo often and ſo ably combated, that I ſhall not dwell on a principle, the truth of which common ſenſe will diſcover. I ſhall only make one obſervation ſufficient to intimidate the conſcience of inquiſitors, and all thoſe who adopt their maxims. The operations of the mind can only be influenced by reaſoning, all the deſigns formed to attain this end by violence are attempts to ſubvert the belief of the ſpirituality of the ſoul, and indirect aſſociations with materialiſts; for we muſt believe in the identity of matter and thought to have

2   a right

a right of prefuming, that the empire exercifed on us by rigorous treatment can
have an influence on our opinions; and
then we muft confider man as a being governed by mechanical laws, to be able to
imagine, that with inftruments of torture
we can excite a fenfation, which, by an
unknown conduit, might act inftead of
judgment and the fentiment of perfuafion.

It is becaufe, the indignant emotions
of a worthy heart are more powerful than
the cool arguments of offended reafon, that
we rife with warmth againft intolerance;
for without this motive it would only deferve our contempt, as indicating a fingular
littlenefs of foul. Who can remember
without pity, thofe diffenfions fo long maintained, in which men, both weak and blind,
united in the name of devotion, actuated by
felf-love, unintelligible decrees, to fome im
portant controverfy? All thefe difputes appear
foolifh when we coolly examine them; and
we have only to confider, abftractedly,
                                        thofe

thofe quarrels, to difcover all their abfurdity.

But as it is only by fpreading knowledge
and diffufing wholfome precepts that we
can hope to cure enthufiafm and intolerance; we ought to be on our guard againft
the dangerous fpirit of indifference, otherwife one evil will be removed only to
introduce another equally fatal; when trying to divert men from fanaticifm, we
deftroy the ideas which ferved as a
foundation for religion. There could
not fubfift any found opinion or eftimable
principle, if the different errors which
creep round them were torn away by an
awkward or violent hand; and if the evil,
which continually mixes with the good,
became the fubject of blind profcription.

Let us loudly acknowledge the benefits
which we have received from diftinguifhed
writers, who have defended with zeal and
energy the caufe of toleration; it is an obligation

ligation, added to many others, which it is
juft to acknowledge, that we have received
from genius and talents united : but permit
us alfo to obferve, that feveral of thofe
writers have loft a part of the applaufe due
to them, by feeking to deprefs religion, in
order to fucceed in their attempt ; fuch a
proceding was unworthy of enlightened
philofophers, who more than others ought
to affign limits to reafon, and never defpair
of its influence. What fhould we think,
if, amongft thofe who juftly attack the
tyranny exercifed over confcience, there
were fome intolerant in the defence of toleration ; and if we had reafon to reproach
them with defpifing, and fometimes hating
thofe who do not concur with them ; and,
by an inconfiderate imputation of pufilla-
nimity or hypocrify, make the characters and intentions of thofe who do not
adopt their fentiments appear fufpicious ?
What a ftrange inconfiftency, in a different
way, do they not exhibit; forgetting, fometimes, their own opinions, and contradict-
ing, without thinking, their acknowledged

incre-

incredulity, they raife a clamour about the miferies to which mankind are fubject, and difplay the pretended diforders of the univerfe, in order, afterwards, to throw an odium on the God whofe exiftence they conteft, to ridicule a Providence they do not rely on ! One would think, that after having overturned the empire of the Deity, that they might remain the only legiflators of the world; they regretted not having any longer a rival, and wifhed to rebuild the temple they have deftroyed, to have again a vain idol to infult. Another inconfiftency appears in their afperity againft thofe who refift their dogmas, whilft, in the fyftem of fate, reafon does not preferve its empire, and the mafter, as well as the difciple, are equally fubject to the laws of neceffity.

To exercife an authority over the mind by the power of eloquence is a great advantage; for fuch an authority is not confined to any place or time; but to have a right to fuch an extenfive reign, we muft renounce

nounce fafhionable opinions, the counfels of vanity and the inftigations of felf-love; and be only actuated by that univerfal and durable intereft, the happinefs of mankind.

I would not wifh to prohibit the wife man or philofopher from treating any fub-ject proper to direct our judgment; for there are abufes and prejudices every where, which we cannot deftroy without making a ftep towards reafon and truth; but as there is a philofophy· for the thoughts, there is one alfo for the actions. I indeed wifh that men ·of an enlarged turn of mind, who per-ceive at a glance the moral order of things, would attack with more caution and mode-ration, and at a proper feafon, that which directly relates to the opinions moft effential to our happinefs; and that a refpect for thefe opinions fhould be manifeft, even when they cenfure fanaticifm and fuper-ftition.

Such a wifh is far from being realized; and· I cannot help lamenting, when I con-

4   fider

fider the defign of the greater part, who have written for fome time paft on religious fubjects: fome feek artfully to deftroy, or, at leaft, relax the band which unites men to the idea of a Supreme Being; and others fhut up in fome myftic idea, as in a dark den, blindly level their anathemas againft every kind of doubt and uncertainty; and confound, in their rigorous cenfures, the acceffary ideas with the principal opinions.

However, in taking a courfe fo oppofite, they unfortunately have an equal intereft in ranking the effential principles of religion with the moft infignificant fymbols: but influenced by very different motives; the former act with a view of making religious zeal ferve to defend every part of the worfhip of which they are the minifters; the latter, guided by a motive of felf-love, readily admit confufion, that they may have an opportunity of undermining religion when they attack its out-works. •

We have need, more than ever, to be directed to religion by wife and moderate difcourfes, by a happy mixture of reafon and fenfibility, the true characterestic of evangelical morality. It is only by thefe means that the authority of falutary truths can be ftrengthened: we are eafily hurried beyond the juft line, when the human mind is not in a ftate to mark any limits; but the daily progrefs of knowledge obliges us to ufe more exactnefs: it is neceffary then to rein in the imagination, and to allow reafon to take place of it: yet it is ftill allowed us to animate reafon, and even ufeful to do fo, but we muft abfolutely avoid difguifing it. Falfe notions only have need of the affiftance of exaggeration; it feems that, fome are very fond of extremes, that common fenfe may not inveftigate them.

I will make another obfervation. Thofe who, to free us from fuperftition, endeavour to relax religious reftrictions; and thofe who, to ftrengthen them, have recourfe to intolerance, equally mifs their aim.

aim. The hatred fo naturally excited by every kind of violence and conftraint, in matters of opinion, creates a repugnance in thofe perfons to religion who are infenfibly led to confider this excellent fyftem as the motive or excufe for a blind fpirit of perfecution. And the direct attacks againft religious opinions engage well-difpofed minds to adhere more ftrenuoufly to every cuftom which appears a form of refpect or adoration; as we redouble our zeal for a friend in the midft of thofe who neglect or flight him.

Let us unite, and it is certainly time, to render to the Supreme Being fincere worfhip; and let that worfhip always be worthy of the dignity of our Creator: let us banifh feverity and fuperftition; but let us equally dread that culpable indifference, the caufe of fo many misfortunes; and when we fhall have ftrengthened the influence of found reafon, let us adhere more clofely to the ufeful opinions which have been refined from errors, and with all our force repulfe

thofe

thofe who wifh us to bury our hopes to free ourfelves from the wanderings of the imagination. Yes, a religion, difengaged from the paffions of men, in its native beauty, ought to dwell with us ; public order and private happinefs equally claim it, and all our reflections lead us to elevate our hearts towards an Omnipotent Being, of whofe exiftence all nature reminds us : religion well underftood, far from being the neceffary principle of rigour or violence, fhould be the foundation of every focial virtue, and of every mild and indulgent fentiment. We are not called to tyrannize over the opinions of others, or to give defpotic laws to the mind; we muft obferve, that a moderate and rational religion only will guide us to the path of happinefs and virtue, by addreffing equally our hearts and minds.

CHAP.

CHAP. XVII.

Reflections on the Morality of the Christian Religion.

I WILL venture a few reflections on a subject which has often been treated; the course of my subject naturally leads to it : but in order to avoid, as much as possible, what is generally known, I shall confine myself to consider the morality of the gospel, under a point of view which seems to me to distinguish its sublime instructions.

The most distinct characteristic of christianity is the spirit of charity and forbearance which pervades all its precepts. The ancients, undoubtedly, respected the beneficent virtues; but the precept which commends the poor and the weak, to the protection of the opulent, belongs essentially to our religion. With what care, with what love, the Christian legislator

returns

returns continually to the fame fentiment
and intereft! the tendereft pity lent to his
words a perfuafive unction; but I admire,
above all, the awful leffon he has given, in
explaining the clofe union eftablifhed between our fentiments towards the Supreme
Being and our duties towards men. Thus,
after having termed the love of God, *the
firft commandment of the law,* the Evange-
lift adds ; *and the fecond, which is like unto
it, is to love thy neighbour as thyfelf.* The
fecond, which is like unto it ! what fimplicity, what extent in that expreffion ! Can any
thing be more interefting and fublime, than
to offer continually to our mind the idea of a
God taking on himfelf the gratitude of the
unfortunate ? Where find any principle of
morality, of which the influence can ever equal
fuch a grand thought ? The poor, the miferable, however abject their ftate, appear
furrounded with the fymbol of glory, when
the love of humanity becomes an expreffion
of the fentiments which elevate us to God ;
and the mind ceafes to be loft in the immenfity of His perfections, when we hope

to

to maintain an habitual intercourse with the Supreme Being, by the fervices which we render to men; it is thus that a fingle thought fpreads a new light on our duty, and gives to metaphyfical ideas a fubftance conformable to our organs.

Juftice, refpect for the laws, and duty to ourfelves, may be united, in fome manner, to human wifdom; goodnefs alóne, among all the virtues, prefents another character; there is in its effence fomething vague and undeterminate which claims our refpect; it feems to have a relation with that intention, that firft idea which we muft attribute to the Creator of the world, when we wifh to difcover the caufe of its exiftence. Goodnefs then is the virtue, or to exprefs myfelf with more propriety, the primitive beauty, that which has preceded time. Thus the preffing exhortations to benevolence and charity, which we find running through the gofpel, fhould elevate our thoughts, and penetrate us with profound refpect; it recals us, it unites us, to a fentiment more

ancient

ancient than the world, to a fentiment, by which we have received exiftence, and the hopes which compofe our prefent happi-nefs *.

But if, from thefe elevated contempla-tions, we, for a moment, defcend to the po-litical principles which have the greateft ex-tent, we fhall find there the influence of a truth on which I have already had occafion to dwell; but I fhall now treat it in a dif-ferent manner. The unequal divifion of property has introduced amongft men an au-thority very like that of a mafter over his flaves; we may even juftly fay, that in many refpects the empire of the rich is ftill more independent; for they are not bound conftantly to protect thofe from whom they require fervices: the tafte and caprice of thefe favourites of fortune fix the terms of their convention with men, whofe only patrimony

---

* I think I perceive the traces of thefe philofophical ideas in the cenfure Jefus paffed upon one of his difci-ples, who called him *good mafter. Why calleft thou me good? there is none good but one.*

is

is their time and ftrength; and as foon
as this convention is interrupted, the poor
man, abfolutely feparated from the rich,
remains again abandoned to accidents; he
is obliged then to offer his labours with
precipitation to other difpenfers of fubfiftence; and thus he may experience, feveral
times in the year, all the inquietudes that muft
neceffarily arife from uncertain recourfes.
Undoubtedly, in giving the fupport of the
laws to a fimilar conftitution, it has been
reafonably fuppofed, that in the midft of
the multiplied relations of focial life, there
would be a kind of balance and equallity
between the wants which oblige the poor to
folicit wages, and the defires of the rich
which engage them to accept their fervices;
but this equilibrium, fo effentially neceffary,
can never be eftablifhed in an exact and
conftant manner, fince it is the refult of a
blind concourfe of combinations, and the
uncertain effect of an infinite multitude of
movements, not one of which is fubject to
a pofitive direction. However, fince to
maintain the diftinction of property they
were

were obliged to leave to chance the fate of the greater number of men, it was indifpenfably neceffary to find fome falutary opinion, proper to temper the abufes infeparable from the free exercife of the rights of property; and that happy and reftoring idea could only have been difcerned in an obligation of benevolence impofed on the will, and a fpirit of general charity recommended to all men : thefe fentiments and duties, the laft refource offered to the unfortunate, can alone mitigate a fyftem, in which the fate of the moft numerous part of a nation refts, on the doubtful agreement of the conveniences of rich with the wants of the poor. Yes, without the aid, without the intervention of the moft eftimable of virtues, the generality would have juft reafon to regret the focial inftitutions, which, at the price of their independance, left to the mafter the care of their fubfiftence; and it is thus that charity, refpectable under fo many different views, becomes ftill an intelligent and political idea, which ferves to blend perfonal liberty and the imperious laws of property.

I know

I know not if ever the chriftian precepts have been confidered under this point of view; but reflecting a little on this fubject, we perceive more than ever of what importance the falutary inftitutions are, which place in the firft rank of our duties the beneficent fpirit of charity, and which lends to the moft effential virtue all the force and conftancy which religion gives birth to. Thus, at the fame time that the doctrines of the gofpel elevate our thoughts, its fublime morality accompanies, in fome meafure, our laws and inftitutions, to fuftain thofe which are really conformable to reafon, and to remedy the inconveniences infeparable from the imperfections of human wifdom.

It is not, however, only to pecuniary facrifices, that the gofpel applies its precepts refpecting charity; it extends to thofe generous acts of felf-denial, that religion alone can render fupportable; and which makes fome defcend with a firm ftep into the dreary abodes, in which the culprit is a

prey

prey to the remorfe that tears his heart;
and when his very relations have abandoned him, he ftill beholds a comforter, whom
religion conducts to pour confolation into
his afflicted foul. The fame motives
and thoughts' induce fome to renounce
the world and its hopes, to confecrate
themfelves entirely to the fervice of the
fick, and to fulfil thofe fad functions with
an affiduity and a conftancy, that the moft
fplendid reward could never excite. O
rare and difinterefted virtue, perfection of
piety! what a tribute of admiration is due
to the fublime fentiment which infpires
fuch painful felf-denial! Men are only fti-
mulated by notions of right and juftice; it
belongs to chriftianity to impofe duties,
whofe bafe is placed beyond the narrow
circle of our terreftrial interefts. I know
not, but it feems to me, that, notwithftanding a diverfity of opinions, we cannot
help being affected, when we contemplate
the fketch of the laft day which the gofpel
delineates: it exhibits a terrific and fublime
picture of that day, in which all actions
are

are to be revealed, and the moſt ſecret thoughts have the univerſe for a witneſs, and God as a judge; and at the moment when we wait to ſee the retinue of virtues and vices which have rendered men celebrated, it is a ſingle quality, a virtue without ſplendour, which is choſen by the Divine Arbiter of our fate, to derive an immortality of happineſs from, and He pronounces theſe memorable words, which contain in a ſmall compaſs our whole duty: —*I was hungry, and ye gave me meat; thirſty, and ye gave me drink; I was a priſoner and ye viſited me. Come ye bleſſed of my father, inherit the kingdom prepared for you,* &c. Men love to contemplate the triumphs of goodneſs—love to exalt it under different forms. We have ſo many wants, are ſo weak; and we are able to do ſo little for ourſelves, that this intereſting virtue appears our ſafe-guard and the myſterious tie of all nature.

The ſpirit of charity, ſo eſſential in its exact interpretation, may be applied to the regard

regard and delicate attention that different degrees of talents, render neceffary: fociety, under this relation, has alfo its rich and poor; and we know the extent of charity and the fecrets of our moral nature, when we practice that general benevolence, which preferves others from feeling a painful fentiment of inferiority, and which makes it a duty to refpect the veil, that a beneficent hand has defignedly placed between the light of truth and thofe imperfections which we cannot entirely correct.

It is always about the generality of men that the author of chriftianity feems to be interefted; the gofpel takes cognizance of their private fentiments, condemning pride, and recommending modefty; and it applies itfelf to level thofe diftances which appear to us fo important, when we only view the little points of gradation which compofe our fcale of vanity. Religion enables us to difcern that haughtinefs and contempt, only difplay our ignorance and folly: *what haft thou, that thou didft not receive? now if*

2   *thou*

thou didſt receive it, why doſt thou glory ?—
What is the pride that does not melt away before theſe awful words? Religion ſeems ever to
tend towards the ſame end, and by continually
reminding us of the brevity of life, to prevent ſtrong illuſions from engroſſing our
thoughts.

The greater part of ancient moral inſtructions were in general addreſſed, either
to man conſidered as an individual occupied
with the care of his deſtiny, or to the citizen connected by his duties to his country,
and none of them had ſufficient extent: it
is neceſſary, when giving counſel to a ſolitary individual, only to try to free him from
thoſe paſſions which would deſtroy his repoſe
and happineſs; and the obligations that are
impoſed on the different members of a political
ſtate, neceſſarily participate of a jealous ſpirit, which the will of the government may
turn into hatred. The Chriſtian religion,
more univerſal in its views, turns its attention
from the contrariety of intereſts which divide

vide men when they belong to different governments; it confiders us indiftinctly as
citizens of a great fociety, united by the
fame origin, nature, and dependencies, and
by the fame fentiment of happinefs. Recommending the reciprocal duties of benévo-
lence, the gofpel does not make any difference
between the inhabitant of Jerufalem and
Samaria; it takes man in the moft fimple
of his relations, and the moft honourable,
thofe which arife from his intercourfe with
the Supreme Being; and under this point
of view, all the hoftile divifions of kingdom againft kingdom, abfolutely difappear;
it is the whole human race which has a
right to the protection and the beneficence
of the Author of Nature, and it is in the .
name of every intelligent being that we credit
the alliance which unites heaven to earth.

The rich and powerful made the firft
laws, or, at leaft, directed the fpirit of
them; it was efpecially to defend their poffeffions and privileges that they extolled juftice: the legiflator of our religion, fpeaking
of

of this virtue, has shown, that the interests of all men were equally present to his thoughts; we might even say, that he made an old obligation a new duty, by the manner in which he prescribed it: *Whatsoever ye would that men should do to you, do ye even so to them,* is a maxim ever remarkable, if we consider the extent of the precept which it contains: there are so many acts of severity and oppression, so much tyranny, which escapes the reach of the law; and the superintendency of opinion, that we cannot too highly value its importance; Christianity indeed affords a simple guide and measure for all our actions.

Religion, beside, in order to fix our determinations, strengthens the authority of conscience: she saw, that every one of us has within himself a judge, the most severe and clear-sighted, and that it is sufficient to submit to its laws to be instructed in our duty; for it is our hidden thoughts that this judge examines, and nothing is excused, no subterfuge admitted.

G g   It

It, is not the fame with thofe cenfures which we exercife towards others, the fimple actions only ftrike us; and the different motives they refult from, the emotions, the conflicts which accompany them, and the regret, the repentance, which follow them, all thefe effential characteriftics escape our penetration : thus religion, always wife, always benevolent in its counfels, forbids our forming hafty and precipitate judgments; and we cannot read, without emotion, that leffon of indulgence fo mildly addreffed to the crowd which furrounded the woman taken in adultery, *he that is without fin among you, let him firft caft a ftone at her.* But how refift being affected by admiration, when we fee religion fo warmly employed about the fate of thofe whom the fufpicions or falfe accufations of men have dragged before their tribunals ?. by declaring that it is. better to let a hundred culprits efcape punifhment, than run the rifk of condemning a fingle perfon unjuftly. This tender anxiety correfponds with every fentiment of our hearts. Innocence delivered to infamy, innocence.

nocence encompaffed with all the horrors of
an execution, is the moft dreadful fight that
the imagination can prefent ; and we are fo
ftruck by it, that we fhould be almoft difpofed to think, that before the Supreme
Being the whole human race is refponfible
for fuch a crime : yes, it is under Thy protection, O my God, that unknown virtue
and injured innocence take fhelter ; men
turn towards Thee for comfort when pur-
fued by men, and it is not in vain that
they truft in that awful day when all fhall
be judged before Thee.

I wifh only to dwell on the particular
character of the Chriftian religion, as it
proportions the merit of our actions, not to
the grandeur or importance of them ; but
to the relation that they have with our
abilities, it is an idea abfolutely new : this
fyftem, which prefents the fame motives
and rewards to the weak and ftrong, remarked the widow's mite, as well as the
generous facrifices of opulence ; this fyftem,
as juft as rational, animates, in fome mea-

fure,

sure, our whole moral nature, and seems to inform us, that a vast circle of good actions and social virtues are submitted to the same rules, as the immense domain of physical nature, in which the simplest flower, or the most insignificant plant, concurs to perfect the designs of the Supreme Being, and composes one part of the harmonious universe.

The superintendence of the Christian religion extends still further than I can point out; and guided by a spirit not to be equalled, it estimates our intentions, obscure dispositions, and internal determinations, often separated from action by different obstacles: it directs men, in some measure, from their first sentiments and designs; it continually reminds them of the presence of God; warns them to watch over themselves, when their inclinations are but dawning, before they have gained strength; in short, at an early hour it forms the mind to the exercise of virtue, by discriminating virtue and vice, and reminding us to cultivate a love of or-

der

der and propriety before the active scenes of life force those sentiments to appear conspicuously displayed in actions.

But the more the methods of meriting the divine approbation are multiplied, the more essential is it that our confidence should not be depressed, every instant, by the sentiment which arises from the experience of our errors; it is necessary, that at the moments, too frequent, when the chain which unites us to the Supreme Being would escape from our grasp, the hope of again seizing it should remain with us: it is then to succour our weak faith, that we see in the gospel that idea at once so excellent and new, that of repentance and the promises which are annexed to it. This noble idea, absolutely belonging to Christianity, prevents our relation with the Deity from being destroyed as soon as it is perceived; the culprit may still hope for the favour of God, and after contrition confide in Him. Human nature, that singular connexion of the spirit with matter, of strength with weak-

G g 3

nefs,

nefs, of reafon with the imagination, perfuafion with doubt, and will with uncertainty, neceffarily requires a legiflation appropriated to a conftitution fo extraordinary :
man, in his moft improved ftate, refembles
an infant, who attempts to walk, and falls,
rifes and falls again ; and he would foon be
loft to morality, if, after his firft fault, he
had not any hope of repairing it ; under
a fimilar point of view, the idea of repentance is one of the moft philofophical which
the gofpel contains.

That preffing recommendation to do
good in fecret, without oftentation, is the
refult of a falutary and profound thought ;
the legiflator of our religion undoubtedly .
had perceived that the praifes of men was
not a bafis fufficiently fteady to ferve for the
fupport of morality ; and he difcerned,
that vanity, allowed to enjoy thefe kind of
triumphs, was too diffipated to be a faithful
guide ; but the moft important part of that
precept is, that morality would be very circumfcribed, if men only adhered to thofe
juft

juft actions which all the world might fee ;
there are not many opportunities to do good
in public, 'and the whole of life may be.
filled by unfeen virtues : in fhort, from that
continual relation with our confcience, a re‑
lation inftituted by religion, there refults an
ineftimable benefit; for it is eafy to per‑
ceive, that if we have within us a clear‑
fighted and fevere judge, this' fame judge
turns confoler and friend every time that
we are unjuftly condemned, or when events
do not anfwer according to the purity of our
intentions ; and we believe then that we
have almoft two fouls, one aiding and fuf‑
taining the other on every occafion in which
virtue unites them.

The fevere cenfure of fuperftition, which
we find throughout the gofpel, is derived from
an idea as reafonable as enlightened; men
are too ' much difpofed to make their
religion confift of little exterior practices,
always eafier than the conflicts with and
triumphs over the paffions: our minds
feize with avidity every extraordinary idea ;

when

when they are in part of our own creating,
they aid our felf-love to fubjugate our imagination; man is not at the age of maturity
terrified by thofe phantoms which annoy his
infancy; but myfteries, occult caufes, extraordinary appearances, continue to make an
impreffion on his mind; and like the wonders of nature, form too large a circle round
his thoughts; it is by ideas more proportioned to his ftrength, by mere fuperftition, that he permits himfelf often to be
led captive: we love trivial commands, ob-
fervances, and fcruples, becaufe we are little
ourfelves, and that in our weaknefs we
would wifh to know every inftant the limits
of our obligations.

Sometimes, perfons terrified by their
imaginations, or by the confufed picture
which they form of the duties of religion,
attach themfelves to fuperftitious practices
as a fafe-guard near at hand which may
quickly guard them from the different anxieties of their minds. The precepts of the
gofpel are defigned to deftroy thefe difpofitions

tions; for on one fide, they facilitate the ftudy of morality, by reducing to fimple principles the entire fyftem of our duties; and on the other, they feek to render our intercourfe with the Supreme Being more eafy, by teaching us that we may unite ourfelves to Him by the expanfion of a pure mind; by informing us, that it is not either on Mount Sion or Gerizim that we are to raife an altar; but that every honeft heart is a temple, where the eternal is adored *in fpirit and in truth*. The Chriftian religion is the only one which, difcarding ceremonies and fuperftitious opinions, leads us to the worfhip more confonant to our nature: Chriftianity indeed, in that grand thought, has pointed out the dictates of our confcience as moft worthy of refpect; benevolence, as the worfhip moft agreeable to the Supreme Being, and all our moral conduct as the moft certain prognoftic of our future ftate. There reigns a profound philofophy in the doctrines of the gofpel, men have only added a vain pageantry, a more founding tone.

I

Let

Let us render homage to Chriftianity, for that facred tie which it has formed, in uniting not for a moment, but for the whole of life, the fate of two beings, one having need of fupport, and the other of comfort: it is religion which refines this alliance by rendering it immutable, and obliges men not to facrifice to the caprices of their imaginations the unity and confidence which fecures the repofe of families, order in the difpofition of fortunes, the peaceable education of the fucceeding generation, and which, in giving to children, for an example, a union formed by fidelity and duty, implants in their hearts the feeds of the moft important virtues; religion has taught us, that the friendfhips of a world, in which felfifhnefs reigns, have need of being cemented by that community of interefts and honours which marriage only gives us an idea of; holy union, alliance without equal, which renders ftill more valuable all the bleffings of life, which feems to augment our hopes, and fortify in us the comfortable thoughts and mild con-

4

fidence

fidence which piety gives birth to : the engagements entered into between men, which
being, for the moſt part, founded on reciprocal ſervices, a time might come,
when our weakneſs would be ſo great,
others having no more intereſt to aſſociate
with us, it might be neceſſary to find a
ſupport in that friendſhip which time has
matured, and of which a ſentiment of duty
repairs the breaches, and which acquires a
kind of ſanctity from the habit and the remembrance of a long and happy union : it
is religion in, ſhort, which has ordained,
that the delicate virtue, the moſt excellent
ornament of a weak and timid ſex, ſhould
only be ſubject to the aſcendency of the
moſt generous and faithful ſentiment.

Theſe principles, indeed, are not formed for
corrupt hearts ; but the ſervice which religion renders, the end which it propoſes, is
to aſſiſt us to combat our depraved diſpoſitions ; it is to point out the errors and the
ſnares of vice ; it is to preſerve, amongſt us,
the ſacred depoſit of principles, which are the
foundation of public order, and ſtill maintain

tain fome light to illuminate the path of wifdom and true happinefs.

Religion recals us continually to thofe univerfal duties which we defcribe under the name of good morals; duties that men would often inconfiderately wifh to fe_parate from public intereft, but which, however, are bound to it by fo many almoft imperceptible and fecret ties. Every act of wifdom and virtue is not of immediate importance to fociety; but morality muft be cultivated by degrees, and fortified by habit, as it is like thofe delicate plants which we rear with a kind of fondnefs to preferve their beauty; if we make a diftinction between perfonal, domeftic, and public manners, in order to neglect, as we find convenient, one part of our duty, we fhall lofe the charm of it, and every day virtue will appear more difficult.

There is, I think, a connexion, more or lefs apparent, between every thing good and worthy of efteem; and it feems to me, that

this

this idea has fomething amiable, which confufedly fatisfies our moft generous difpofitions and moft comfortable hopes: and if, to fuftain a truth fo important, I was permitted to interrogate the young man, whofe virtues and talents are the moft remarkable in Europe, I fhould afk him, if he did not experience that his filial tendernefs, the regularity of his domeftic life, the purity of his thoughts, and all his rare private qualities, are not united to the noble fentiments which make him appear with fo much fplendour as a ftatefman? But without dwelling on fuch inftances, who has not been fometimes ftruck with the beauty attached to that fimplicity and modefty of manners which we often find in an obfcure fituation? We then manifeftly difcover, that there exifts a kind of agreement and dignity, I could almoft fay, a kind of grandeur, independent of refined language, polifhed manners, and all thofe advantages due to birth, to rank, and fortune.

I have

I have only glanced over the benefits arifing from the Chriftian religion; but I
cannot avoid obferving, that we owe to it a
confoling idea, that of the felicity referved
for innocent babes; interefting and precious
hope for thofe tender mothers, who fee flip
from their embraces the objects of their
love, at an age when they have not acquired
any merit before the Supreme Being, whom
they cannot have any relation with; but
through His infinite goodnefs. I feel that
I involuntarily mix with the elogiums of
Chriftianity a fentiment of gratitude for the
mild and paternal ideas which are diffemi-
nated with its inftructions; and there is fomething remarkable in thofe inftructions, that
they are continually animated by every thing
which can captivate our imagination, and
affociate with our natural inclinations. Sen-
fibility, happinefs, and hope, are the ftrong-
eft ties of a heart ftill pure; and all the
emotions which elevate towards the idea of
a God exalt in our minds the doctrine of
morality, which recals us continually to the
fublime

fublime perfections of Him who was its author.

In fhort, we cannot avoid admiring the fpirit of moderation, which forms one of the diftinct characteriftics of the gofpel; we do not always find, it is true, the fame fpirit in the interpreters of the Chriftian doctrines; feveral conftrained by a falfe zeal, and more difpofed to fpeak in the name of a. threatening mafter, than in that of a God, full of wifdom and goodnefs, have frequently exaggerated and multiplied the duties of men; and to fupport their fyftem, they have often obfcured the natural fenfe, or the general import of the precepts contained in the fcriptures; and fometimes alfo, collecting a few fcattered words, they have formed a body of divinity, foreign in feveral refpects to the intention of the apoftles and firft Chriftians. Servants always go further than their mafters; and as the firft thought does not belong to them, they only act by adding fomething heterogeneous: the fpirit of moderation confifts, befide, in a kind of proportion,

portion, which mere imitators have only
an imperfect knowledge of; fortitude is
even neceſſary to impoſe limits on virtue
itſelf; and to determine the preciſe and
exact meaſure of the multiplied duties of
men requires a profound and ſublime intelligence. 'It was by his ſublime precepts
that the inſtitutor of a univerſal morality
ſhewed himſelf ſuperior to that age of ignorance in which extremes reigned; when
piety was changed into ſuperſtition, juſtice
into rigour, indulgence into weakneſs; and
when, in the exaggeration of every ſentiment, a kind of merit was ſought for incompatible with the immutable laws of
wiſdom : it was by thoſe ſublime precepts,
in ſhort, that a legiſlator roſe above tranſi-
tory opinions to command all times and ages,
and that he appears to have been deſirous to
adapt his inſtructions, not to the inſtantaneous
humour of a people, but to the nature of man.

We ſhall, beſide, find eaſily in the goſ-
pel ſeveral characteriſtics proper, eſſentially
to diſtinguiſh it from philoſophic doctrines;
but

but in an examination fo ferious and important I avoid every obfervation which might
appear to the greater number a fimple refearch of the underftanding ; it is the grand
features only which belong to grand things,
and any other manner would not agree with
a fubject fo worthy of our refpect. I muft
fay, however, that when I am left alone to
reflect with attention on the different parts
of the gofpel, I have experienced, that, independent of general ideas and particular
precepts which lead us every inftant to profound admiration, there reigns, befide, in
the whole of that fublime morality, a fpirit
of goodnefs, of truth, and wifdom, of
which all the characters can only be perceived by our fenfibility, by that faculty
of our nature which does not feparate objects, which does not wait to define ; but
which penetrates, as by a kind of inftinct,
almoft to that love, the origin of every
thing, and that indefinite model from which
every generous intention and grand thought
has taken its firft form.

Hh   CHAP.

C H A P. XVIII.

Conclusion.

WHAT a time have I chosen to en-
tertain the world with morality and
religion! and what a theatre is this for such
an undertaking! Only to conceive it is a
great proof of courage; every one is employed about his harvest; lives in his affairs;
is lost in the present instant, all the rest appears chimerical. When I was formerly
engrossed by cares for the public welfare,
and writing on my favourite subject, I could
draw the attention of men by a series of reflections on their own fortunes and on the
power of their country; it was in the name
of their most ardent passions that I engaged
them to listen to me; but in treating the
subject I have now made choice of, it is
their natural dispositions, now almost effaced, that I must address: thus I feel the
necessity of re-animating the sentiments
which I wish to direct, and giving birth to
the interest I desire to enlighten. And
when I fix my attention on the actual course

of

of opinions, I fear to have for judges, either men who are indifferent to the subject, or who are too severe in their censurers; but the reflections of vanity are trivial to the motives which have guided me; and provided any of my thoughts have agreed with the inclinations of feeling minds, and added something to their happiness, I shall enjoy the sweetest reward. Such a wish I formed, when, with a weak hand, I ventured to trace some reflections on the importance of religious opinions.

The more we know of the world, its phantoms, and vain enchantments, the more do we feel the want of a grand idea to elevate the soul above discouraging events which continually occur. When we run after honours, fame, and gratitude, we find every where illusions and mistakes; and it is our lot to experience those disappointments which proceed from the infirmities or the passions of men. If we leave our vessel in the harbour, the success of others dazzles and disturbs us; if we spread our sails, we are the plaything of the winds: activity in action, ardour,

and

and indifference, all have their cares and difficulties; no perſon is ſheltered from the caprices of fortune, and when we have reached the ſummit of our wiſhes, when we have
by chance attained the object of our ambition,
ſadneſs and languor are preparing to fruſtrate
our hopes, and diſſipate the enchantment:
nothing is perfect except for a moment;
nothing is durable but change: it is neceſſary then to have intereſt in with thoſe immutable ideas which are not the work of
man, which do not depend on a tranſient
opinion: they are offered to all, and are
equally uſeful in the moment of triumph
and the day of defeat; they are, as we need
them, our conſolation, our encouragement,
and our guide. What ſtrength, what ſplendour, thoſe ideas would ſoon have, if, con-
ſidered as the beſt ſupport of order and
morality, men would try to render them
more efficacious, in the ſame manner as we
ſee the citizens of a political ſociety concur,
in proportion to their faculties, to promote
the welfare of the ſtate. A new ſcene
would open before us; men of learning, far

from

from following the counsels of vanity, far
from searching to destroy the most salutary
belief of men, would, on the contrary, allot
for their defence a portion of their no-
blest powers; we should see the penetrating
metaphysician eager to refer to the common treasure of our hopes, the light which
he perceives through the continuity of his
meditations, and the perspicacity of his
mind: we should see the attentive observer
of nature occupied with the same idea, animated by the same interest; we should see
him, in the midst of his labours, seize with
avidity every thing which could add any
support to the first principle of all religions;
we should see him detach from his discoveries,
appropriate, with a kind of love, all that tended to steengthen the happiest persuasion and
most sublime of thoughts. The profound moralist, the philosophic legislator, would concur in the same design; and in such a grand
enterprize, men, merely endowed with an
ardent imagination, would be like those
wanderers, who, when they return home,

talk

talk of some unknown riches. There are ways in the moral, as well as in the physical world, which lead to unknown secrets; and the harvest which may be gathered in the vast empire of nature is as extensive as diversified. How excellent would be the union of every mind towards this magnificent end! In this view, I represent sometimes to myself, with respect, a society of men distinguished by their character and genius, only employed to receive and place in order the ideas proper to augment our confidence in the most precious opinion. There are thoughts conceived by solitary men which are lost to mankind, because they have not had the talent to connect a system; and if those thoughts were to be united to some other knowledge, if they were to come like a grain of sand, to strengthen the banks raised on our shore, the following generations would transmit a richer heritage. We sometimes register with pomp a new word, introduced into the language, and men of the most exalted genius of the age are called to be present at

2   that

that ceremony : would it not be a more noble enterprize to examine, to choose, and confecrate the ideas or obfervations proper to enlighten us in our moft effential refearches? One of thofe refearches would better deferve a wreath, than any work of eloquence or literature.

Let us fuppofe, for a moment, that in the moft ancient empire of the world there might have been priefts, from time immemorial, who guarded the depofit of all the original ideas which ferved to fupport the opinion of the exiftence of a God, and the fentiment of the immortality of the foul; and that, from time to time, every new difcovery, calculated to increafe the confidence due to thefe moft neceffary truths, was infcribed in a religious teftament, called the book of happinefs and hope; how highly fhould we value it, and how eagerly defire to be acquainted with it; and with what refpect fhould we approach the ancient temple, in which thofe fuperb archives were depofited. But, on the contrary, could we imagine another re-

treat,

treat, where fubtle arguments and artificial difcourfes were collected, by which fome endeavour to deftroy or fhake thofe holy opinions which unite the univerfe to an intelligent thought, to a fublime wifdom; and the fate of men to infinité goodnefs, who amongft us would wifh to enter into that dark abode? who would wifh to explore that fatal regifter? Let us learn to know our nature better, and through the delirium of our blind paffions difcover its wants: it is a God we feel the want of, a God, fuch as religion prefents; a God, powerful and good, the firft fource of happinefs, and who only can fecure it to the human race: let us open all our faculties to that fplendid light, that our hearts and minds may welcome it, and find pleafure in widely diffufing it. Let us be penetrated in our youth, by the only idea ever neceffary to our peace: let us ftrengthen it when in our full vigour, that it may fupport us in the decline of life. Ravifhing beauties of the univerfe, what would ye be to us without this thought? Majeftic power

of

of the human mind, astonishing wonders of the thinking faculty, what could it represent if we separated it from its noble origin? Souls affectionate and impassioned, what would become of you without hope? Pardon, O Master of the world, if not sufficiently sensible of my own weakness, and abandoning myself only to the emotions of my heart, I have undertaken to speak to men of Thy existence, Thy grandeur, and Thy goodness! Pardon me if, lately agitated by the tumultuous waves of passion, I dare to raise my thoughts to the realms of eternal peace, where Thou more particularly exhibits Thy glory and sovereign power. Ah! I know more than ever that we must love Thee, we must serve Thee. The powerful of the earth exalt and depress their favourites capriciously; there is no relying on them; after profiting by the talents devoted to them, they forsake the victim, or crush him like a reed. There is in the universe but one immutable justice; but one perfect goodness and consolatory thought: yet we go continually towards other coasts, where

we

we call for happinefs, but it is not to be
found: there are phantoms accuftomed to
deceive men, who anfwer when they call:
we run towards them, and purfue them,
and we leave far behind religious opinions,
which only can' lead us back to nature,
and elevate us to its author. The blind
paffions of the world, and the devouring
defires of fame and fortune, only ferve to
harden us; every thing is felfifh and hoftile in them. Ambitious men, who only
wifh for a vain name, a childifh triumph,
acknowledge your features in this fketch;
a fingle object engroffes you, a fingle end
fixes your views: the heavens may be obfcured; the earth covered with darknefs;
and the future annihilated before you; and
you are fatisfied if a weak taper ftill permits
you to difcern the homage of thofe who
furround you; but how is it poffible to expect thus to pafs a whole life? how be able
to retain that homage which appears fo neceffary to your dream of happinefs? how
can you make ftationary what fo many
concur to demand? We have a more rational

tional certainty of happinefs, when a fentiment of piety, enlightened in its principle
and action, foftens all our paffions, and
bends them, in fome meafure, to the laws
of our deftiny. Piety, fuch as I form an idea
of, may be properly reprefented as a vigilant
friend, tender and rational. It lets us fee
the various bleffings of life; but it recals
us to the idea of gratitude, in order to augment our happinefs, by referring it to the
moft generous of all benefactors : it allows
us to exercife our faculties and talents; but
recals us to the idea of morality and virtue,
in order to affure our fteps, and fhield us
from regret : it allows us to run the race
of glory or ambition; but recals us to the
idea of inconftancy and inftability, to preferve us from a fatal intoxication : it is always with us, not to difturb our felicity, not
to impofe ufelefs privations, but to blend itfelf with our thoughts, and to unite to all
our projects thofe mild and peaceable ideas
which attend wifdom and moderation : in
fhort, in the day of adverfity, when our
ftrength is broken, in which we have placed
our

our confidence, piety comes to fuccour and confole us; it fhows us the nothingnefs of vanity and worldly illufions; it calms the remorfe of our fouls, by reminding us of a particular providence; it foftens our regrets, by prefenting more worthy hopes than any earthly object can afford, in order to engage our intereft and fix our attention.

I am not led to thefe reflections by a temporary melancholy; I fhould be afraid of it, if I had not always had the fame thoughts, and if the various circumftances of a life, often perturbed, had not led me to think of the neceffity of attaching myfelf to fome principle independent of men and events. Almoft entirely alone at this inftant, and thrown into folitude by an unforefeen accident, I experience, it is true *, more than ever, the want of thofe rational ideas, the reprefentations of all that is great, and I approach with renewed intereft the truths which I always loved; grand and fublime truths, which I have recommended to men at the moment when I fee them more than

* For I had begun this chapter during my exile.

ever

ever inclined to neglect them. How miftaken are they in their calculations, they
truft to-day in the ftrength of their minds,
to-morrow they will find their weaknefs;
they imagine, that in turning their views
from the termination of life they remove the
fatal boundary; but already the hand trembles on the dial to give the fignal of their
laft moment. What a dire facrifice we
fhould make, if we gave up thofe confoling
truths which ftill prefent to us a future,
when all the buftle of life is over! We
fhould again demand them, fearch for them
with the moft diligent anxiety, if ever the
traces of them were unfortunately effaced.

All thefe ideas, fome may fay, are vague,
and do not agree with the humour of the
age; but at a certain diftance from the field
of ambition and vanity, is there any thing
to every one of us more vague than the
paffions of others? Are men employed about
our intereft? do they dream of our happinefs? No, they are like ourfelves; they feek
for precedency; now and then indeed they

I pronounce

pronounce the name of public good; but it is only a watch word which they have stolen, to be able to run over our ranks without danger. Where shall we find then a real tie? Where shall we find a universal rendezvous, if not in those unalterable ideas which are so consonant to our nature, which should equally interest us all, being suited to all without distinction; and which are ready to welcome us when we see the folly of earthly pursuits? They may not, indeed, gratify the childish wishes of the moment; but they relieve our anxiety about to-morrow, they are allied to objects of meditation which belong to our whole life, and above all, they unite us to that spirit which constitutes our true grandeur, to that sublime spirit, a few of whose relations only are yet discovered by us, and the full extent of whose power and goodness can be but faintly guessed at by finite beings.

F I N I S.

I WAS engrossed by the last Cares which the Publication of this Book occasioned, when M. de CALONNE's Second Memorial made its Appearance. I have read it; and I here publicly engage to answer this new Attack, and fully to support the Credit which is justly due to the Account I presented to the King in 1781.

NECKER.

Lightning Source UK Ltd.
Milton Keynes UK
UKHW012247110219
337137UK00006B/941/P